POSITIVE THINKING

for *Every Day*
of *the Year*

NORMAN VINCENT PEALE

PEALE CENTER
FOR CHRISTIAN LIVING

The Outreach Division of Guideposts
66 East Main Street, Pawling, N.Y. 12564-1409

Published by
PEALE CENTER FOR CHRISTIAN LIVING
66 East Main Street
Pawling, NY 12564-1409

Printed in the United States of America
January 2001

JANUARY

Seek the Lord and his strength, seek his face continually.   I CHRONICLES 16:11

James Russell Lowell made a remark one time which has always fascinated me. He said, "Mishaps are like knives that either serve us or cut us, as we grasp them by the blade or the handle." If you grasp the blade of a difficulty it will cut you, but if you grasp the handle of a difficulty, then you can cut your way through all manner of obstructions.

The Russians have a proverb which I like: "The hammer shatters the glass, but forges steel." If you're glass, if you're superficial, if there's no faith in you, adversity will crack and shatter you. But if you have in you the victory that overcomes the world, then the hammer of circumstance hitting you forges you into a strong person. God knew what He was doing when He constructed this world so that there was difficulty in it. That is what makes it possible for us to grow in strength and understanding. There is conflict in the universe and that is what makes life go.

PRAYER: *Our Heavenly Father, help us to believe that even though great difficulties come against us, we can overcome them because You will help us. And help us so to give of ourselves that we may be in harmony with the great flow of good. Through Jesus Christ, our Lord. Amen.*

<table>
<tr><td>

DAY

2

</td><td>

O LORD, I know that the way of man is not in himself: it is not in man that walketh to direct his steps.   JEREMIAH 10:23

</td></tr>
</table>

Once while in San Francisco I climbed into one of the cable cars alongside the grip man—the man who runs it—and the car filled up with people. We were traveling down the Powell Street hill at high speed. It looked as though at each moment we were in imminent danger of destruction, but this made it a more exciting ride. I asked him, "Don't you ever get nervous when this car starts plunging down this grade?"

"Nervous?" he replied. "Never. Because, you see, I know I'm in control of this car. So why should I be nervous?"

As we careen down the steep grades of our lives, we sometimes have dark apprehensions of what may happen. But if you know you are in emotional control, you then can handle any situation. It is when we finally relax in God that we find health and well-being and deep joy.

LIFE LIFTER: *God's promises mean that no matter what happens, nothing can separate you from His love and protection. The secret is to build up in your mind, day by day, the knowledge and realization of God's presence and His love for you. Dwell on this mentally until it becomes an unshakable fact.*

DAY 3

And the Lord said unto Joshua, See, I have given into thine hand Jericho, and the king thereof, and the mighty men of valour. And ye shall compass the city, all ye men of war, and go round about the city once. Thus shalt thou do six days.

JOSHUA 6:2,3

The Bible just bubbles over with spiritual food for getting a new heart when disheartened. Dig into the New Testament and you come up with light and music and singing, health and hopefulness and faith and love.

An important thing to realize is it doesn't make any difference how much difficulty there is—there are always great possibilities in any situation. Generally, when people are disheartened, they can't see the possibilities. They see only the difficulties that are involved, not the solution. They magnify the difficulties, to blow them up, to make them bigger than they actually are. The thing to do when you are disheartened is the very opposite: go hunting around in your situation for the bright possibilities that are surely there.

PRAYER: *Our Heavenly Father, we thank You for the vibrant life with which You have surrounded us. Revitalize us, bring us into the newness of life, that we may thrill to the world and the great issues thereof and the people thereof and live with vitality and excitement all our days. Through Jesus Christ, our Lord. Amen.*

<table>
<tr><td>DAY
4</td><td>*Having therefore, brethren, boldness to enter into the holiest by the blood of Jesus, By a new and living way, which he hath consecrated for us, through the veil, that is to say, his flesh.*
HEBREWS 10:19,20</td></tr>
</table>

Several years ago, I was to speak at a dinner and was seated next to the United States Senator from New Jersey, Warren Barbour. He seemed fidgety and he surprised me by remarking, "I'm glad you're speaking first. Having to speak still scares the wits out of me."

"But why, if you were so afraid of speaking," I asked him, "did you run for public office?"

"Actually," he confided, "my fear of speaking was one reason I decided to run. I was determined I wasn't going to go through life reeling because I was afraid to speak. I find that the more I do it, the less I fear it."

You and I, experiencing fear, should remember to have a holy boldness. I call it that because it is of God. He put potential boldness into you. We cannot do it of our own unaided strength, but with God's ever-present help, we can.

PRAYER: *Our Father, help us to return to You our Creator and ask You to cleanse and reestablish and retool this wondrous instrument, the human mind, that we may live without anxiety and abnormal fear. Through Jesus Christ, our Lord. Amen.*

DAY
5

Then I looked on all the works that my hands had wrought,...and, behold, all was vanity and vexation of spirit, and there was no profit under the sun. ECCLESIASTES 2:11

Truth is the wisdom of God in the mind and in the soul of man. So many people have so little grasp of truth that they are constantly plagued by mistakes. A gentleman who was really concerned about himself asked me a question. As he put it, "Why am I so dumb? Why do I do so many dumb things?"

His IQ was very high. He was a graduate of a celebrated university. But this man had lost six jobs in ten years and in every instance it was because he did something stupid. "Now," he said, "Tell me what is wrong with me."

I remarked, "You aren't really stupid." And I pointed him to the answer that will help anyone in that situation: "Jim, if you will commit your life to Jesus Christ so that He takes over your thought processes, you will be guided and will not make all these mistakes."

PRAYER: *Our Heavenly Father, we ask You to look in tender mercy on us all. You know our faults and our many failures. But we feel within us the God-inspired life in our souls. Make it manifest in each of us so that we may go into the society of which we are a part and break down evil impossibles and bring to pass the great glorious possibles of God. This we ask through our Lord, Jesus Christ. Amen.*

<table>
<tr><td>DAY
6</td><td>*Watch ye, stand fast in the faith, quit you like men, be strong.*   I CORINTHIANS 16:13</td></tr>
</table>

I used to sit down in the first pew, when I was still so small that my feet wouldn't touch the floor, and watch my father up in the pulpit and hear him quote these familiar words: "Be firm in your faith. Stay brave and strong." I haven't heard a sermon on I Corinthians 16:13 in years. But in the old days of rugged Protestant Christianity in this country, when ministers still had the idea that their function was to help develop great souls, you used to hear such texts designed to fan up the strength in human beings.

Accept Jesus Christ as your Savior, receive Him as your Divine Redeemer, let yourself be washed clean by Calvary's atonement, let your life be changed. Then you will be able to handle anything life brings. I don't mean to say it's going to be easy. It never will be easy. The Bible tells us we will face tribulation. You'll have trouble to the end. But you can be master of it in the name of Jesus.

PRAYER: *Our Heavenly Father, we give thanks for our faith. Help us to believe more deeply and with more dedication. Help us to be more committed. We are pledged to get our lives changed and through our changed lives to change the life of the world. It is a big order, but we can do it by drawing on Your great power. For this we dedicate ourselves. Through Jesus Christ, our Lord. Amen.*

<table>
<tr><td>DAY
7</td><td>I sought the LORD, and he heard me, and
delivered me from all my fears.   PSALM 34:4</td></tr>
</table>

Some years ago I met a man named Oelroyd. He was the curator of the house in Washington across from Ford's Theater to which Abraham Lincoln was carried after the assassin shot him, and where he died. Mr. Oelroyd showed me a Bible which he said had been used by Abraham Lincoln during the critical days of the Civil War. Opening it to Psalm 34, he pointed to the fourth verse and to a slightly soiled indentation alongside it near the edge of the page, which looked as it might have been made by a finger. Mr. Oelroyd liked to think that this was evidence that Abraham Lincoln frequently turned to that verse, which says: "I asked the Lord for help, and he saved me from all my fears."

Now the psalmist doesn't say that God delivered him from some of his fears, but from all his fears. I've always been impressed by the outgoing promises the Bible makes. There is nothing halfway about it. It offers you everything—including, here in Psalm 34, deliverance from all your fears.

PRAYER: *Our Heavenly Father, it is a fact that we are living in a world of difficulty and all manner of trouble, hardship, confusion, and discouragement. But we have Jesus Christ in us, and You in us, and the ability to think, and the courage to handle anything and see it through. We thank You, through Jesus Christ, our Lord. Amen.*

<table>
<tr><td>

DAY

8

</td><td>

And God said unto Noah, This is the token of the covenant, which I have established between me and all flesh that is upon the earth. GENESIS 9:17

</td></tr>
</table>

Do you think Christianity could have lasted for nearly two thousand years on its promises unless the Lord could deliver on them? Why, it would have been forgotten long since. Christianity still maintains its ancient power in today's world because there are always people who find out that these things are true. So whatever your problem may be—poor health, a confused mind, wrong relations with people, unhappiness in the home, business problems— whatever they may be, put them in the hands of Jesus Christ, who knows more about such problems than you or I ever could. You may say this is claiming a lot. It certainly is. But it is not half of what we could claim. If we had the time, hundreds of people could be brought to pulpits everywhere who could bear witness as to what happens in human lives when Jesus Christ takes over, when the God of the impossible is given control.

LIFE LIFTER: *When you have done all that you can do, don't try to do any more, just follow the path to God's peace. Relax, stop, be quiet, don't fuss about it; you have done everything possible; leave the results to God.*

<table>
<tr><td>

DAY

9
</td><td>

And besought him that they might only touch the hem of his garment: and as many as touched were made perfectly whole.

MATTHEW 14:36
</td></tr>
</table>

The key to becoming what we want to be is found in the fourteenth chapter of Matthew. In it we find a description of Jesus moving amid the multitude on the shores of Lake Galilee. Instinctively the people knew that He had the answer to their lives. They weren't going to go to school to learn the ways of faith. They were just going to touch His garment. And the passage goes on to say, "Everyone who did was healed."

Don't feel you have to understand so much or do so many things. It isn't so complicated. I don't want to oversimplify, but what this passage says is: If you want to be a better person, just get hold of something of Him, even if it's only the hem of His garment. If your desire is real, you will be made perfectly whole. Think of that. You'll no longer be defeated by your fears, or torn asunder by inner conflict, or be defeated by evil in your nature. You will be made perfectly whole.

LIFE LIFTER: *To revitalize the spirit is a necessity. Every longing of the human spirit finds enduring satisfaction in the life-giving message of Jesus. It becomes a perpetual well of self-renewing inspiration. From the water of life, our spirit is endowed with continuous refreshment. We never thirst again.*

<table>
<tr><td>

DAY

10

</td><td>

...I am come to show thee; for thou art greatly beloved: therefore understand the matter, and consider the vision.　　DANIEL 9:23

</td></tr>
</table>

For many years I never experienced an operation firsthand. But my turn came. My doctor told me he had to remove my gall bladder. On the appointed morning, I told my wife that I loved her. And she told me the same. Then I asked the Lord to forgive me for any sins that I had committed. And I thanked Him for all His goodness. I looked out at the beautiful Dutchess County hillside and I said, "I love this world, Lord, and I'd like to go on and do a good job."

Now this is a simple thing I'm telling you. But what I did was to let go. I committed my soul to God. Have you ever really done that? It's a tremendous experience. Friends, I want to tell you that in that one minute I had an experience of the Presence. I felt a sustaining power. I had a sense of reality. And it is going to live with me all the rest of my life. You don't have to wait for an operation or an illness to commit your life to Him. You can do it now.

LIFE LIFTER: *The spiritual formula of prayer tells us to ask and then immediately conceive of ourselves as receiving. For example, to be free from fear, ask the Lord to free you. Then believe that He has immediately done so. The minute you express your faith by sincerely asking Him for a blessing and believe your prayer is answered, your prayer is answered.*

DAY 11

He layeth up sound wisdom for the righteous: he is a buckler to them that walk uprightly.
PROVERBS 2:7

Phyllis Simolke was in New York City on a buying trip. After a happy reunion, she went with a friend to the subway and waited until a train came. Her friend got on, and they waved to each other as the train moved off. She started toward the exit. All at once, five thugs appeared and blocked her passage. The young woman froze. Mrs. Simolke had a committed faith. So she prayed to the Lord, saying, "For the sake of my two little boys and my husband, help me." And He did.

She walked straight up to the leader, a tall fellow with a scar on his face. Standing tall, she said gently but firmly, "Let me pass, please."

Like the parting of the Red Sea, they broke ranks. As she passed, one punk hissed, "You walk tall, woman. Walk tall!"—as though in his mind there glimmered a respect for the immense power available to renewed people. Phyllis Simolke is the kind of person who lives with unchanging truth in a changing world.

> **PRAYER:** *Our Heavenly Father, we ask Your blessing for every individual. May the love of Christ be so real to us that we shall never henceforth be afraid, never be defeated, never be overcome by the sorrows and woes of human life. And for the wonder of His love we give You thanks. Through Jesus Christ, our Lord. Amen.*

DAY
12

And God wrought special miracles by the hands of Paul.   ACTS 19:11

Prayer is the contact of the soul with God through the mental processes whereby the individual conquers his own weaknesses and enters into life abundant. If you have the idea that it is merely the mumbling of a few words, I almost think you're better off not to use it at all, for that is a degradation of this great process. True prayer requires discipline, it requires pain, it requires the agony to think. But when you do think prayerfully, with Jesus as your guide, you break free from the defeats which have encompassed you. I do not believe there is any problem, any defeat, any difficulty that cannot be overcome through prayer. I do not believe there is any disease from which prayer cannot bring deliverance. One of the most devastating enemies of man is disease, but one reason it devastates is because we just accept it as inevitable. I believe in the power of Jesus Christ to resolve any difficulty, to remove any weakness, to heal any disease.

PRAYER: *Our Heavenly Father, we give You thanks for Your great power which can operate in human life, and we pray for all who today are suffering and feel defeated in the presence of great difficulty. Let them know, we pray, that with God, all things really are possible. And for this we give You thanks, through Jesus Christ, our Lord. Amen.*

<table>
<tr><td>DAY
13</td><td>*And he answered, Fear not: for they that be*
with us are more than they that be with them.
II KINGS 6:16</td></tr>
</table>

You may be full of fear. You have had fears all your life. You are so sick of these fears that you just don't know what to do, but you are in the habit of saying to yourself, "I've always been a fearful person. My grandfather was a fearful person, my mother was a fearful person—so I am a fearful person. That's just the way it is. That's just the way I'm made." What an evaluation of yourself!

Say instead: "Dear Jesus Christ, I believe that You came to give me power. I hereby repudiate these fears. I am from this minute on a person of courage." Then you will go out and live with courage. You'll do things you formerly were afraid to do. You'll live dangerously. And after a while you will find that your fears are gone.

The same thing is true of excitement and enthusiasm. Live on the basis of enthusiasm and excitement and you'll have them. And they will make a different person out of anyone who does it.

> PRAYER: *Our Heavenly Father, we pray that a deep spiritual experience may come to everyone. Help us so to yield ourselves that God with all His power may take hold of us and thereby we may have life in depth, life in full vitality, life which is life indeed. Through Jesus Christ, our Lord. Amen*

DAY **14**	*Praise ye the Lord for the avenging of Israel, when the people willingly offered themselves. Hear, O ye kings; give ear, O ye princes; I, even I, will sing praise unto the Lord God of*

Israel. JUDGES 5:2,3

At a luncheon I was seated next to a distinguished woman who asked me what extra thing I was doing now. "Writing a book," I said. "The working title is *Enthusiasm Makes the Difference.*"

"I want to congratulate you on your audacity and your courage," she said, "that you would actually write a book on enthusiasm in a day and age like this."

Well, I was surprised to know that this required courage and audacity. But I shall persevere in encouraging people to sing in their spirit.

How does one have enthusiasm in his life? It is as simple as this: Cultivate the ability to love living. Love the people who live, love the sky under which you live, love the season in which we pass these days, love all of the facets of living. Jesus taught that the person who loves becomes happy. The person who loves everything becomes enthusiastic, filled with the zest and the joy of life. It is just that simple.

> **PRAYER:** *Our Heavenly Father, we thank You for the immense possibilities You have given all of us. Help us to realize our high possibilities and live as is Your will for us, in fullness and joy. Through Jesus Christ, our Lord. Amen.*

<table>
<tr><td>DAY
15</td><td>*Buried with him in baptism, wherein also ye are risen with him through the faith of the operation of God, who hath raised him from the dead.*   COLOSSIANS 2:12</td></tr>
</table>

Paul says that we have been raised to life. What does that mean? It means we are supposed to get rid of all the old barnacles that have encrusted us for so long: our hates, our lusts, our dishonesties, our rationalizations, our fears, our weaknesses. These must all go, so that we may experience the power of Christ.

And how can you and I become new? The only way is to have contact with the power of God so that, like a lightning bolt, it may burst into our lives and change us. Maybe people have shaken their heads about me and said, "This man is becoming an old-time evangelist." Well, I'm not old-time, but I am an evangelist. An evangelist is a person who is trying to bring people the good news. And the good news is that we have been raised to new life in Christ.

PRAYER: *Our Heavenly Father, we ask Your blessing. Come into us out of Your great goodness and help us really to take the radiant gospel of Your Son Jesus Christ and live by it. Remind us that You have made us good not merely for time but for eternity. And for this we give thanks. Through Jesus Christ, our Lord. Amen.*

DAY **16**	*But ye shall receive power, after that the Holy Ghost is come upon you: and ye shall be witnesses unto me both in Jerusalem, and in all Judea, and in Samaria, and unto the*

uttermost part of the earth. ACTS 1:8

We use words rather loosely because we repeat them so frequently. One such word is "power." I decided to consult the dictionary on the subject. The Latin word from which "power" derives is the equivalent of the Greek word *dynamis,* a word used all through the New Testament. And from *dynamis* is derived the English word dynamite.

The Bible is filled with the most powerful ideas in this world. By substituting the word "dynamite" for the word "power," you can begin to understand the greatness of it. Take Acts 1:8: "The Holy Spirit will come upon you and give you dynamite." When the Holy Spirit comes upon you, you will experience an explosion that will change your whole life and, through you, help to change the world. It's really tremendous.

PRAYER: *Our Heavenly Father, we thank You that as weak as we seem to be, this doesn't truly represent the measure of ourselves, for You have put within us potential power. Through faith and humble dependence upon Jesus Christ, we can have power over difficulties. For this we give great thanks, through Jesus Christ, our Lord. Amen.*

DAY
17

And there was great joy in that city. ACTS 8:8

You were not made to live a dull life. You were not put into this exquisite world, filled with beauty and fascination, to be less than an interested, excited human being. It may seem strange to you that a minister of the gospel should talk about having an interesting and exciting life. A crime has been perpetrated against Christianity in the assumption, built up over many years, that the religion of Jesus Christ is dull, formalistic, something apart from vibrant life.

The most alive Person who ever came into human existence was a man named Jesus Christ. He had an impact upon human beings as no other person who ever walked the earth. Could a nice, quiet, lifeless person have jolted humanity as He did? He was and is the personification of interest and excitement. The story of His life is told in only a small section of the total Bible. But in those pages there is more life than in any book or stack of books ever written.

LIFE LIFTER: *This promise runs counter to the modern materialistic conception that to have, one must get and keep. But people who live only for themselves find that life shrinks and finally withers. But for those who give generously, who help other people in Christ's name, life grows ever richer. Lose yourself in big things outside yourself, and you will find yourself. The more you give, the more you receive from life.*

DAY
18

Then said David to the Philistine, Thou comest to me with a sword, and with a spear, and with a shield: but I come to thee in the name of the Lord of hosts, the God of the armies of Israel, whom thou hast defied. I SAMUEL 17:45

The story of David and Goliath might be told in this fashion. The Philistines had a giant named Goliath. He would yell at the Israelites, "Come out and fight. If your giant defeats me, we will be your slaves; but if I defeat him, you'll be our slaves."

David, a clear-minded boy, went to the king and said, "If you will let me, I will take care of this fellow." This went over with the king. He said, "If you want to take on the giant you may do it."

David collected five smooth stones and proceeded in the direction of the giant. He swung his slingshot and the stone smacked the giant right on the forehead. And Goliath toppled over, dead.

What a story! And what does it teach? A simple truth. You are faced with a Goliath. Everybody is. But no difficulty is bigger than you are when you are united with God. Together you and God have the power to do mighty things which you know not.

> **PRAYER:** *Our Heavenly Father, help us never to be frightened or discouraged, but to know that by faith we gain power for dealing with the problems we must face. For this we thank You, through Jesus Christ, our Lord. Amen.*

<table>
<tr><td>DAY
19</td><td>*But Jonah rose up to flee unto Tarshish from the presence of the Lord, and went down to Joppa; and he found a ship going to Tarshish: so he paid the fare thereof, and went down*</td></tr>
</table>

into it, to go with them unto Tarshish from the presence of the Lord.   JONAH 1:3

When you are up against a tough situation, the first essential is to stand up to it. Face it, think about it, study it, pray about it; then hit it and keep after it. You have within you enough force, put there by Almighty God, to overcome situations that seem overwhelming. If you practice faith constantly, if you keep in His spirit, if you stay in tune with Him, you can bring the necessary strength into play against all difficulties.

Don't ever think you're weak. Don't ever say you're weak. Don't ever believe you're weak. You're not weak. Draw upon your strength. And maybe it seems you have very little strength, but you can bring it into play against difficulties and overcome them.

LIFE LIFTER: *A cure for fear that will absolutely work is to get close to God in your thoughts. That may be done by spending fifteen minutes every day thinking about God. You can split this up into five-minute periods, but never let a day pass without spending fifteen minutes thinking about God. Each day declare to yourself, "I surrender myself into the hands of God, and I trust Him." Three times every day, thank God for all His goodness. Soon your life will be filled with God and emptied of apprehensions.*

<table>
<tr><td>DAY
20</td><td>*Then said David, O Lord God of Israel, thy
servant hath certainly heard that Saul
seeketh to come to Keilah, to destroy the
city for my sake.*   1 SAMUEL 23:10</td></tr>
</table>

I believe a person should pray for courage as he prays for his daily bread. God will give it to you, because He will give you Himself. Let me illustrate.

At a prayer breakfast in Washington, General Harold K. Johnson, Chief of Staff of the United States Army, related an instance from his life. Fourteen years before, during the Korean War, General Johnson found himself in charge of a handful of men holding a dreary stretch of deserted road to cover a retreat.

"I was very troubled," he said, "so I just shut my eyes and talked to God, right there on that cold, frozen road. I asked His help. And out of the night, as if from a great distance, came God's voice saying, 'Be strong, have no fear, I am with you.'" From that moment he had no fear, only a deep sense of peace. And he and his men had the courage they needed to fight their way out of that situation.

> PRAYER: *Our Heavenly Father, we thank You for the great gift of courage which comes to us as we think of it; of courage which comes to us out of acting courageously; and of that courage which we receive from You, the Author of courage, through our prayers. Help us to be valiant. Through Jesus Christ, our Lord. Amen.*

> DAY
> **21**

When thou goest out to battle against thine enemies, and seest horses, and chariots, and a people more than thou, be not afraid of them: for the Lord thy God is with thee, which brought thee up out of the land of Egypt.

DEUTERONOMY 20:1

My wife and I were in England and went to Chartwell, Winston Churchill's home where he lived during the war. Outside the house we were shown where he stood every evening during the Battle of the Britain, watching the German bombers coming over in great waves. I asked our guide, "Did he ever lose hope?"

She laughed, "Churchill? No. Hope was built into him. He never expected anything but ultimate victory." That is why some men become immortal. They have hope and expectation built into them.

Well, you may think, I'm not Churchill; I'm just a plain human being. Certainly you are! But don't say you are going to let these things defeat you. Not when you have God who will put such a glow of victory and health in you that it will be a thrill.

LIFE LIFTER: *Realize the power that is within you. Cast out doubt. Affirm faith, think positively, visualize achievement. Believe in the power of God, who can do anything. If you set this firmly at the center of your thought pattern, you will never again be the victim of low spirits.*

DAY 22

For they all saw him…And immediately he talked with them, and saith unto them, Be of good cheer: it is I; be not afraid.   MARK 6:50

The two greatest forces in the world, ceaselessly contending with each other, are fear and faith. But faith is stronger than fear.

I am reminded of a talk I had with J. Edgar Hoover, who was head of the Federal Bureau of Investigation. In his early career, he was famous for his fearless pursuit of vicious criminals. I said to him, "When you were hunting those gangsters, were you ever afraid?"

"Of course I was afraid," he answered. "There were many times when I might have been shot to death at any moment. Of course I was afraid."

"How did you overcome your fear?" I asked.

Instantly he replied: "I lost my fear in the power of my Lord." He added, "Get the power of the Lord in your heart and you overcome your fear."

PRAYER: *Our Heavenly Father, You know us and You love us so much that You sent Your Son Jesus Christ to tell us that if we put our faith in Him and do as He says, we can have an abundance greater than we could think of having, because He gives us power over everything that would destroy. And for this we thank You, through Jesus Christ, our Lord. Amen.*

DAY
23

And when the Gentiles heard this, they were glad, and glorified the word of the Lord: and as many as were ordained to eternal life believed.   ACTS 13:48

I consider it a travesty of the gospel of Jesus Christ to insist that there should be no expression of joy in this world. It was said of the first Christians that they had within them the song of the skylark and the babbling of brooks. But today that lilt seems, for the most part, to have gone out of Christian preaching. And this is a tragedy.

Now, of course, if you see only clouds you naturally are not going to say, "It's good to be alive." But believe me, friends, there is much more in this world than clouds. And if that's all you see, then you should have a change of vantage point. Take flight within yourself. It is a wonderful thing to have altitude in your thoughts. You can have it if you just take it. And altitude of the spirit makes all the difference in the world.

LIFE LIFTER: *Whoever embarks upon the Christian life will have periods of testing. However strong his faith, he will experience down moments. He will not be spared opposition. He will be criticized, mistreated, misunderstood. The way will be far from easy. When such times come, fall further back on God, pray more earnestly, surrender more completely.*

<table>
<tr><td>DAY
24</td><td>*Also now, behold, my witness is in heaven,*
and my record is on high.   JOB 16:19</td></tr>
</table>

William Lyon Phelps, who in the early years of the 20th century was one of the most famous of American professors at a great New England university, once wrote, "The happiest people are those who think the most interesting thoughts."

One morning in New York City as I left my apartment for the day, the doorman, with a dour expression on his face, said to me, "This is one of the most miserable days I've ever seen."

For a moment it dashed my spirits, but I rose to the occasion and replied, "This is the day which the Lord has made; we will rejoice and be glad in it." A new expression came over the man's face, so maybe I gave him a different idea. That's the way you've got to think. Your happiness in life depends upon how you think about everything. How do you think about your future? Do you see it gloomy? If you do, it will be so. Don't see it that way. See it happy. See God in it. See God controlling your mind, and happiness will come.

LIFE LIFTER: *The quality of your disposition depends upon your inner spirit. If you have allowed it to deteriorate, Almighty God, who created you, can recreate and renew in you the fine balance, the controlled spirit. Let no day pass that you do not say many times, "Create pure thoughts in me and make me faithful again."*

| DAY
25 | *And let us arise, and go up to Bethel; and I will make there an altar unto God, who answered me in the day of my distress, and was with me in the way which I went.* |

GENESIS 35:3

Your mind is a powerful instrument. If it controls you, you'll not be victorious. But if you control it, you will be. However, I don't believe that a human being by his own unaided strength can accomplish this. Something else needs to be added.

I once knew a distressed man who held steady and made his way back up with the help of a wonderful dynamic thought that changes everything. Given what little I know about human beings and about God, I will guarantee that this thought can help anybody under any circumstances to keep on keeping on. Everybody would do well to hold it in consciousness until it absorbs into the unconsciousness and live by it. It's found in Philippians, the fourth chapter, thirteenth verse. And this is it: I can do all things through— myself? No. "Christ gives me the strength to face anything." Christ will help you keep on keeping on.

PRAYER: *Our Heavenly Father, we thank You for the wonderful gospel, for the clear mind of Jesus Christ, for the power which he possesses and for the fact that He makes this power available to us to set us free from defeat and fear. We give You thanks. Through Jesus Christ, our Lord. Amen.*

DAY
26

*The Lord also will be a refuge for the
oppressed, a refuge in times of trouble.*

PSALM 9:9

When you get turned on to the gospel—not just
intellectually in agreement with it, but experiencing it
really deep within you—then, no matter what you have
to face or deal with, you have the power to do it. The
Bible promises us this. Psalm 9:9 says God is "a refuge
in time of trouble." That means there is no time, ever,
when He isn't there to help you, if you are there to turn
Him on inside you. Now how do you go about getting
the help of God in this great way? You begin by having
what we call spiritual experience. "Spiritual
experience." What does that mean? It means a personal
awareness of the presence and work of Jesus Christ in
your life.

LIFE LIFTER: *A human mind can stand only so much
weight. Fortunately you do not need to carry your
burdens without assistance. God will help you carry them.*

*But how is this done? It is accomplished in the mind.
Practice thinking that God is actually with you. Form a
picture of yourself as shifting your burdens to Him. He is
willing to assume them and is perfectly able to do so. But—
and this is most important—don't give Him just part of
them. And don't take them back. Let God handle them. Leave
them with Him.*

| DAY
27 |

And she said unto the men, I know that the Lord hath given you the land, and that your terror is fallen upon us, and that all the inhabitants of the land faint because of you.

JOSHUA 2:9

A university put out a questionnaire among six hundred psychology students and asked them, among other things, to say what they thought was their most pressing, painful, personal problem. Seventy percent of them said that it was lack of courage or self-confidence.

What, then, is the secret of self-confidence and courage? It hinges on the kind of thoughts you think. Your subconscious is very accommodating. If you keep on sending it fear thoughts and self-inadequacy thoughts, that is what it will feed back to you.

When you come right down to it, the secret of courage and self-confidence is to fill your life with God. Of course, you expect me to say that. And you are not going to be disappointed, because I've said it. And why do I say it? Because it's true. You were created by God and He made you right. If you haven't walked with God, you are making yourself wrong.

> **PRAYER:** *Our Heavenly Father, we thank You so much for the greatness that You have put into us. Help us really to draw upon it, upon this unused strength. Help us to grow and to outgrow until we finally become what we were really destined to be. Through Jesus Christ, our Lord. Amen.*

DAY
28

But let him that glorieth glory in this, that he understandeth and knoweth me, the I am the Lord which exercise lovingkindness, judgment, and righteousness, in the earth: for in these things I delight, saith the Lord. JEREMIAH 9:24

Your physical body is a marvelous instrument. Most everybody has a hand, and it seems to be an ordinary appliance. But consider the positions and motions you can make with your fingers and your hand. Think of the angles, the joints, the engineering that goes into the one small member of your body known as a hand! And that isn't all there is about you. But your wonderful body isn't the greatest thing about you.

There is in you that indescribable thing called God's power. It is a power over yourself, a power over situations, a power over circumstance. If you exercise this power, amazing things can be done with it. Now you must be humble about it. It isn't your power. It is God living within you. This is why we constantly urge people to come into a closer relationship with Jesus Christ. Because what does He do? He releases power whereby anyone can transform himself or herself.

LIFE LIFTER: *Live by the sayings of Jesus Christ and become like that wise man who built his house upon the rock. You can have an inner serenity, strength and courage that defies all the storms of life. Christ makes you strong. You can be undefeatable. How your spirit will rise!*

DAY
29

Thus saith Cyrus king of Persia, The Lord God of heaven hath given me all the kingdoms of the earth; and he hath charged me to build him an house at Jerusalem, which is in Judah.

EZRA 1:2

The Holy Bible contains some remarkable statements. It is probably a good thing that the canon of the Scriptures was written and settled generations ago. It was produced by men who were more naïve than we are today, men whose faith was simpler, and they were not afraid of the great claims and promises which were written into the holy text.

What if leaders of religion today were to write the canon on the basis of traditions such as were given to the early Biblical writers? I am sure that, with their more sophisticated scholarship and their smaller concepts, they would produce a Bible which, while it might be meticulously perfect from a literary point of view, wouldn't posses the rugged power and greatness of faith which this book possesses.

PRAYER: *Our Heavenly Father, we give You thanks for Jesus Christ the Son of God who takes away the sins of the world. Help us not to forget You or turn away from You but to love You passionately and give You our undying devotion. Through Jesus Christ, our Lord. Amen.*

DAY **30**	*Jesus said unto him, If thou canst believe, all things are possible to him that believeth.*

MARK 9:23

I call to your attention a text in the New Testament, it is Mark 9:23, and it is probably one of the greatest gems of truth you will find. It says: "Anything is possible for someone who has faith!" Notice that there is a condition. You are offered something tremendous, but only if you have faith. In-depth belief requires giving your whole self to it. It isn't the glib recital of a creed. But if you can overcome your doubts and your negative thinking and really, deeply believe, you will thereby enter into a life transformed. This is the magic of believing. Belief is factual, it is truth. The magic of believing is a manifestation of one of the greatest powers in the universe, the power of thought. By our thoughts we either create or destroy. You can tear your life down by destructive thinking, but you can build your life up by thinking constructively.

PRAYER: *Our Heavenly Father, we ask Your blessing for us and all Your children. We pray that we may hold in mind our great expectations in You and that we may live with You. And for this we give You thanks, through Jesus Christ, our Lord. Amen.*

| DAY 31 | *The Spirit of Lord is upon me, because he hath anointed me to preach the gospel to the poor; he hath sent me to heal the brokenhearted, to preach deliverance to the captives, and* |

recovering of sight to the blind, to set at liberty them that are bruised, To preach the acceptable year of the Lord.

LUKE 4:18–19

"The Lord has sent me to preach deliverance to the captives ..." What captives? Those who were in jail? Jesus meant far more than that. People build their own prisons, forge their own chains. Held by self-imposed limitations, they are captives who wither and die.

But Jesus sets us free. He implies to each of us, *There is a giant within you.* Have you ever seen the giant within you? Have you ever felt him trying to burst out of the prison you have made for him? Let Jesus help you let him out. No child of God should ever be a slave either to his passions or his ambitions or his hates or his weakness or his self-depreciation. Accept the truth that Jesus Christ has come to set the prisoners free. There is glorious joy in true freedom. Don't settle for your limitations.

PRAYER: *Our Heavenly Father, how can we ever thank You for the wonderful things You do for us! Inspire us to seek You, knowing that You will hear us and deliver us from all our fears. For this wonderful blessing we give You thanks through Jesus Christ, our Lord. Amen.*

FEBRUARY

<table>
<tr><td>DAY
1</td><td>And God gave Solomon wisdom and understanding exceeding much, and largeness of heart, even as the sand that is on the sea shore.   I KINGS 4:29</td></tr>
</table>

We live in the midst of the greatest scientific civilization in the history of the world. But the greatest wisdom walking our streets is not that of any laboratory scientist, but the wisdom of Jesus of Nazareth. When you have to solve perplexing problems and handle tough situations, He will give you the calm, quiet, orderly mind without which no solution can emerge. So the first thing is: Don't panic. Second thing: Think. That's what Jesus Christ enables a person to do. He teaches you to think.

Write all the parts of the problem out. Talk it over with people whose intelligence and understanding you respect. Then do something about it. Do anything you can think of to find an answer. And never, never give up. Because there is an answer and in God's leading, you will be guided to the answer if you keep on thinking, keep on working at it.

> **LIFE LIFTER:** *When you are filled with self-doubt, and in the grip of your inferiority complex, don't give up. You have the kingdom of God within you. God has placed in your personality all the ability you need. You have only to believe and the strength within you will be released. In saying the text, try it this way, "God's abundance, peace and power are within me. I lack for nothing."*

DAY 2

Bless the Lord, O my soul, and forget not all his benefits.   PSALM 103:2

Psalm 103:2 is packed full of wisdom. It is another way of telling us to thank God and be sure that you do not forget all that He has done for you.

It is fitting and proper that we should have a special day of thanksgiving each year. But it would be most unfortunate if we were to limit our thanksgiving to one day. Thanksgiving is one of the most important, most creative capacities of the human mind. As we practice it assiduously and constantly, we develop a deep joy in living despite the fact that life is filled with all manner of suffering and difficulty.

I truly believe that the individual who learns to practice thanksgiving activates within himself and around himself continuous victories and blessings from God. Become a practitioner of thanksgiving, and victory and joy and satisfaction will fill your life and will contribute to the happiness of those who touch your life.

PRAYER: *Our Heavenly Father, we thank You for the great principle of thanksgiving. May we as a people find it more deeply embedded in our life. May we as individuals know and practice the law that thanksgivers indeed become blessing receivers and so live. And for this, accept our humble gratitude. Through Jesus Christ, our Lord. Amen.*

| DAY 3 | *And they said, Thou hast saved our lives: let us find grace in the sight of my lord, and we will be Pharoah's servants.*   GENESIS 47:25 |

What is the hope of the world? Is it in the military? Is it in money? Is it in diplomacy? I would say that the diplomacy of the world hasn't succeeded too well, although without it we might be worse off by far than we are. Military force will never save the world. Education won't save it either. If all the people in the world are able to read, that is not going to guarantee anything, because what will they read? I tell you, the hope of the world is in Jesus, because He alone can bridge the gap between people. He alone can establish a fellowship that is basic. He alone brings people together as brothers. You do not see people's race any longer, nor their color, nor their background, nor their present condition; you see only a human soul, a child of God, under Jesus. If we could just get this world full of Jesus.

PRAYER: *Our Heavenly Father, how great You are. And the greatest thing You've ever done for us was to give us Your Son Jesus, who came to this earth and took the form of a man, that He might live with the humble poor and downtrodden and the mixed-up and the sinful of this earth, amongst whom we must include ourselves. When we have looked into our hearts and seen our weakness and then looked into His face and seen the strength we can have, we have fallen in love with Him. Bring us finally to Him, that we may be like Him. This we ask in His holy name. Amen.*

| DAY 4 |

And from Jesus Christ, who is the faithful witness, and the first begotten of the dead, and the prince of the kings of the earth. Unto him that loved us, and washed us from our sins in his own blood. And hath made us kings and priests unto God and his Father; to him be glory and dominion for ever and ever. Amen.   REVELATION 1:5–6

The most astonishing force that has been let loose in this world is Christianity. It is positively amazing what the Christian faith offers to its followers. They are offered peace of mind; victory over every defeat of the human spirit; a deep pulsating joy in their inmost souls; and, finally, the immortality of the soul.

These things are not offered cheaply. Christianity is not a superficial religion. You have to pay for everything it gives you. And what is the price? It is yourself. But if you give yourself to Jesus, He will give Himself to you, and life will be so wonderful that there is no describing it. You will be given the opportunity to be what Dostoyevsky, the great Russian writer, referred to as a citizen of eternity.

PRAYER: *Our Heavenly Father, we give You thanks for the greatness and the glory and the power of Jesus Christ, who gives that deep and true contentment by which we know that life is good. He also gives that driving discontent to make it ever better until finally, in His name, it is perfect indeed, through Jesus Christ, our Lord. Amen.*

DAY
5

(Beforetime in Israel, when a man went to inquire of God, thus he spake, Come, and let us go to the seer: for he that is now called a Prophet was beforetime called a Seer.)

I SAMUEL 9:9

Part of having meaning in your life is to get lifted out of yourself, to get high, so to speak. Everybody needs a high experience once in awhile. You can't live adequately on a level of no great experience. You must have great experiences at intervals. For instance, you can be caught up by some great music or be lifted by some beauty in nature or have some marvelous experience of love with other human beings. You need these elevated experiences. Christianity tells us this. Jesus said, "I came so that everyone would have life, and have it in its fullest" (John 10:10). In other words, that we might have it high. That is, have meaning in your life.

PRAYER: *Our Heavenly Father, we thank You for the marvelous facts of the Gospel, for the teachings of Jesus and for Jesus Himself, who shows us how to have life that is tremendous, fabulous, wonderful. Help us no longer to fool around with living, but to put into our life the depth and breadth and height and wonder that it ought to have, and to let ourselves go in every good thing and have high experiences that change everything and pack life full of meaning. Through Jesus Christ, our Lord. Amen.*

DAY
6

Then spake Jesus again unto them, saying, I am the light of the world: he that followeth me shall not walk in darkness, but shall have the light of life.
JOHN 8:12

Everyone wants to make a new start. How can this be done? The formula is very simple. One sentence gives the answer to the whole matter. Put this thought at the center of your consciousness, stay with it, and you will keep it right every day: "I am the light of the world. Follow me, and you won't be walking in the dark. You will have the light that gives life."

How many more years do you think you are going to have? Are you going to have fifty more? Thirty more? Ten more? One more? Very seldom does anybody have more than a hundred. Most people do not even have as many as eighty-five. It would seem that since we have so few years we ought to figure out what is the best procedural wisdom to apply to them. I believe it is contained in the text, "I am the light for the world! Follow me, and you won't be walking in the dark. You will have the light that gives life."

PRAYER: *Our Heavenly Father, we give You thanks for the love and the truth of Jesus Christ. Help us to see Him as One who is alive and vital, who walks the pathway of life with us, who sustains us in sorrow, who gives us moral greatness, who helps us to live meaningfully. Bless us, Your human children. Through Jesus Christ, our Lord. Amen.*

DAY 7

On the left hand, where he doth work, but I cannot behold him: he hideth himself on the right hand, that I cannot see him.   JOB 23:9

Howard M. LeSourd was a dean of one of the colleges of Boston University. He is not emotional toward religion, yet he brings God into the little activities of life. He wrote me a note saying, "Thank you for the Sunday morning services which have brought comfort and inspiration to us," and went on to tell of this incident: "Last night our car stalled on 42nd Street. It would not start." His wife began to pray for help. "When she opened her eyes a man was standing by the car saying, 'If you have a pair of pliers I think I can help you.' I produced the pliers. He raised the hood, released the choke, and the engine started immediately." Isn't God wonderful?

That is a very simple illustration, but God always has His eyes on you. He notes the fall of a sparrow; even the very hairs of your head are numbered. So He is big enough to be interested in everyday human life.

LIFE LIFTER: *Always remember that you will receive as a result of prayer exactly what you think, not what you say. If you pray for achievement but think defeat, your words are idle because your heart has already accepted defeat. Therefore, practice believing that even as you pray you are receiving God's boundless blessings, and they will come to you.*

<table>
<tr><td>

DAY
8

</td><td>

Turn ye unto him from whom the children of Israel have deeply revolted.   ISAIAH 31:6

</td></tr>
</table>

It may be that as a child you had experiences which made you doubt yourself, made you shy, withdrawn, bashful. If you developed such a state of mind as a child, what you need to do is to take charge of your mind and begin to fill it with the healthiest, most powerful, most vital thoughts ever formulated. And where do you find them? In the Bible. The Bible is full of healing thoughts which, if put into your mind, will change your whole condition and fill you with courage and self-confidence.

You can always come back to God, and He will remake you. He remakes you in such a way that you no longer are a phony, but honest and real. If you try to become someone other than yourself, you do a bad job. When you are yourself—just the way God made you—real, honest and whole—then courage will flow into you and confidence, because you are right.

PRAYER: *Our Heavenly Father, how many times have we given up, retreated, been defeated, because we were depending upon our own strength alone! We pray that all of us may build into our personalities a living relationship with Jesus Christ, by which always, under all circumstances, we can keep on keeping on. For this we give You thanks. Through Jesus Christ, our Lord. Amen.*

DAY 9

And that lord answered the man of God, and said, Now, behold, if the Lord should make windows in heaven, might such a thing be?
II KINGS 7:19

Years ago, a member of Marble Collegiate Church played guard on the Northwestern University football team. Apparently he wasn't exerting himself to the fullest, for the coach kept him back one day and told him, "You have it in you to be the greatest guard Northwestern ever had. But you've got to think bigger than you're thinking; you've got to believe bigger than you're believing." He added something the man says he never forgot—and which I have never forgotten since he told me. "Okay boy," said the coach, "go out there on the field running tall." What a phrase!

So I urge you as I urge myself: Get out there on the field running tall, thinking big, believing big, setting your goal high enough for the good that Almighty God has created for you. Think that good, believe that good, work for that good.

LIFE LIFTER: *Trust in God's promises and commandments, Christ's whole message of love and salvation. Believe these promises, live upon them, and you shall have peace and assurance, even if the world is full of trouble. Through faith in Him the world may also be full of the overcoming of trouble. So, regardless of difficulty, be of good cheer for victory is yours through Him.*

| DAY **10** | *But Jesus beheld them, and said unto them, With men this is impossible; but with God all things are possible.* |

MATTHEW 19:26

One of the most dynamic thoughts ever uttered in the history of mankind is found in Matthew 19:26, where it says: "God can do anything."

Ours is no little faith. If a person will receive this thought, believe it and incorporate it in one's consciousness, there is a power, a vitality and a force never felt before. Do you imagine that Christianity would have survived had it been based on little innocuous truths? The Christian faith was hewn out of truth itself. And it tells us: "God can do anything."

With man lots of things are impossible, but not with God. You should hold to this truth if you want to live a life that is filled with power.

PRAYER: *Our Heavenly Father, we thank You for what You have put into us. If we have hidden it deep within some recess, afraid to let it out, touch us now with Your releasing power and let us be free of ourselves, that we may have consciousness of our own inherent worth and greatness and that we may dare to live on the highest level, knowing that we will be sustained in this and strengthened, because the Lord is the strength of our lives, and in this will we be confident. Through Jesus Christ, our Lord. Amen.*

DAY 11

Favor is deceitful, and beauty is vain: but a woman that feareth the Lord, she shall be praised. PROVERBS 31:30

I once met a lady who lives in Mississippi who said, "I thought my husband would provide for me so that when he died I wouldn't worry. But his estate was eaten up, and I've got to go to work or go on relief."

I didn't know what to suggest. So I prayed, "Lord, give us an insight for Miss Lou." At the end of the prayer I hit on it. I asked, "Can you make candy?"

"Now that is something I can do," she answered.

"You go home," I said, "and make me a pound of it. Send it to me."

Actually she sent me a two-pound box and it was marvelous candy. So I wrote her saying, "Get busy merchandising that candy."

If you go to Edwards, Mississippi, you will find a shop there called "The Sweetest Spot." Miss Lou found that by thinking creatively she could change her life. And by serving others, she became a great influence for good in the area where she lives.

PRAYER: *Our Heavenly Father, we ask Your blessing upon all people, that the hearts of Your children may be filled with the glory of enthusiasm and that they may go out into the life if our time with faith and courage and an open mind to live gallantly and with power. Through Jesus Christ, our Lord. Amen.*

<table>
<tr><td>

DAY

12

</td><td>

Now faith is the substance of things hoped for, the evidence of things not seen. HEBREWS 11:1

</td></tr>
</table>

The Bible tells us that the great days of the Christian faith were when rugged believers preached to the people, giving them great Biblical examples of strong faith so that they would know that, if they would let God help them, they could overcome any difficulty they ever had to face.

We're dealing with something big. The Lord our God is with us to help us if we let Him. And how do you let Him? It is very simple: you put everything in His hands, you surrender to Him, you take your problem whatever it is—and you say, "Lord, here it is. You tell me what to do with it. I'll do anything You say. I'm completely Yours." You let go and you let God. Then God either relieves you of the problem or He gives you the ability to handle it. In either case you have a victory.

LIFE LIFTER: *Perhaps today you have a problem which has baffled you. Try allowing God's Word to penetrate your mind and it will do some important things for you. It will make you understand that there is an answer to every problem, and that God is thinking along with you. It will bring to bear upon your problem that keen and sharp perception of wisdom called insight. If you put every problem in God's hands, ask Him to give you the right answer, believe that He is doing just that, and take the guidance that comes, your decisions will turn out right.*

<table>
<tr><td>DAY
13</td><td>*Then took Haman the apparel and the horse,
and arrayed Mordecai, and brought him on
horseback through the street of the city, and
proclaimed before him, Thus shall it be done*</td></tr>
</table>

unto the man whom the king delighteth to honor.

ESTHER 6:11

God in His wisdom isn't going to give you and me everything we want, because He knows what we need. I am reminded of Rabindranath Tagore, the great Indian mystic and poet, who said, "I have often been saved by God's hard refusals."

Not getting something you greatly desire isn't pleasant. It can be painful. It can be very bitter. But sometimes the greatest thing that ever happens to us is when God says, "No. I want it another way." Infantile people complain and say that God is cruel or that there is no God. Mature people, however, know that there is wisdom and sometimes an eternal kindness in God's refusals.

PRAYER: *There are many things about You, Lord, that we do not understand. Why shouldn't it be so? You are infinite and we are finite. Your mind is vast. But we shouldn't want a small god such as we've often made You in our imaginations. We want You as You are, a God so great that we can never begin to understand You, but can stretch our lives up against You and make ourselves greater. Amen.*

DAY **14**	*All things were made by him; and without him was not any thing made that was made. In him was life; and the life was the light of men.*

JOHN 1:3–4

Jesus was so vital that they said of Him, "Everything that was created received its life from him, and his life gave light to everyone." Light, fire, power.

Have you ever gotten excited about Christianity? Have you ever gotten excited about life itself? Are you ever thrilled by the mere fact that you are alive? It is a great thing to be alive. It means that you can feel, you can sense, you can dream, you can think, you can love, you can have relationships with other people. Yes, it's a great thing to be alive. But there are lots of people walking around who are only half-alive. Yet they can come alive. You can come alive right now, today. You can throw off all your darkness, your dullness, your dreariness, your negativism, and really live, if you open your mind and heart and receive Jesus.

LIFE LIFTER: *The Scriptures suggest how to obtain the values which make life rich and full with peace, quietness, material necessities, and right relationships: We are told to have God's righteousness or right-mindedness. Develop a right thought pattern. Right thinking, governed by intelligence, is positive not negative, unselfish not self-centered, creative not destructive, kindly not hateful. Employ these attitudes and everything that you need for the good life shall be multiplied for you.*

| DAY 15 | *And if his oblation be a sacrifice of peace offering, if he offer it of the herd; whether it be a male or female, he shall offer it without blemish before the Lord.* LEVITICUS 3:1 |

Not long ago I met a man whom I hadn't seen for a while. When I first knew this man he always seemed to be only half alive and he complained continually of not feeling well. At one time he had a partial nervous breakdown. When I saw him later I could hardly believe it was the same man. He had come alive.

His method consists of spending fifteen minutes every day filling his mind full of God. And how do you go about it? You think about God, you read or repeat to yourself Scripture statements about God, you talk to Him, you let Him bring you into a God-centered state of mind. Health and happiness are available to everyone. But they are gifts of God, for He is the source of health and happiness.

LIFE LIFTER: *Without a deep inner state of quietness, one becomes prey to tension, worry, and ill health. A song, a sunset, moonlight, the sea washing on a sandy shore, these administer a healing balm. But they lack the power to penetrate the inner recesses of the soul. When tense or restless, sit quietly and allow these words to pass unhindered through your thoughts: "It is good that a man should both hope and quietly wait for the salvation of the Lord" (Lamentations 3:26). Think of them spreading a healing balm throughout your mind.*

<table>
<tr><td>

DAY

16

</td><td>

And Moses built an altar, and called the name of it Jehovah-nissi　　EXODUS 17:15

</td></tr>
</table>

A woman tells this story of hope: "During the Depression, we had a terrible time. Only my married daughter's help—which she could ill afford— was keeping us alive. Things got to a point where I even thought of suicide as a way out. Then I thought, 'If I can depend on my daughter's love, why can't I depend on God's?' I got down on my knees, telling God I would leave everything in His hands. Then I prayed for those whose actions I had resented because they had injured us. And I arose from that prayer with joy in my heart.

"The next day my husband got temporary work. I went back to college to get my degree so I could teach. And it wasn't long before my husband had a permanent job and I became a regular teacher. We gradually paid off all our debts. When my husband was incapacitated we were able to retire on pension.

"My own strength was not enough, but when I admitted it to God and put myself in His care, His strength was made perfect in my weakness."

> PRAYER: *Our Heavenly Father, so touch us all today, we pray You, that we may turn to Jesus, Lord and Savior, risen Christ, with whom we may live now in dignity and greatness and with whom we may live eternally in joy and in life. This we ask through Jesus Christ, our Lord. Amen.*

DAY 17

And the Lord said unto Joshua, Be not afraid because of them: for tomorrow about this time will I deliver them up all slain before Israel: thou shalt hough their horses, and burn their chariots with fire.

JOSHUA 11:6

One of the worst things you can do is to permit a continuous trickle of worry across the mind, because like water it will ultimately dig a huge trench. Then every thought you think will be drained into this channel of fear and worry and come up tinctured with anxiety. You will be a person full of fear and worry.

The way to obliterate this is to start another stream. Let a stream of faith run across the mind and go deeper and deeper as you absorb faith thoughts into your consciousness—and after a while it will undercut the channel of fear and worry which will then fall into the channel of faith, and a great river of faith will surge through your mind so that every thought will come up bright and resplendent, optimistic and hopeful, and life will be good, very good. Cultivate a channel of faith to give you the deep security which you need.

PRAYER: *Our Heavenly Father, we thank You for the great power of Christ. We pray that it may come now, in this moment of time, into the mind and the body and the soul of each of us, that we may learn how to find real inner security and how to turn off worry. Through Jesus Christ, our Lord. Amen.*

| DAY **18** | *In those day the Lord began to cut Israel short: and Hazael smote them in all the coasts of Israel.* II KINGS 10:32 |

You may constantly think scarcity. I have observed that people who think scarcity tend in a strange way to manifest scarcity. The word scarcity is related to the word scarce. And there is only one letter difference between scarce and scare. It just could be that if you think scarcity you scare money and prosperity away. This is, as I say, a little harder to demonstrate than the other correlations between attitudes and outcomes, but you might consider trying it out. Instead of saying, "How difficult everything is for me; how poor I am," instead affirm how God is helping you, how blessed you are. Avoid manifesting scarcity by thinking scarcity thoughts.

By the same token, if in our minds we entertain thanksgiving we manifest blessings. The more thankfulness a person cultivates, the more, I do believe, he will open to himself the power flow, the vast wealth of heaven, and blessings will pour out upon him.

PRAYER: *Our Heavenly Father, You have put us into this world in the midst of troubles. You have also given us assurance that You are our refuge and our strength and our very present help in time of trouble. Therefore, by following Your guidance and by living with You, we can become experts in the handling of troubles. And for this we give thanks through Jesus Christ, our Lord. Amen.*

| DAY **19** | *And God heard their groaning, and God remembered his covenant with Abraham, with Isaac, and with Jacob.*   EXODUS 2:24 |

Some time ago I received a telephone call from a stranger who said, "I heard your talk tonight. I'm having a bad time. I know that my main problem is myself, but what I want to ask is, will you pray for me?"

"Of course," I said. "And I will do it right now." When I concluded the prayer, his reverent "Amen" echoed my own. After a moment he said, "Thanks a lot. I will get busy and follow through on that prayer."

When he had rung off I asked myself: Do I follow through on my prayers? How often have I prayed "gimme" kind of prayers or desperation kind of prayers or bewildered prayers with no results? Having prayed, do I believe God has heard? Do I leave it with Him? Or do I shut out answers by continuing to expect the worst? Do I try to do something about the thing myself? I think everyone could ask these same questions. When you pray do you follow through?

LIFE LIFTER: *In Bible times the shield was used to protect the heart; the helmet to protect the head. So we must protect our hearts and minds against negativism, pessimism, evil thoughts, hate. The mind must be kept clean. Take the sword of God's word, and put it to fight those enemies of the good life: wrong thinking and wrongdoing. Thus armed we can win in the battle of life.*

DAY 20

He that hath the Son hath life; and he that hath not the Son of God hath not life.

I JOHN 5:12

Jesus said "I came so that everyone would have life, and have it in it fullest" (John 10:10, CEV). Life. What is life? Life is vitality. It is excitement. It is enthusiasm. It is motion. And the Bible says, "His life gave life to everyone." Jesus was the most alive being who ever walked the earth. Even death couldn't crush Him. He said, "And because I live, you will live" (John 14:19, CEV). And that statement in I John 5:12 (above)—that is really tremendous, a ringing message to anybody who wants to live.

Christianity is an either/or business. It lays it on the line. Either you have it, or you don't have it. Christianity tells us that if you want to have life, real life, life so exciting that you can hardly stand it, so thrilling that you never can erase it, so glorious that you can never get over it, then have the life that is in the Son. If you don't have this, you're not really alive.

PRAYER: *Our Heavenly Father, we give You thanks for the greatness, the ruggedness, the power in Christianity. Bring us near, we pray, to Jesus, who frees us from defeat and fear and makes us strong so that we may indeed acquit ourselves. This we ask in His name. Amen.*

| DAY **21** | *Then I arose, and went forth into the plain: and, behold, the glory of the Lord stood there, as the glory which I saw by the river of Chebar: and I fell on my face.* EZEKIEL 3:23 |

How wonderful life would be if we could just hold on to mystical experiences with perpetual enthusiasm! And some people do—like a man I met who told me, "I hate to go to bed at night, I'm so afraid I will miss something. I can hardly wait to get up in the morning, I am so happy. Since I met Jesus Christ and surrendered my life to Him it just seems that He pours His power and glory into me every day. I am so wonderfully alive."

Are you alive? The Father wants to give you the kingdom, so that you will delight in life. How is that done? By transferring life to you. This is the greatest thing about the Christian religion. Jesus wants to give us abundant, overflowing life. Because He lived it, you and I can live it too, if we pay the price to get it.

PRAYER: *Our Heavenly Father, You brought every one of us into being. You endowed us with capacities which we so often fail to use. Free our minds, we pray, from tension, fear, and worry, hate and prejudice, and every other thing that inhibits our powers. Help us to live grandly and greatly and joyously and victoriously, and to serve You better all our lives. Through Jesus Christ, our Lord. Amen.*

DAY 22

Jesus Christ the same yesterday, and today, and for ever. HEBREWS 13:8

I was brought up on revival meetings, those of Billy Sunday and other evangelists. In every church every winter they had what were called "Protracted meetings." These strung out over many nights and the whole impact and effort was to win people to Christ and away from their evil and indifferent living.

While naturally I changed my approach because I was living in a modern age, I felt that the gospel preached in 1840, 1890 and 1940 is the same gospel that the American people need today. I believe that Jesus Christ, Lord and Savior, divine Son of God, who died on the cross for our redemption, is the chief message of the church in any age. Christianity is timeless.

The only figure in history who has no date is Jesus. Great statesmen arise, but they are a dim memory twenty years after they die. Their principles seem antique to the modern ear. Only Jesus is everlastingly modern. His gospel is as fresh as today's newspapers. That is why He lives while others fade into oblivion.

PRAYER: *Our Heavenly Father, we thank You for the simplicity of the gospel of Christ, the wonderful teachings which He gave us, that the way to live is to live with love and faith and trust, to care for people and to commit our lives to You, to let go and let You take over, so that the power may come to us. Through Jesus Christ, our Lord. Amen.*

| DAY **23** | *For thus saith the Lord God, the Holy One of Israel; In returning and rest shall ye be saved; in quietness and in confidence shall be your strength: and ye would not.* ISAIAH 30:15 |

Dwell on this tremendous thought from Isaiah: "I will make you strong if you quietly trust me." One of the basic, fundamental ingredients of the Christian religion is strength. Those who built Christianity knew how the onslaughts of circumstance, difficulty, pain, sorrow, opposition and resentment can break a human being down. But the prophets and apostles and, most of all, Jesus Himself built into the structure of our faith a power that can make us men and women who handle life majestically. Your job and mine is to handle life. if you don't handle life, it will handle you. So the issue is who handles what. You are created in the image of God. Go home and look in the mirror and tell yourself that through Him this strength can be yours.

LIFE LIFTER: *Philippians 4:13—"I can do all things through Christ which strengtheneth me"—is an antidote for every defeat feeling. If you feel discouraged, this statement will remind you that you do not need to depend upon your own strength entirely, but that Christ is with you and is now giving you all the help you need. As you continue this affirmation, you will actually experience Christ's help. You will find yourself meeting problems with new mental force. You will carry heavy burdens with ease. Your new "lifting" power will amaze you.*

| DAY 24 |

But the Lord said unto him, Go thy way: for he is a chosen vessel unto me, to bear my name before the Gentiles, and kings, and the children of Israel.   ACTS 9:15

I have a letter from a woman who told me that if I wished to share her story I could. Here is what she says.

"They tell me I have heart disease and only one year to live. I don't believe they always know, especially about us Irish Christians, who are made of pretty tough stuff! I have buried two sons. I've had nine operations and rheumatic fever, in addition to this heart disease. You're probably thinking, 'That poor woman!' But don't you dare. Save your pity for some poor soul who isn't tough-minded and optimistic.

"I'm forty-five years young and I'm going to live to be ninety if the Lord wills it. I've never been in need since I found the Lord. I'm proud that God has chosen me to bear these crosses, and grateful that He gave me a strong back to bear them.

"I'm happy. My friends tell me I'm a character. I'm never quite sure just how they mean it. But if I'm a character because I can laugh and enjoy God's wonderful world we live in, then I'm a character."

PRAYER: *Our Heavenly Father, what a wonderful faith this is! Set us free, Lord, that we may walk out into the clear light of life and live with You all the days of our lives. Through Jesus Christ, our Lord. Amen.*

| DAY 25 | *Be ye strong therefore, and let not your hands be weak: for your work shall be rewarded.*
II CHRONICLES 15:7 |

I believe the faithful following of these five rules will revolutionize the life of any person.

First: Be bold and mighty forces will come to your aid. The person who is afraid cuts himself off from the flow of power, but when you venture boldly, there comes a flow of power in response.

Second: Deny adverse conditions. Don't go around saying or thinking: "Conditions are against me." Face facts, but realize it often happens that a person is defeated not so much by the facts of a situation as by his negative interpretation of the facts. In every problem there is an inherent good. Believe that.

Third: Picture good outcomes. By envisioning good things you actually bring good influences into play, both within yourself and in the world around you.

Fourth: Pray for every person you meet with by name, that he or she may benefit from the dealings you have with him or her.

Fifth: Practice Christian love toward everybody.

PRAYER: *Our Heavenly Father, we give You thanks for the greatness, the ruggedness, the power in Christianity. Bring us near, we pray, to Jesus, who frees us from defeat and fear and makes us strong. This we ask in His name. Amen.*

DAY
26

The Lord God is my strength, and he will make my feet like hinds' feet, and he will make me to walk upon mine high places. To the chief singer on my stringed instruments.

HABAKKUK 3:19

When you have experienced a defeat, you should promptly make a new endeavor. Otherwise you'll get the idea that life's too much for you and will keep defeating you. When you experience a defeat, take it to Jesus and say, "Lord, I messed this one up badly."

He'll say to you, "Just take more of Me into your heart and into your life."

That's the message which poor, defeated humanity needs to hear and heed. You cannot handle everything with just your own strength. But with Jesus Christ we become "more than conquerors." God will not let us be tempted beyond our strength, which means we shall be equal to any circumstances or conditions we may encounter. And if we stay in contact with Jesus Christ, we continue to receive this power.

PRAYER: *Our Heavenly Father, we rejoice in Your strength. We know it can happen in the lives of all Your children. We pray that everyone who is defeated by a condition, a situation, a personal relationship or anything else may experience the magic of a positive mental attitude and of the transformed mind. Through Jesus Christ, our Lord. Amen.*

DAY **27**	*Let the priests take it to them, every man of his acquaintance: and let them repair the breaches of the house, wheresoever any breach shall be found.* II KINGS 12:5

A couple consulted a minister in California and said, "We don't understand why we have money trouble all the time. You talk about the boundless generosity of God, but we never see anything of it." And they asked, "Will you pray for us?"

The minister gave them a strange task. "Tomorrow I want you to go to the beach. See if you can calculate how many grains of sand the Lord made. When you get tired of considering the sand, walk through the park and count all the leaves on the trees."

"I want you to realize," the minister told them, "that this God who has put all the sand on the beach and all the leaves on the trees is trying to put blessings into your life. But you're closed. Your belief is too little."

The couple went and talked it over with God. And they began to reappraise their lives. They started an enterprise that brought new values and prosperity into their lives. They learned to believe big, pray big, think big, and built themselves a full, rich, satisfying life.

PRAYER: *Our Heavenly Father, we thank You for the marvelous blessings that Jesus Christ gives to us: continuing vitality, vigor, enthusiasm, dedication and energy of body, mind and soul. Through Jesus Christ, our Lord. Amen.*

DAY **28**

And the Lord said unto him, Who hath made man's mouth? or who maketh the dumb, or deaf, or the seeing, or the blind? have I not the Lord?

EXODUS 4:11

God will help you if you let Him. Even God, with all His power, cannot help you unless you will allow Him to do so, for He has made man a free agent, with power of choice. But one of the greatest of all facts is that God is ever ready to help you with whatever difficulty you may have, however great it may be. With His help you will either solve your problem, overcome your difficulty, or learn to live with it and get along with it.

Take any sizable group of people and you can find the whole range of human problems represented to one degree or another among them. There will be people who are very sad, laboring under a weight of grief; there will be people who are very discouraged, for whom things haven't gone well, who have encountered much resistance and to whom life seems very hard. But God will help them all if they will let Him.

PRAYER: *Our Heavenly Father, we thank You for the problems and difficulties of this life. We mean this prayer, Lord. It is sometimes a hard prayer to pray. But we know it is a proper prayer, for at the heart of problems and difficulties lies the bright and glorious good You have prepared for those whom You love. For this we give You thanks in the name of Jesus Christ, our Lord. Amen.*

DAY **29**	*Look unto me, and be ye saved, all the ends of the earth: for I am God, and there is none else.* ISAIAH 45:22

Once in Miami Beach I spoke to a large audience of businessmen. Among those present was a man named Ford Philpot, who was one of the greatest demonstrations of power I have ever encountered. Ford was a young man with all kinds of personality, but he became an alcoholic. And in the grip of that complicated disease he sank lower and lower. He was expelled from school and spent all his time in bars.

Everybody—family, friends, doctors, everybody—had tried to help him with no success. Then one night he unaccountably decided to reach for a power that could save him. Later the same night he knelt in prayer with a group of dedicated men, and by midnight was so completely delivered from his old weakness that it never again controlled him. He became a minister who helped and inspired many other human beings.

PRAYER: *Our Heavenly Father, You have put into us all a very great potential that we have often inhibited by the error which we have built up in us by thought, word, and deed. Help us to open ourselves so completely to the truth that the error may be flushed out and truth may prevail, so that walking uprightly, with head and heart in harmony with Almighty God, we may enter into richness of life. Through Jesus Christ, our Lord. Amen.*

MARCH

DAY 1

But there came a man of God to him, saying, O king, let not the army of Israel go with thee; for the Lord is not with Israel, to wit, with all the children of Ephraim. But if thou wilt go, do it, be strong for the battle: God shall make thee fall before the enemy: for God hath power to help, and to cast down.   II CHRONICLES 25: 7–8

You don't have to stand up to your problem alone, for God is with you. And this is really the great thing. If we had to stand up to tough problems alone, life would be very bitter. In the end, it would be a losing battle, for man isn't that big. The greatest among us is small in the presence of some problems of human life. So we should forever be mindful, and grateful, that we are not alone.

The secret, then, is to stand up to your problem by taking it and doing all you can about it. Then put it in God's hands, turning it over to Him. Turn away from the problem and turn to God. When you pick the problem up again, it will be the way He wants it. And that means it will be right. And you'll get your answer. It may be a "no," it may be a "wait a while," it may be a "yes," but it will be the right answer.

> **LIFE LIFTER:** *If we do our part, and have faith, God will see that all of our real needs are supplied. How the spirit rises when one develops confidence that he will be cared for, that all will be well, that the future is bright with promise.*

| DAY **2** | *They are all plain to him that understandeth, and right to them that find knowledge.* |

PROVERBS 8:9

If you are troubled, spend half an hour doing nothing but reading the Bible. Open to the Psalms, Proverbs, or to Matthew, Mark, Luke or John. Let God give you quietness. Then, whatever anybody may be doing to trouble you, or what you have been doing to trouble yourself, it can trouble you no longer; you are above it.

A man who heard me preach a number of times said to me, "You know? You only have one sermon—just one message. You come at it a little differently each time, but it's the same message."

"What is it?" I asked.

"It is this," he replied. "Whatever the problem, surrender your life into the hands of Jesus Christ."

"I'll settle for that," I said. "It is the answer."

We have minds and we are supposed to use them. And heaven help us if we don't. God does help those who help themselves; but there are problems we cannot handle without a greater wisdom and power than our own.

PRAYER: *Our Heavenly Father, You offer such big things to such little people. Help us to be big enough to take the big things You offer and live the big life You intend for us. Help us to know by Your grace that we can do anything with ourselves. Through Jesus Christ, our Lord. Amen.*

DAY 3

And he walked in all the ways of Asa his father; he turned not aside from it, doing that which was right in the eyes of the Lord: nevertheless, the high places were not taken away; for the people offered and burnt incense yet in the high places.

I KINGS 22:43

I was on friendly terms with Jesse L. Lasky, a pioneer of the motion picture industry and a wonderful spiritually minded man. One evening at his home, he said to me, "Before dinner I want you to spend fifteen minutes in my silence room." I was intrigued, of course. He took me to a room fitted out as a place to practice creative silence. On the table there was a Bible; also a stack of cards on which he had written texts from the Bible which had to do with silence and peace.

"I will leave you here," he said, "to commune with God's silence." He was gone for fifteen minutes. It was a delightful, renewing experience.

Are you aware of inner silence even now? You can spend this very moment in the temple of silence, acquainting yourself with Him and becoming peaceful. So practice creative silence.

PRAYER: *Our Heavenly Father, grant that each of us may experience Your peace that passes all under-standing and by means of it gain control over situations and over ourselves and live effectively and with joy. Through Jesus Christ, our Lord. Amen.*

| DAY 4 |

For I am with thee, saith the Lord, to save thee: though I make a full end of all nations whither I have scattered thee, yet will I not make a full end of thee: but I will correct thee in measure, and will not leave thee altogether unpunished.

JEREMIAH 30:11

A physician told me that as a boy he was full of fear, anxiety, nervous tension, and apprehension. Perhaps because of his own emotional frailty, he decided that he wanted to help the sick find health again. But when he began his practice, he was stymied. There was no health in him; how could he give health to other people?

He went to one of his old professors and poured out his problem. The older doctor said, "Son, there is only one Physician who can heal you and His name is Jesus Christ. You put your life in His hands and He will heal you of your fears."

The young doctor found healing in the words of the Bible. They sank into his consciousness and into his subconscious mind, and drove out the disease of fear. He became a strong man of faith and a great healer.

PRAYER: *Our Heavenly Father, we thank You for the simple truth that as we forget the past, seek forgiveness for our errors, and live with a consciousness of the greatness of life, we may trust tomorrow, for You are there and, if we are there with You, then tomorrow will be wonderful. For this we give hearty thanks. Through Jesus Christ, our Lord. Amen.*

<table>
<tr><td>DAY
5</td><td>The law of the Lord is perfect, converting the soul: the testimony of the Lord is sure, making wise the simple.
PSALM 19:7</td></tr>
</table>

Things go well when you get in tune with the Lord. Get on His side. Live His way. We can, I believe, take comfort in what may be called the law of opposites. This whole world is filled with opposites. There is up and its opposite, down. There is light and its opposite, dark. There is wet and its opposite, dry. There is heat and its opposite, cold. There is a problem and there is its opposite, a solution.

But the question is: How do you find this answer to every problem? Psalm 19:7 states: "The law of the Lord is perfect; it gives us new life. His teachings last forever, and they give wisdom to ordinary people." There you have it in a capsule. You overcome your difficulties, you solve your problems, by understanding in depth, which you obtain from the precepts of God.

LIFE LIFTER: *This is how to do an "impossible" thing. Size up your problem, pray about it, do all you can about it. If it seems impossible, don't give up, but affirm, "The things that are impossible with humans are possible with God." Keep relaxed. Don't worry. Avoid getting panicky. Never think "This can't be done." Declare: "It can be done, it is being done because God is doing it through me." Affirm the process is in operation. The final outcome may not be entirely what you now desire. But, handled in this manner, the solution will be what God wants it to be.*

<table>
<tr><td>DAY
6</td><td>And they set the altar upon his bases; for fear was upon them because of the people of those countries: and they offered burnt offerings thereon unto the Lord, even burnt offerings</td></tr>
</table>

morning and evening.　　　　　　　　　　　EZRA 3:3

There are plenty of people who experience fear continually without even having any notion what it is they are afraid of. Now, what can you do about the problem of fear? You can do either one of two things. One is to give in to your fears and permit yourself to be dominated by them all your life. And many people do just that. They carry their fears with them all the days of their lives, suffering misery and inner conflict until the very end of their days. And that is a piteous thing.

The other course—the only alternative—is to rise up in the full stature of your manhood or womanhood and, with all the help of Almighty God and of the Lord Jesus Christ, dominate your fears. If you do that, you will have gained a victory that will make you worthy of eternal life. And that kind of greatness is potential in every human being.

PRAYER: *Our Heavenly Father, we give You thanks that we are not alone in this world, but that You are always here and at any time we may put out our hand in the darkness or in the cold and feel the warm, reassuring touch of the Greatest Friend any of us ever had, our Lord and Savior Jesus Christ. In this will we be confident. In His name. Amen.*

<table>
<tr><td>DAY
7</td><td>Give therefore thy servant an understanding
heart to judge thy people, that I may discern
between good and bad: for who is able to
judge this thy so great a people? I KINGS 3:9</td></tr>
</table>

A man once gave me an insight to overcoming problems. "My mother," he told me, "used to say, 'When you have a problem and you've worked as hard as you can at it and still haven't solved it, the thing to do is just walk away and think about God. But don't talk to God about the problem. Tell Him how much you love Him, thank Him for all He has done for you, tell Him you want to be His faithful follower. Have fellowship with God and with Jesus.'"

How wise that woman was! An irreligious person might advise you to put the problem aside and play a game of golf. But there is a vast difference between playing a game of golf and talking to Jesus—Jesus lifts you way up, so that when you go back to the problem you have grown and the problem shrinks. Then prayerfully you can break it open and find the answer.

PRAYER: *Our Heavenly Father, we are very grateful that there has never been a time when You have departed from us. We admit that there have been many times when we have departed from You. But even this You forgive, and when we came back humble and contrite You take us once again to Yourself. You are wonderful, O Lord. Amen.*

<table>
<tr><td>

DAY

8
</td><td>

In the body of his flesh through death, to present you holy and unblameable and unreproveable in his sight: If ye continue in the faith grounded and settled, and be not
</td></tr>
</table>

moved away from the hope of the gospel, which ye have heard, and which was preached to every creature which is under heaven; whereof I Paul am made a minister.

COLOSSIANS 1:22–23

A friend of mine reads the Bible every morning. He always reads something from Paul, he says, because he thinks Paul has the most acute and profound mind he knows. He says, "I like to sharpen my mind on the great keen mind of Paul."

I did this myself once, and it did me good. I was in my study working on a sermon. It was raining and the rain was beating against the windowpane. I love the sound of the rain, and because I wasn't getting anywhere with the sermon, I turned around and watched the rain. Suddenly I asked myself: "Why are you preaching sermons?" I thought it over and I came to an answer. It is because I believe with all my heart in the immense power of Jesus Christ to change the life of the entire world. This is my greatest enthusiasm.

> **LIFE LIFTER:** *You can possess within yourself all the power you will ever need in life. The essence of the formula is surrender to God's will and Christ's way. When this is sincerely done, you will in turn receive power.*

<table>
<tr><td>

DAY

9

</td><td>

And Naomi said unto her daughter-in-law, Blessed be he of the Lord, who hath not left off his kindness to the living and to the dead. And Naomi said unto her, The man is near of kin

</td></tr>
</table>

unto us, one of our next kinsmen.   RUTH 2:20

I recall the wisdom of the man from whom I first heard of the law of supply. He went through fire and flood and depression and panic and made out all right. He used to say, "The law of supply never failed me once."

"What is this law of supply?" I asked him. I had never heard of it in the highfalutin schools I went to.

"It is an inclination of the universe to sustain you if you're in harmony with the flow of rightness. And you get in harmony with it by letting your thoughts open up big. Let the soul flower out," he said. "Speak big, pray big, ask big, give big, believe big, love big, and bigness will flow to you."

Now this doesn't mean that by being in harmony with the law of supply that you will necessarily get rich. God isn't going to line your pockets, but He will give you all you need if you are in harmony with His will, loving and serving others and forgetting yourself—in other words, if your soul gets big.

LIFE LIFTER: *Develop and maintain an attitude of faith and expectancy—dreaming, believing, praying, working. Fill your mind with the positive power of spiritual expectancy, and God and His good will flow toward you.*

| DAY 10 | *Now when he had left speaking, he said unto Simon, Launch out into the deep, and let down your nets for a draught.* LUKE 5:4 |

I was reading in the Gospel of Luke about the time when Jesus told his disciples to launch out into deep water if they wanted to get any fish. It's a message to anyone who wants to pack meaning into his life. Get away from yourself. Don't be tied up with yourself. Don't hang on to yourself. "Row…into the deep water and let your nets down…"—and you'll pull up more values than you could imagine. One of the ways you launch out into the deep is to embrace the profound principle that abiding, joyous life comes only through giving. The people who throw themselves into some great social issue, forgetting themselves, being willing to suffer hurt if necessary for their convictions and ideals, become the happiest people in the world because they are growing bigger. When you give, you get bigger, you grow, your personality expands. You become a far greater individual by giving yourself, your time, your money.

LIFE LIFTER: *It never fails. Give God His biblical share (at least one-tenth) and He will give you far more than your share. Indeed, He will overwhelm you with His blessings. Tithing is the stimulator of prosperity in all aspects of life, material and spiritual.*

| DAY 11 | *Concerning this house which thou art in building, if thou wilt walk in my statutes, and execute my judgments, and keep all my commandments to walk in them; then will I* |

perform my word with thee, which I spake unto David thy father: And I will dwell among the children of Israel, and will not forsake my people Israel.   I KINGS 6:12–13

Many years ago I knew the president of a great corporation who told me, "For years I have made decisions on problems and made them fast. Now I live in fear of making decisions. You're a spiritual doctor. Can you give me a prescription to cure me of this?"

So I gave him this prescription: "When you get up in the morning, say, 'Thank You, Lord, for giving me a good night's sleep. Now I'm going to go to work. And each time I have to make a decision I'm going to talk with You about it. I can't go wrong with You helping me.' Before you go to sleep say, 'Thank You, Lord, for all the decisions we made today.'"

He assured me he would follow the prescription. And he did. He became a strong, effective man again having discovered that if you seek the Lord He will hear you and will deliver you from all your fears.

> PRAYER: *Our Heavenly Father, help us to know that the answer to the upset which agitates our lives consists in saying "Yes" to You. For this we give You thanks. Through Jesus Christ, our Lord. Amen.*

| DAY 12 | *For verily I say unto you, That whosoever shall say unto this mountain, Be thou removed, and be thou cast into the sea; and shall not doubt in his heart, but shall believe* |

that those things which he saith shall come to pass; he shall have whatsoever he saith. Therefore I say unto you, What things soever ye desire, when ye pray, believe that ye receive them, and ye shall have them. MARK 11: 23–24

Confidence is a vital ingredient of living. The Bible regards confidence—faith in God—as necessary to our well-being. One day you may notice a huge obstacle in your pathway. You can't get around it and you don't know what to do about it. That is your mountain. It has you licked. But you can knock it down if you have faith, if you believe.

You can overcome gigantic obstacles and have a life more wonderful than you ever imagined if you recondition your mind. Learn to reject small thinking. Never admit a negative thought. Never give utterance to defeatist fears. Talk it up, think it up, believe it up! As you think big, big results will come.

> **PRAYER:** *Our Heavenly Father, we thank You for showing us that You are big; for sending a big Savior to this world to make big people of us; for giving us big opportunities and the capacity for big faith, big love, big hope, big life. Thank You, Lord. Help us to take it and grow with it. Through Jesus Christ, our Lord. Amen.*

<table>
<tr><td>DAY
13</td><td>*And Moses spake before the Lord, saying, Behold, the children of Israel have not hearkened unto me; how then shall Pharaoh hear me, who am of uncircumcised lips?*</td></tr>
</table>

EXODUS 6:12

After a speech one evening a young man told me his story: "I was a salesman, but I couldn't sell," he said in a booming voice. "I knew the trouble was that I had clamps on me of shyness and self-doubt. These things held me tight and I couldn't get free. I went to my pastor and he said, 'Bill, turn to Jesus and ask Him to free you of these things. If you give your life to the Lord, He will give Himself to you.'

"So," Bill said, "I did and those clamps fell away and I was able to sell. But I realized that the big thing that had happened was that I was free inside. It was as if I had moved out of a little cell into the big wide world."

The man's face glowed. People who had stood listening had misty eyes, for they were seeing one of the greatest things in the world: a man who had been set free by the power of Jesus Christ.

PRAYER: *Our Heavenly Father, help us turn from disorganization of mind and emotion into the healing quietness of Your presence and, feeling Your quieting hand on our hot and fevered lives, may hereafter keep our minds on You that we may live in peace, masters of the tensions of life. This we ask through Jesus Christ, our Lord. Amen.*

| DAY **14** | *Call unto me, and I will answer thee, and show thee great and mighty things, which thou knowest not.* JEREMIAH 33:3 |

The Christian religion is far greater than anyone realizes. It tells weak people they can become strong. It tells defeated people they can become victorious. It tells unhappy, mixed-up people they can become organized. It teaches that we can become great persons. There is nothing else like it in the whole wide world.

Listen to just this one statement from Jeremiah: "Ask me, and I will tell you things that you don't know and can't find out." Call upon God, it says, and He will answer; He will show you tremendous things. And yet we make something small and indifferent out of our religion.

There is a very profound law of human nature which says that we become to a very large degree what we think. If you think little and believe little and act little, the results are likely to be little. If, on the other hand, you think big, believe big, act big, the results are very likely to equate with bigness.

PRAYER: *Our Heavenly Father, we ask You to bless us and give us that insight and that greatness of spirit by which we can stand up to life's problems. We give You thanks. Through Jesus Christ, our Lord. Amen.*

DAY **15**	*And the Lord spake unto Moses, saying, Speak unto all the congregation of the children of Israel, and say unto them, Ye shall be holy: for I the Lord your God am holy.*

LEVITICUS 19:1–2

Think what might be accomplished in the United States if only a few of the best young people among us would have the revolutionary spirit their forefathers had and would determine, "This great fair land shall not be destroyed. We'll make it clean, so that high leadership for the future may be certain and sure."

"Well," you may think, "I'm not a young person." Maybe not; but if all the men and women in this country who profess belief in God would live clean lives and would set those lives against the decay of our time, they would be contributing to a moral revolution. I believe the time has come for greatness. That is what built this country's splendor, power and prestige. That is the only force that can hold its future secure. So get into the fight against evil. "Some people accepted Him and put their faith in Him so He gave them the right to be the children of God." That's the difference between a little life and a tremendous life.

> PRAYER: *Our Heavenly Father, help us to know that Jesus walks the thronging streets of our world. Help us to be true to Him and to follow Him to remake this world according to Your will. Through Jesus Christ, our Lord. Amen.*

<table>
<tr><td>DAY
16</td><td>*Give glory to the Lord your God, before he cause darkness, and before your feet stumble upon the dark mountains, and, while ye look for light, he turn it into the shadow of death,*</td></tr>
</table>

and make it gross darkness. JEREMIAH 13:16

A man wandering outside on a moonless night decided to take a short cut through the cemetery. He stepped in some loose dirt and fell to the bottom of a newly dug grave. He tried to get climb out, but couldn't and decided to just take it easy until morning.

He was half asleep when a second man slipped in the dirt and also fell into the grave. He struggled to get out and couldn't. In the darkness, the first man said, "You'll never get out of this grave." But the second man did get out. Fear sent him over the top.

Faith, however, is an even greater force. A ball will roll downhill, a flower will come out of a seed, and faith will cancel out fear. So the secret we must all master, if our lives are to be as effective as we want them to be, is how to get our faith built up, how to protect it, how to live by it.

PRAYER: *Our Heavenly Father, we thank You for the great power of Christ. We pray that it may come now, in this moment, into the mind and the body and the soul of each of us, that we may learn how to find real inner security and how to turn off fear. Through Jesus Christ, our Lord. Amen.*

DAY 17

For I am the Lord your God: ye shall therefore sanctify yourselves, and ye shall be holy; for I am holy: neither shall ye defile yourselves with any manner of creeping thing that creepeth upon the earth. For I am the Lord that bringeth you up out of the land of Egypt, to be your God: ye shall therefore be holy, for I am holy. LEVITICUS 11:44–45

You can't have a sound mind unless you have a clean mind. Any dirtiness in the mind will send out spiritual and intellectual disease and will create a pathological condition. There have probably been more worries and fears started and grown big by guilt than by any other thing. An unclean mind grows fear, anxiety, and conflict. Here again is where the Gospel comes in. By the grace of Jesus Christ the mind can be cleansed. And when it is cleansed it becomes sound once again.

So have a sound mind in which there is no guilt, in which there is statistical common sense, in which there is control of the spasm of emotions that grasp an obsessive idea. Do you see why Jesus Christ is called the Great Physician? He understands the intricacies of human nature as nobody else does. And in His touch there is wondrous healing of fear, anxiety, and worry.

PRAYER: *Our Heavenly Father, help us to give our minds a new mental and spiritual guide living on the great teachings of Jesus which have the power to change thinking, to change everything. Amen.*

DAY
18

So that we may boldly say, The Lord is my helper, and I will not fear what man shall do unto me.　　　　HEBREWS 13:6

Fear is tenacious. It gets down into the intricacies of your consciousness. So, how can you get it out? The first step is to know that fear, like every other deficiency of human personality, is removable. God didn't give it to you. You took it onto yourself or it was put upon you by your environment. But it is removable.

Don't think that you've got to live with fear. Don't imagine that because your father or your mother had it, or your grandfather had it, you've got to have it. You only have to have what you're willing to have. If you want to live with fear you can. But it is removable.

Once you know that it is removable, then comes the process of removing it. And this involves something which isn't very popular with this generation, but which this generation needs to relearn, namely: self-discipline. You can do anything you want to with yourself if you have what it takes to discipline yourself.

PRAYER: *Our Heavenly Father, we thank You that though there is fear in the world there is also faith and that faith is stronger than fear. Help us truly to receive faith into our minds and hearts and lives and be victorious over fear. Through Jesus Christ, our Lord. Amen.*

DAY 19	*And now come I to thee; and these things I speak in the world, that they might have my joy fulfilled in themselves.* JOHN 17:13

Would you like to have a sense of well-being? Would you like to be filled with energy, vitality, eagerness, enthusiasm, even excitement? That is a healthy person. How enthusiastic are you? How thrilled are you? How excited are you?

One January night, I looked out the window at midnight to see a glorious snowstorm. I became so excited that I rushed back to the bedroom where my wife was sound asleep and said, "Ruth, get out of that bed. Let's get dressed and take a walk in the snow!"

Don't get to the point where you do not thrill to feel blood surging through your system. Don't get so you cannot breathe pure cold air down into your lungs and feel sheer exhilaration. Don't become withdrawn. Live with vitality and energy and excitement.

The Bible is full of life. Life is a big word in this Book. And one of the things life includes is to have the blessings of health, to be a whole integrated, organized, enthusiastic human being.

> **PRAYER:** *Our Heavenly Father, we thank You for the simple, yet powerful laws that lie embedded in the New Testament, by which we can overcome our weaknesses, our defeats, our poverty, our failures, and live with greatness and in abundance. Through Jesus Christ, our Lord. Amen.*

| DAY **20** | *Be not afraid of their faces: for I am with thee to deliver thee, saith the Lord.* |

JEREMIAH 1:8

The Democratic convention that nominated Grover Cleveland for President declared, "We love him for the enemies he has made." During the campaign, advisers kept reminding Cleveland that, in order to be elected, he would have to carry New York state. When his campaigning brought him to New York City, he attended a dinner at which two bosses of the notorious Tammany Hall political machine were present. After dinner these men wanted to know, "What will you give us?" "I will not give you one single, solitary thing," Cleveland answered. The Tammany Hall bosses respected Cleveland's bluntness and integrity. They got behind him and helped him carry New York.

In a similar way, the presence of God helps us resist fear and intimidation. You are not alone in this great big universe. God is with you. You can stand in the presence of difficulties, pain, onslaughts, resistance, criticism, anything, and not be afraid. God is with you.

PRAYER: *Our Heavenly Father, we ask Your blessing upon us all. Help us to hold up a standard, fight the good fight, finish the course, keep the faith and know the deep joy that comes to those who win victories over their weaker selves and live in the freedom of cleanness and goodness. Through Jesus Christ, our Lord. Amen.*

<table>
<tr><td>DAY
21</td><td>*For the vision is yet for an appointed time, but at the end it shall speak, and not lie: though it tarry, wait for it; because it will surely come, it will not tarry.*
HABAKKUK 2:3</td></tr>
</table>

I've noticed that the non-enthusiast, the pessimist, has a remarkably high score for faulty judgment. For example, in 1806, William Pitt, one of the greatest statesmen in history, declared, "There is scarcely anything around us but ruin and despair." In 1852, the Duke of Wellington, on his deathbed, stated, "I thank God I shall be spared from seeing the consummation of ruin that is gathering about us in this world."

Well, friends, do these comments strike you as familiar? Some people spend their lives insisting that the world is going to pieces. But the world blunders along, striving for something nobler. And the world will attain it if it keeps enthusiasm working for it. Enthusiasm! It is a word that is built deeply into the victorious spirit of humans. Enthusiasm literally means "full of God." God will help you overcome all difficulties, all tragedies, all sorrows, all heartaches, all defeats, and will give victory.

LIFE LIFTER: *Faith, the greatest power in this world. Hope, the attitude of expectancy. Love, one of the greatest qualities of all—a heart of compassion. Let these three shine in your life, and your spirit will be uplifted always.*

DAY 22	*But the hand of the Lord was heavy upon them of Ashdod, and he destroyed them, and smote them with emerods, even Ashdod and the coasts thereof.* I SAMUEL 5:6

There is no power in the world equal to spiritual power. I really mean that. Some people think atomic power is the greatest power in the world. Well, it is certainly an enormous, explosive power—there is no getting around that. A terrible power. But call to mind the sight of spring sunshine streaming through a window. There is more power there than there is in atomic energy, because within a period of a few weeks the earth awakens to that power and soon grass and flowers cover the earth, powered by something that makes no noise. That is more than atomic power can do. Just think about it. Don't judge power by the noise it makes. Judge it by the results it achieves.

LIFE LIFTER: *Re-slant your thoughts for happier living. Picture yourself dropping out every destructive thought, every fear, every inferiority feeling. Visualize your mind as completely empty. Then fill it with thoughts of God, and of Christ, thoughts about every good and pleasant thing. Practice this new habit twice every day, morning and evening, to counteract the negative habit of allowing unhappy things to occupy your mind. In due course, unhappy thoughts will not feel at home in your mind and happy thoughts will transform you.*

| DAY **23** | *For I am not ashamed of the gospel of Christ: for it is the power of God unto salvation to every one that believeth; to the Jew first, and also to the Greek.* ROMANS 1:16 |

I think one of the most heroic episodes in the human story is Paul standing at the gates of the Eternal City with a smile on his lips. Probably he threw back his shoulders as he said to mighty Rome, "I, not you, have the lasting power." Rome, the city of the Caesars, was for its time the personification of earthly power. Nobody could take it; but Paul did. Three centuries after he passed through its gates, the Emperor Constantine declared the new faith of Christianity the religion of the Roman empire. Multitudes were baptized into the faith called by the name of the lowly Nazarene.

Paul declared in a sentence that shall live as long as life lasts: "I am proud of the good news! It is God's powerful way of saving all the people who have faith, whether they are Jews or Gentiles." So won't you believe, really believe? If you have never given your heart to Christ, never allowed Christianity in depth to take root in your heart, I beseech you to do so now.

PRAYER: *Our Heavenly Father, we thank You for the great truth that Jesus is full of life and that as we come to Him He touches us and we become full of life. We thank You. Through Jesus Christ, our Lord. Amen.*

> **DAY 24**
>
> *And an angel of the Lord came up from Gilgal to Bochim, and said, I made you to go up out of Egypt, and have brought you unto the land which I sware unto your fathers; and I said, I will never break my covenant with you.* JUDGES 2:1

In 1907, Frank Bettger was playing baseball for Johnstown, Pennsylvania. Suddenly one day the manager fired him because he was too lazy. He said, "Whatever you do next, for heaven's sake put some enthusiasm into your work."

Bettger took the first job he could get, playing in a fourth-class league. He decided to begin acting enthusiastic and this had an interesting result. An old ballplayer perceived that this boy had possibilities and persuaded New Haven, Connecticut, to give him a try. "From the minute I appeared on the field," Bettger would say, "I acted like a man electrified."

The next day the newspaper said, "This new player is a barrel of enthusiasm." They nicknamed him "Pep" Bettger. From there he went on to big league baseball, playing third base for the St. Louis Cardinals.

PRAYER: *Our Heavenly Father, we thank You for this thing we call enthusiasm. Help us to try enthusiasm, that we may help elevate the whole world into new beauty, new love, new righteousness. Through Jesus Christ, our Lord. Amen.*

DAY 25

And when Pharaoh drew nigh, the children of Israel lifted up their eyes, and, behold, the Egyptians marched after them; and they were sore afraid: and the children of Israel cried out unto the Lord.
EXODUS 14:10

We modern, civilized people live in a fear-ridden world. What things are we afraid of? We are afraid of money problems, of the boss, of the job; we are afraid of other people; we are afraid of ourselves—afraid that we will not have what it takes to do what we ought to do. Children are afraid of their parents and, heaven help us, parents today are oftentimes afraid of their children. There is a veritable plague of fears concerning health. We are afraid of cancer; of viruses; of being awakened in the middle of the night and having to be hurried off to the hospital.

As you go about your day, say to yourself, "I am strong in the Lord. I am not afraid. 'God's Spirit doesn't make cowards of us. The Spirit gives us power, love, and self-control.'"

PRAYER: *Our Heavenly Father, we are all pilgrims on the pathway of the years. Life on earth is insecure, uncertain. But there is one thing that is sure: Jesus is the light of the world, and whoever follows Him will have the light of life and will never walk in the darkness. Help us to follow all the way. Through Jesus Christ, our Lord. Amen.*

DAY 26

Therefore turn thou to thy God: keep mercy and judgment, and wait on thy God continually.
HOSEA 12:6

Christians should never lack confidence. They, of all people, should be confident, for they are not like those who have no hope. Their lives are based upon something unshakable, something enduring, something completely secure—Almighty God, the Father of our Lord Jesus Christ, and on our Savior Himself. Therefore, if you feel weak, defeated, and insecure, I call upon you to return to Jesus Christ and build Him into the center of your life. Then you will never be lacking in sound confidence.

Remember this great affirmation from Romans 8:38–39: "I am sure that nothing can separate us from God's love—not life or death, not angels or spirits, not the present or the future, and not powers above or powers below. Nothing in all creation can separate us from God's love for us in Christ Jesus our Lord!"

 PRAYER: *Eternal Everlasting God, Creator and Sovereign of the universe, we ask You today to make better people of us, to take away our weaknesses, our mixed-up ideas, our superficiality, and help us to be bigger people in every way, not merely living from day to day enjoying the pleasures of this life, but making our lives useful. Accept our dedication for the days that lie ahead. Bless us all and help us to become new people—the kind of people who can make a whole world new. Through Jesus Christ, our Lord. Amen.*

DAY **27**	*Then Gideon built an altar there unto the Lord, and called it Jehovah-shalom: unto this day it is yet in Ophrah of the Abi-ezrites.*

JUDGES 6:24

Perhaps you've read the story about John Wesley, the famous religious leader, who came from England to Georgia in the eighteenth century, on a small ship. They encountered an enormous storm and Wesley, by his own admission later, was petrified.

There was a group of religious people on board, known as Moravians. They were calm and unaffected by the storm. When it was all over, Wesley asked the Moravian leader, "How did you manage to have such composure and such faith? How can I have faith?"

The man told him, "Act as though you have faith and by and by you will have faith."

So if you want to have enthusiasm, say to yourself, "The Lord God gave me enthusiasm. But this thing that God built into me has somehow escaped me. I know that potentially I have it. Therefore, I will act as though I were enthusiastic." By and by that which God gave you at birth will reassert itself.

LIFE LIFTER: *What is the secret of energized life? Christ is the answer. It is said of Him, "In him was life" (John 1:4). Fill your mind with Christ, fill your heart with Him, and inevitably energy, vitality, exuberance, delight, and eagerness will well up within you.*

DAY 28

And Samson called unto the Lord, and said, O Lord God, remember me, I pray thee, and strengthen me, I pray thee, only this once, O God, that I may be at once avenged of the Philistines for my two eyes. JUDGES 16:28

God helps you when you can't help yourself. Let's face it. You are strong and you can do lots of things, but there come times in life when you haven't got what it takes to do any more, you struggle with things and they won't come right and you face difficulties and you can't overcome them. Then, you should turn and say, "Dear God, why am I doing it wrong? Why can't I handle it? I turn it over to You. I put it in Your hands."

God can do for us what we can't do for ourselves. So the principle, as Paul said, is "when the battle is over, you will still be standing firm" (Ephesians 6:13). Having done everything you can do, then just put it in the hands of God and let it go. Of course, this is one of the most difficult things—to let something go. But let Him take it. Don't strain and strive and be under stress with it so much. Let it go! "Let go and let God."

LIFE LIFTER: *If your mind is filled with defeat thoughts, fear thoughts, or resentment thoughts, there can be no inner peace. Practice thinking about God, keep your mind "stayed," or fixed, not upon your troubles, but upon God. This may be difficult at first, for you are unused to spiritual concentration. Practice will make it easier.*

| DAY
29 |

*Seek ye the Lord, all ye meek of the earth,
which have wrought his judgment; seek
righteousness, seek meekness: it may be ye
shall be hid in the day of the Lord's anger.*

ZEPHANIAH 2:3

Christianity provides the techniques for becoming
strong in life. Christianity provides the formulas and
principles by which a person can really live with
certainty, conviction, and confidence in all the
circumstances of this life. One must have a simple,
humble and active faith in God, not as an inscrutable
idea, as the far-removed Creator of the universe, but as
a friend and Helper who is with you all the time.

The greatest truth in this world, in many respects,
is this: We are not alone. Whoever develops simply and
humbly this confidence in the intimate presence of
God will have one great shining word made real:
confidence.

LIFE LIFTER: *Uncertainties can be frightening, but
these reassuring words— "And, behold, I am with thee,
and will keep thee in all places whither thou goest, and will
bring thee again into this land; for I will not leave thee, until
I have done that which I have spoken to thee of" (Genesis
28:15)—show that God will be with you wherever you go or
in whatever situation you find yourself. You are never alone.
He will always see you through.*

<table>
<tr><td>DAY
30</td><td>*Deliver me, I pray thee, from the hand of my brother, from the hand of Esau: for I fear him, lest he will come and smite me, and the mother with the children.*   GENESIS 32:11</td></tr>
</table>

Sometimes when I stand in the pulpit and look out at the congregation, I could almost swear that everybody present is inwardly confident and calm. But I know that if you could gather together all the fears lurking behind all those impassive faces, you would have a great load of fear. I've often thought it would be wonderful if we could have two collections at each church service. The first would be the usual collection of money. Then I would ask everybody to come up and lay his fear on the altar and leave it there with God. Or maybe we could have the ushers go down the aisles and take up all the fears. Then I would say, "Let's stand and sing." Nobody would have to be told what to sing. Everybody would feel so free and released that the whole congregation would burst out singing "Praise God from whom all blessings flow" so joyously it would knock the church roof off.

PRAYER: *Our Heavenly Father, we give You thanks that from the practice of thankfulness comes a never-ending flow of blessings. We thank You, God, for Your blessed Son, who came to set us free, that we may enter into the heritage of this vital principle ever bursting into new and more wonderful forms. Through Jesus Christ, our Lord. Amen.*

| DAY **31** | *The Lord is my light and my salvation: whom shall I fear? the Lord is the strength of my life; of whom shall I be afraid?* PSALM 27:1 |

Those many, many thousands, even millions, of people for whom life is very hard are asking themselves, "How can I have what it takes?" Christianity has an answer to this problem. When the going is hard, when difficulties mount up, when the stresses are great, when the resistances are overwhelming, Christianity tells us that through faith in God and through commitment to Jesus Christ we have within us all that is needed to handle anything that confronts us. Psalm 27:1, for instance, shows that Christianity is the most rugged, vital, powerful faith ever to come among men. It says, "You, Lord, are the light that keeps me safe. I am not afraid of anyone. You protect me, and I have no fears." Does anybody have more strength than the Lord does? No. this faith is so toughening that we can develop what it takes to stand up to anything life may hand us.

PRAYER: *Our Heavenly Father, we thank You for all the days that have gone by, the hard ones as well as the easy ones. We ask You to forgive us for the wrong days we've lived. Help us to know now that we have this present day to deal with and that if we give ourselves to You wholeheartedly You will lead us by Your grace into increasingly wonderful and glorious tomorrows. And for this we give thanks, through Jesus Christ, our Lord. Amen.*

APRIL

<table>
<tr>
<td>DAY
1</td>
<td>And he said unto me, My grace is sufficient for thee: for my strength is made perfect in weakness. Most gladly therefore will I rather glory in my infirmities, that the power of</td>
</tr>
</table>

Christ may rest upon me.   II CORINTHIANS 12:9

Do you think Christianity would be such a dynamic force in the world if it were not an extraordinary adventure for human beings? Just let it into your life. If you really let it in, not just as an idea, but as a power, you will experience the sure cure for depressive feelings and for every other ailment of the human spirit. You really will. What I have told you is the truth.

We find the secret stated many times in the Bible. I find it, for example, in 2 Corinthians 12:9, in the wonderful words: "My kindness is all you need." That is to say, nothing can ever happen to you that you cannot meet with faith in Him, because His kindness is sufficient. The text goes on to say, "My power is strongest when you are weak." That is to say, if in your weakness, you will turn to God, His strength will be manifested through that weakness. You have the kindness of God, which provides everything you need.

PRAYER: *Our Heavenly Father, we thank You that there is great good in life. Help us never to lose faith in our human existence. Grant that we may know that there is wondrous opportunity awaiting us each day of our lives. For this we give thanks, through Jesus Christ, our Lord. Amen.*

| DAY 2 |

And at the evening sacrifice I arose up from my heaviness; and having rent my garment and my mantle, I fell upon my knees, and spread out my hands unto the Lord my God. And said, O my God, I am ashamed and blush to lift up my face to thee, my God: for our iniquities are increased over our head, and our trespass is grown up unto the heavens.   EZRA 9: 5–6

Do you ever consider your life? Does it need changing? Are you in control of yourself? Are you the master of yourself and of your life? Are you proud of the life you live or are you ashamed of yourself? Have you fallen for the notions of those who maintain that the morality of the Lord Jesus is outmoded? Do you listen to those who want to set Jesus aside? Why, time will set them aside. The ages don't set Him aside. "The sky and the earth will not last forever, but my words will (Mark 13:31).

What did He tell us? Be good, be honorable, be pure, be righteous, be loving. Well, have you lost the way? Many people do. But the wise person comes back to Christ and finds the way again.

PRAYER: *Our Heavenly Father, this is the message of the gospel of Jesus, who is so powerful when He gets into a human mind that He completely revitalizes that mind. He fills the mind with hope and eagerness and newness of life. We pray that this glorious experience may come to us all. Through Jesus Christ, our Lord. Amen.*

<table>
<tr><td>DAY
3</td><td>Thou hast made known to me the ways of life;
thou shalt make me full of joy with thy
countenance.   ACTS 2:28</td></tr>
</table>

Why are you depressed? Why are you discouraged? Isn't it because your mind is full of shadows, full of gloom, full of ghosts? Most fears are ghosts, and they build up in the mind. I venture that if I could open your mind I would cut through layer after layer of gloom and doubt and darkness. Maybe that is what we ought to do with our minds at very frequent intervals—open them up.

It's too bad, really, that we have such thick skulls. What the mind needs is ventilation to let out all the dark shadows. Naturally, you can't go around cutting holes in your head, but by the use of creative thought and prayer, you can ventilate your mind. How would you feel right now if every dark shadow and apprehension were lifted out of your mind? Why, let me tell you, people would meet you and they would say, "What in the world has come over you?" and you would be so excited and alive that you could scarcely contain yourself.

LIFE LIFTER: *God is the source of all energy. Through the pipeline of spiritual thought, He will pour new energy and strength into you. You will feel it physically, emotionally, and mentally. Imagine our Lord touching you. Affirm that He is sending into your being His illimitable strength. Repeat this Life Lifter. You will feel new strength.*

<table>
<tr><td>

DAY

4

</td><td>

Insomuch that they brought forth the sick into the streets, and laid them on beds and couches, that at the least the shadow of Peter passing by might overshadow some of them.

ACTS 5:15

</td></tr>
</table>

I follow the line of thought given to me by a gentleman I knew who was told by a competent doctor that he could not live more than a year. The doctor said, "There isn't anything specifically wrong with you and yet everything seems to be wrong with you. Your whole organism seems to be deteriorating and I believe it will give out within a year unless you get a tremendous infusion of faith into your mind. Affirm life. Say to yourself, 'I affirm that life is operating in me. Life is going through my nerves, my bloodstream, life is in me. I shall live by the life which is from God.'" The man took the doctor's advice and recovered from his illness.

Some cynic may say, "I don't believe in all that." Well, that is okay by me. The man I refer to is still alive and he does believe in it. Whatever works is legitimate, if it's in harmony with the will of God. In any case, many medical professionals today believe that the cultivation of harmony between the spirituality of man and his physical being is the future of healing.

PRAYER: *Our Heavenly Father, help us to let go of our straining and overpressing and gain peace and wisdom and power. Through Jesus Christ, our Lord. Amen.*

| DAY 5 |

And the king answered and said unto the man of God, Entreat now the face of the Lord thy God, and pray for me, that my hand may be restored me again. And the man of God besought the Lord, and the king's hand was restored him again, and became as it was before.   I KINGS 13:6

A woman telephoned me and said, "My problem is belligerence. Underneath I'm a friendly person. But I have a quarrelsomeness in me and a lot of irritability." Then she told me about a time on the highway when her belligerence had caused an accident. She said it was a miracle that nobody was hurt. "Talk about getting in your own way!" she said. "That sure is me!"

Christianity has an answer to this problem, many answers. If you accept the teachings and guidance and help which Jesus Christ offers you, you will be made free. You will be freed from your anger and hate, your depression, your discouragement, from whatever it is that gets you in your own way. You may be blocked by some defect, some failure in your personality. All can be healed by bringing the truth of God to bear upon it.

PRAYER: *Our Heavenly Father, we humbly give You thanks that there is no problem in this life that is greater than our Lord Jesus Christ, even the problem of ourselves. Grant that today we may so yield ourselves that the great healing power of Jesus may harmonize us inwardly and outwardly, giving us victory. Amen.*

DAY 6	*And the Levites were purified, and they washed their clothes; and Aaron offered them as an offering before the Lord; and Aaron made an atonement for them to cleanse them.*

NUMBERS 8:21

When you think of the world, how evil it seems to have become, how the old standards seem to have broken down, how mankind has reverted to the filth of Roman Empire days and wallows in it, remember also that there are beautiful mountains and rushing rivers and sounding seas and magnificent forests and that the stars come nightly to the sky and that the sun still goes down in the west in an effulgence of beauty.

Remember also that there are good people, people reaching for the good, people who will not let anything overwhelm them, people who see the surging fountains of the waters of life and who wash themselves in them and become clean and fresh and restored. Be glad that you have life. It is a precious thing. It is awfully good. Keep it good as long as you have it.

PRAYER: *Our Heavenly Father, we give You thanks for the great power that comes to us from You through Jesus Christ. We are children of God, and to us is given dominion and the power to overcome. Help us to enter truly into our inheritance and exercise our power of standing up creatively to any and every tough situation. Through Jesus Christ, our Lord. Amen.*

<table>
<tr><td>

DAY

7

</td><td>

But God commendeth his love toward us, in that, while we were yet sinners, Christ died for us.   ROMANS 5:8

</td></tr>
</table>

I went to Belfast to make three speeches. There is no central heating in Belfast. Every room has a fireplace or stove and its separate chimney. They are all smoking all the time and everything is grimy. It was raining and the smoke had no way to be lifted. Talk about smog in Los Angeles! You should see Belfast.

I stood at my window looking down at all the grimy houses. Then I saw something that changed the whole picture for me. As far as my eye could see there were dozens of tall, soaring, graceful steeples. Why would any architect ever build a church without a steeple? A steeple is a symbol of the upthrust of faith in the midst of the smoke and grime and the sin in human life, as if to say, "We believe in something higher, and this higher something must be visible to all the world." Jesus came to put the slender soaring steeple into our souls, and to get us to dedicate ourselves to the continuity of Christian idealism and faith.

LIFE LIFTER: *The pressure of modern living draws on our energies. But we have a renewal method. Every day, visualize yourself as "plugged" into the spiritual line. Affirm that God's re-creative energy is restoring strength to every part of your body, mind, and soul. This brings vitality and energy and constant replenishment into your being.*

> **DAY 8**

Having therefore these promises, dearly beloved, let us cleanse ourselves from all filthiness of the flesh and spirit, perfecting holiness in the fear of God.

II CORINTHIANS 7:1

We must be careful, friends, not to be always basking in what Jesus does for us without ever asking what we can do for Him. He is at the forefront of a struggle going on continuously in this world. Some people call it the struggle between good and evil. Others call it the struggle between freedom and slavery or the struggle between crass materialism and spiritual philosophy. It is a struggle between the weakness of humanity and the greatness of humanity.

And Jesus persistently holds before us ideals which we believe in, but only half accept and hardly follow. H.G. Wells said once, "This Galilean is too much for our small hearts." And there is a great deal of truth in that. But, unless we have His greatness to pull us up, we sink down.

LIFE LIFTER: *Through his pain, the dying thief heard the jeers of the crucifying crowd. Suddenly, he knew that this noble character on the cross was truly God's Son. He believed and he asked for forgiveness and admission to God's kingdom. No sooner was it asked than it was granted. So, too, when we believe and ask for pardon it will be granted. When our hearts accept Him, Christ admits us to paradise.*

<table>
<tr><td>

DAY

9

</td><td>

So they came up to Baal-perazim; and David smote them there. Then David said, God hath broken in upon mine enemies by mine hand like the breaking forth of waters: therefore

</td></tr>
</table>

they called the name of that place Baal-perazim.

I CHRONICLES 14:11

In the old days, Syracuse University had one of the greatest crews in the whole United States. Freshmen would watch them on the lake and they would go out for crew. The coach, Jim Ten Eyck, had them meet him at the football stadium. "You see all those aisles going up and down between the seats?" he would say. "I want you to walk up and down every one of those aisles." When they protested, he said, "You can't row until you've got good solid legs. You've got to have good lungs, lots of wind, deep diaphragms. You've got to be able to think, too. I'll teach you how to think later on."

A man who had rowed on one of Jim's crew's told me, "It paid off. I'll never forget the day when we pulled ahead of every other crew and won. We broke through into that power because we had practiced the work and the thinking and the discipline."

> **LIFE LIFTER:** *The negative principle accepts defeat. The positive principle goes for victory. Keep alert to the magic motivational word that forms an inspiring idea for you. It can reactivate and change you from indifferent to dynamic living.*

DAY
10

Then shall ye call upon me, and ye shall go and pray unto me, and I will hearken unto you. And ye shall seek me, and find me, when ye shall search for me with all your heart.

JEREMIAH 29:12–13

How deeply do we believe? Do we just believe superficially, without depth or commitment? In the book of Jeremiah we read, "You will turn back to me and ask for help, and I will answer your prayers. You will worship me with all your heart, and I will be with you." Nobody ever made anything great out of his life who didn't do it with his whole heart.

I remember talking years ago to a celebrity. I knew that she had had a great deal of trouble in her life. I asked, "How come you keep at it with such enthusiasm?"

"Why," she answered, "because I love it. I give my whole self to it." And she did; she threw everything she had into it. If with all your heart you give yourself to your business, to your children, to your marriage, to your future, to your hopes, you are going to come out with something that is lasting and strong.

PRAYER: *Our Heavenly Father, we know that we are flesh and blood and, as such, are weak. But we know that we are also mind, and mind is powerful; that we are spirit, and spirit is more powerful yet. Help us to live in dignity and in power. Through Jesus Christ, our Lord. Amen.*

<table>
<tr><td>DAY
11</td><td>*And Jesus answered and said unto him, Blessed art thou, Simon Barjona: for flesh and blood hath not revealed it unto thee, but my Father which is in heaven.*   MATTHEW 16:17</td></tr>
</table>

One time I crossed the Atlantic during hurricane season. I was lying in bed, seasick and feeling helpless as the ship pitched mercilessly. Suddenly, the door opened and a cheery fellow popped in. "What are you lying there for?" he said. "Let's go up on deck."

Well, that shamed me into it. We went up on deck and it was glorious. The waves were like horses with white manes thrown back. The wind drove streams of spray at us. My friend exclaimed, "Isn't this great?"

"It really is!" I agreed. I wasn't seasick at all after that. "You were lying there thinking error," observed my friend, "and up here you're thinking truth."

I realize there are some serious diseases that may be difficult to handle in this way. Yet, I have seen evidence that if you don't limit the power available to you, but allow it to move up and up, you can achieve tremendous results. Remember you are called to be a disciple and to take power and authority over all devils and cure diseases—within you as well as in others.

PRAYER: *Our Heavenly Father, we thank You that we have a Lord Who is master of death, disease, weakness and sin. Let His healing touch be upon any who need it. We give You praise, through Jesus Christ, our Lord. Amen.*

<table>
<tr><td>DAY
12</td><td>*Commit thy works unto the Lord, and thy thoughts shall be established.*</td></tr>
</table>

PROVERBS 16:3

How can a better tomorrow be brought to pass? The real wisdom that answers this question is found in the greatest book of wisdom ever written. The book of Proverbs, chapter 16, verse 3, contains this gem of truth: "Share your plans with the Lord, and you will succeed."

Now what does that mean? Dedicate to God everything you are doing. Place your activity, give all your works, into His hands. Your plans will work out; your hopes, your dreams, your ideals, your objectives, your goals will be realized. Your thoughts will be translated into actualities. This is an astonishing promise. This is worth its weight in gold. Commit what you are doing today and again what you are doing the next day, and again every day after that, into the hands of God. Let God have everything and yourself along with it.

PRAYER: *Our Heavenly Father, we give You thanks for this great benefit given to us by You whereby we may have the great power of faith working within us. And we thank You that the power of love is all around us, and that by the grace of Jesus Christ we can have sound, undistorted minds to grapple efficiently with any of the problems of life. Bless us all, that we may live truly unafraid. Through Jesus Christ, our Lord. Amen.*

DAY
13

When Jesus heard it, he saith unto them, They that are whole have no need of the physician, but they that are sick: I came not to call the righteous, but sinners to repentance.

MARK 2:17

A physician once told me that he was convinced that countless thousands of people are ill from what he called "dammed up anxiety." When anxiety can't find any outlet, it infects a person's whole psychology and his whole physical condition.

There is, however, healing in God's touch. This healing comes through Jesus Christ. If you want to get on top of your worries for good, you can do it best by surrendering your life to Jesus Christ, by identifying yourself with Him, and by giving your all to Him and having that most glorious of all experiences in this world, a spiritual experience. People afflicted with discouragement, weakness, sickness, sinfulness, hate, prejudice, fear have found a cure in the touch of Jesus.

Say, "Dear Lord Jesus, You take me, I take You." And in this partnership comes healing.

PRAYER: *Our Heavenly Father, we give thanks for Jesus Christ, without whom our lives would be poor indeed. Help us to be more faithful to Him throughout our lives, as He continues to heal the damaged areas in our natures, until we are made whole so that we can help to make the world whole too. Through Jesus Christ, our Lord. Amen.*

<table>
<tr><td>

DAY

14

</td><td>

Then cometh Jesus with them unto a place called Gethsemane, and saith unto the disciples, Sit ye here, while I go and pray yonder. MATTHEW 26:36

</td></tr>
</table>

Years ago I was asked to speak to a gathering of advertising and sales people, a very sophisticated and dynamic audience. I remarked to the man who was sitting on my right, that I felt power in the room. I thought it must be from the quality of those people.

"Oh," he said, "don't be so sure. I've been praying," he informed me, "for this meeting." This remark startled me; I hadn't expected to encounter such ardor.

The man then said to me, "I found two things in life that made everything different for me. The first—and it was the greatest single experience I ever had—was finding Jesus Christ and committing my life to Him. The second was that I learned to pray. These two things revolutionized my life."

This is what Jesus has been saying to us through the years. Really astute people make this discovery. Christ can change your life. Prayer can change your life.

LIFE LIFTER: *If you are not getting answers to your prayers, check whether you have any resentments in your mind. Spiritual power cannot pass through resentment. Every time you pray, add this phrase, "Lord, take from my thought all ill will, grudges, hates, jealousies." Practice casting these things from your thoughts.*

DAY 15

It is a night to be much observed unto the Lord for bringing them out from the land of Egypt: this is that night of the Lord to be observed of all the children of Israel in their generations.

EXODUS 12:42

While we can sometimes do a great deal on our own to turn our defeats into victories, the supreme change in a defeated individual is not brought about by that individual of himself—or herself—but is effected by the grace of God through Jesus Christ. We refer to Jesus Christ as the Savior. That is a great term. It has not been used nearly enough or properly enough. The Savior.

If you are in a boat at sea and you're lost, you send out an S.O.S. Well, there are people lost on the sea of life. They have lost control of themselves and of their circumstances. They are defeated. Then they will call upon Jesus. And He saves them. He gives them power over their defeats, their sins, their weaknesses. This is the great message in the Bible. You have a Savior who will do for you what you can never do for yourself. The wonderful things that He can do would fill volumes. Indeed, they have filled volumes.

> **PRAYER:** *Our Heavenly Father, we thank You for the great truth that if we receive Jesus as our Savior we shall experience such joy, such release, such victory as is not known in this world. Help us to commit ourselves in depth and obtain spiritual power. In Christ's name we pray. Amen.*

DAY 16

Incline not my heart to any evil thing, to practise wicked works with men that work iniquity: and let me not eat of their dainties.

PSALM 141:4

What do you want? See it clearly in your mind. Then check it with God, for if it isn't right, it's wrong and no wrong thing ever turned out right. Then believe, and you will create. You want a happy life? You want a useful life? You want to be a part of the movements of our time for human good? Do you want to rise above all your sins, weaknesses, and fears? Faith will lead you on. Because faith leads to belief and belief creates. Have faith in the Lord and you will be established.

Keep dreaming dreams, having visions, having faith, and you'll create. Faith also helps in another way, by taking out of us that which holds us back. I tell you right now, on the authority of God's Word—and you can check it later on—that if you do a wrong thing you will get a wrong result. But if you let God take wrong out of you, take fear out of you, and hate out of you, He will put life into you.

LIFE LIFTER: *The forces of sin and disease do not necessarily go together—but sometimes they do and that causes real trouble. Those who accept true forgiveness are saved from the destruction of sin, and those who are healed of disease attain that wholeness which God desires for each of His children.*

DAY 17

And be renewed in the spirit of your mind.
EPHESIANS 4:23

The Bible, in Ephesians 4:23, tells us "Let the Spirit change your way of thinking." This is an extraordinarily interesting injunction. Paul tells us there should be an upbeat to the mind, an uplift. This verse embraces attitudes, perceptions, ideas. Keep the spirit of your mind high. Raise it high—high up to Jesus Christ himself. Then you will be renewed. Christianity works to help people who want to overcome their tendency to make mistakes. If you have the mind of Jesus in you, you will not be error prone.

There is an old truism to the effect that we learn by our mistakes. And sometimes this is the case. But you also may reinforce a dangerous tendency: If you concentrate upon being educated by your mistakes, you may get to dwelling on them too much. You may come to believe that making mistakes is the only teacher you have. Instead, whenever you make a mistake, you should extract from it all the know-how it may offer and then put it immediately out of your mind.

PRAYER: *Our Heavenly Father, we give You thanks for Your Son, Jesus Christ our Lord, who has such skill that He can bring the best self out of each of us and cause miracles to happen in our lives. Let this happen to each of us now. Through Jesus Christ, our Lord. Amen.*

<table>
<tr><td>DAY
18</td><td>*For whether is easier, to say, Thy sins be
forgiven thee; or to say, Arise, and walk?*
MATTHEW 9:5</td></tr>
</table>

One evening, Mrs. Peale and I were sitting on the terrace of a hotel overlooking Lake Galilee. We were rereading parts of the Gospels and it was not difficult to sense the Holy Presence. I was startled upon this occasion by the emphasis which Jesus and the Gospel writers put on healing. My sense of the importance of this emphasis grew on the following day as I walked along the shores of Lake Galilee where Jesus walked and I tried to mark the spots where He had healed people. His was a healing ministry.

How the church in the nineteenth century ever chose to neglect healing is beyond my comprehension. Healing came to be seen as a solely physical process and the effect of mental and moral conditions upon states of health was ignored completely. Nowadays, fortunately, there is a great new movement for healing in the church. We are bringing back the healing ministry of Jesus in a modern application.

PRAYER: *Our Heavenly Father, touch, we pray, each of us with the healing of Your grace, bringing peace and quiet where there is stress and turmoil. This we ask, that we may be whole people, effective, able to take our place and do our part in a disturbed world that needs peace. Through Jesus Christ, our Lord. Amen.*

DAY
19

And Sarah said, God hath made me to laugh, so that all that hear will laugh with me.
GENESIS 21:6

Each of us was born as a baby—that is the only way we get into this world—and when God gives birth to a baby He does a wonderful thing: He wraps up this adorable little package and packs him, or her, full to overflowing with enthusiasm. It is the one thing that characterizes an infant.

Life is thrilling, exciting, and fabulous for a baby. The world is his oyster. He simply loves it. Everything is fresh and vital. Everything is fascinating and glorious. He has the time of his life. It's too bad, isn't it, we cannot always remain as babies? The writer Huxley said that the spirit of genius is to carry the attitude of the child into old age: to keep perpetual enthusiasm.

PRAYER: *Our Heavenly Father, we give You thanks for the fact that at our creation You filled us full of enthusiasm. If we have lost it, help us to recover it. Help us to live throughout our lives strengthened by the glory and the wonderment that is possible to a human being in this world of wonders. Open to us the kingdom. Make us wise and perceptive enough to take it. Through Jesus Christ, our Lord. Amen.*

| DAY 20 | *Heal me, O Lord, and I shall be healed; save me, and I shall be saved: for thou art my praise.* JEREMIAH 17:14 |

A woman from Minneapolis wrote: "I had migraine headaches for years. One evening I had to take the children to the library. I had a terrible headache. I thought I would read some books on the power of the mind. I saw your book and read it and liked it. You told me that with God's help I could have health.

"I gave myself unreservedly into His care. Even though things in my life were upsetting, I began to get well. After about six months I could tell others that I was rid of the headaches. I didn't say anything at first because I didn't want others to think He had failed me in case it was His decision that I continue to have the headaches. As for myself, I had made up my mind that if I still had them, I would accept it because now that I had Him nothing would be too hard to bear."

This woman couldn't solve her problems herself, so she went to the Lord and surrendered the problem to His care. If you have a difficult problem, you can get help by surrendering it to the Lord.

PRAYER: *Our Heavenly Father, we thank You for the great truth that when Jesus fills our minds, though difficulties come, the shadows can never remain, for You have filled us full of the joy of Your countenance. And for this we thank You. Through Jesus Christ, our Lord. Amen.*

DAY 21

And on the day that the tabernacle was reared up the cloud covered the tabernacle, namely, the tent of the testimony: and at even there was upon the tabernacle as it were the appearance of fire, until the morning. NUMBERS 9:15

The attitude you take toward the day—when the day begins—determines the day. If you wake up and say to yourself, or to the people near you, "Oh, this is going to be a tough day. This is going to be one of the worst days I've ever been through. I can just feel it coming." You will find that you are absolutely right—because you are bringing it on yourself.

But if you are a person of prayer, the first thing you will do in the morning is to thank God that He watched over you and your loved ones during the night and brought you to the light of another day with all its opportunity. God gave you this day and it is a day to rejoice in. In the course of my life I have often observed that the more spiritually minded a person is the more beautiful the day becomes, the more replete with opportunity it is. So if you want to have a good day every day, get your life changed by Jesus Christ and every day will be a great one.

PRAYER: *Our Heavenly Father, we thank You for this day. Help us this day to walk with Jesus, to think as Jesus thinks, to love as Jesus loves, and make it a wonderful day. Through Jesus Christ, our Lord. Amen.*

<table>
<tr><td>DAY
22</td><td>*And God remembered Rachel, and God
hearkened to her, and opened her womb.*
GENESIS 30:22</td></tr>
</table>

I was in a meeting not so very long ago where they were talking about various difficulties and problems, both of our society and of individuals. They called upon a man to pray. I knew this man had had much difficulty and even then was having a lot; and I was astonished by his prayer. He did not ask the Lord for a single thing except His presence. And he quickly affirmed His presence.

The prayer was full of the giving of thanks and of affirmation of God's goodness. It was an entrancing prayer and I said to him, "Jim, I know something of the difficulties you face. How come you never ask God for anything?" "Oh," he replied, "I've learned that the best way to pray is to thank God. He knows what I need. Why should I ask Him for anything? Let me just tell you all the wonderful things I have." And he began to enumerate his blessings. No matter how much difficulty you have, and there may be lots, he emphasized that you still have many, many things for which to be thankful.

LIFE LIFTER: *One way to lift your spirits is to think and talk and pray with people who, like yourself, are seeking a deeper relationship with Jesus. The warmth and uplift this fellowship will bring to your heart is impossible to describe.*

<table>
<tr><td>

DAY

23

</td><td>

And he laid it upon my mouth, and said, Lo, this hath touched thy lips; and thine iniquity is taken away, and thy sin purged.

ISAIAH 6:7

</td></tr>
</table>

One of the main principles of the Japanese religion Tenrikyo is that disease begins in the mind and that if you get the mind clean you'll be at peace, happy, creative, and an asset to society. I especially like the way they have constructed their temples. Each altar is open to the elements. The rain falls on it, the snow falls on it, the wind blows on it, the sun shines on it. Everything— rain, snow, wind, and sun—is a cleansing agent and the lesson is that if you let the rain and snow and wind and sun of the good God into your mind, He will cleanse you of that which destroys your peace of mind.

This same idea reaches its glorious fulfillment in Christianity. Not only does it cleanse, but it makes old creatures new. I've seen defeated people become victorious people, soiled people become clean people, dull people become excited. God doesn't merely create you, He repeatedly re-creates you.

PRAYER: *Our Heavenly Father, we thank You for the creative vitality that You have given us. May we have within us Your peace, the peace of God which passes all understanding, that we may overcome and master tension and stress and live with power. Through Jesus Christ, our Lord. Amen.*

<table>
<tr><td>DAY
24</td><td>*But as many as received him, to them gave he power to become the sons of God, even to them that believe on his name.*   JOHN 1:12</td></tr>
</table>

People have often asked me, "Why is it I do not have a sense of power that stays with me when the going gets hard?" Well, the Bible says that "some people accepted Him and put their faith in Him. So He gave them the right to be children of God." It is all there. Everything is offered to you. To as many as receive Him—that is, accept His guidance and help—to them He gives the power to become—that is, to grow, expand—to become children of God.

Now what is a child of God? We believe that Jesus is the Son of God. But in some degree we all become children of God. God at his creation breathed into man the breath of life, and he became a living spirit. Humans are more than flesh and blood. They are of the divine. They come, as Wordsworth said, "trailing clouds of glory…from God, who is our home." And when they pass from this world, they pass to an eternal glory with God.

PRAYER: *Our Heavenly Father, we give You thanks that into a world of conflict, cruelty, and hate came this fragile flower of love. It will grow strong because it is based on everlasting law. And the same law operating in human affairs will bring us to the high purpose of God in building this world. Amen.*

DAY 25

And Isaiah said, Take a lump of figs. And they took and laid it on the boil, and he recovered.
II KINGS 20:7

People are troubled by illness. They are either ill themselves or have loved ones who are ill. But God is the master of illness. He has the power to heal. And He has the power to give us understanding if it be His will that a loved one be taken from us. There is no problem I can conceive of, either individual or social, that God cannot help us with if we have the faith to let Him.

Now there is where the trouble is. How much faith have we? Christian faith in earlier times was a very rugged thing. We are the descendants of a great breed of men and women who had strong, uncomplicated faith. They believed in God and that was that. They believed that God would help, that He would bring to their support an enormous power. And the Bible tells of people who are mature, not children; adults carrying out a challenging job. These people in the Bible had enormous faith. That is why they overcame enormous odds.

PRAYER: *Our Heavenly Father, we know that when the clouds come we see only darkness. Help us to realize that there is everlasting battle between cloud and light, but that light always wins if we are in harmony with Jesus Christ. For this we give You thanks. Through Jesus Christ, our Lord. Amen.*

<table>
<tr><td>DAY
26</td><td>*And it came to pass, when they were gone over, that Elijah said unto Elisha, Ask what I shall do for thee, before I be taken away from thee. And Elisha said, I pray thee, let a double*</td></tr>
</table>

portion of thy spirit be upon me.　　II KINGS 2:9

T.E. Lawrence once took some Arabs to London; what interested them more than anything else were the faucets in the bathrooms in their hotel. They would turn the water on and watch the enormous stream gushing out and exclaim "Look! All you have to do is turn that thing and you have all the water you want!"

When it was time to leave, Lawrence found these men trying to remove the faucets. Astounded, he asked them what they were doing. "We will take these back to the desert and then we will never lack for water." So Lawrence had to explain that the faucets had to be attached to a source of water.

Christians oftentimes do just the same thing. We try to get a flow from faucets that are not attached. Our faucets are all the little forms of faith and tradition: going to church regularly and all the rest.

LIFE LIFTER: *If the peace of God passes all understanding, it also defies all description. When it enters our hearts, the old haunting fears give way to feelings of courage and confidence. The restlessness of life is quieted. What a promise! The ineffable peace of God offered by Christ is yours for the taking.*

<table>
<tr><td>DAY
27</td><td>*And it came to pass, when I heard these words, that I sat down and wept, and mourned certain days, and fasted, and prayed before the God of heaven.* NEHEMIAH 1:4</td></tr>
</table>

Christianity survives because it faces all of life, including the evil and the wickedness in humans. It paints the whole picture, but nevertheless affirms that in the midst of all this trouble, pain, and confusion there is a good outcome, a way out of sorrow. The bright, pure lily comes up through the mud. There has never been a philosophy of life like Christianity. It deals realistically with all of the hardships of the human condition, but it comes out with victory.

At the heart of Christianity there is a great splintery blood-spattered cross. You can't laugh that off: the sorrow and the suffering of life. But the lilting note of victory is never absent. That is why it was said of early Christians that there was something in them akin to the song of the skylark and the babbling of brooks. Optimism, hope, freshness, newness. One Bible text after another reminds us of these truths. Freshness, newness. That is Christianity in its essence. Newness.

> **PRAYER**: *Our Heavenly Father, bless us all so that the message of joyous, victorious Christianity may wing its way into our hearts. May we live in fullness, that every day with gratitude we may say, "It's good to be alive." And for this we give thanks. Through Jesus Christ, our Lord. Amen.*

| DAY **28** | *Be watchful, and strengthen the things which remain, that are ready to die: for I have not found thy works perfect before God.* |

REVELATION 3:2

Nobody can live successfully in this world without being strong. You may be pampered and protected when you are a child, but you have to learn to be strong as you mature, because sooner or later life will throw the book at you. Sometimes it will throw the whole book at you all at once. You have to get adjusted so you won't collapse under the trouble, or give way under difficulty, or fold under the blow of adversity. I sometimes think that the greatest virtue of all is to be strong.

Christianity is a way of life that makes people strong. You can have all the strength you will ever need if you build into yourself the love of God and stay close to Jesus until He becomes part of you.

PRAYER: *Our Heavenly Father, we thank You for making human beings whom You have created great human beings, to whom You have given authority. By Your grace, they can control themselves. We give thanks for this, that they who are controlled are joyous, knowing that nothing whatsoever can defeat them or upset their equilibrium. Grant that all of us may let Your peace rule, dominate, control our hearts and minds. Through Jesus Christ, our Lord. Amen.*

DAY 29

Knowest thou the ordinances of heaven? canst thou set the dominion thereof in the earth?
JOB 38:33

This world is a wonderful place. We were put into it by a God who loved us and wanted to surround us with that which would develop us, so that ultimately He could take us out of this world of the temporal into the world of the eternal.

Certain theological circles have put forth the notion that too much enjoyment of the physical world is pantheistic, even pagan, but I reject this attitude completely. I believe that the hills, the seas, the stars, the sky, the sun, the rain, the snow reflect a greater spiritual world. The purpose of material forms is only to give substance and reality to the world of the spirit. The person who associates with the natural world, thinking of it spiritually, will find his spirit refreshed, his mind cleansed, he will be stimulated and inspired.

PRAYER: *Our Heavenly Father, we are so grateful to You for all the wonderful blessings You pour upon us. You gave us life and the chance to live in this wonderful world. But so often we spoil our opportunities through living by something superficial rather than by something in depth. Give us, we pray, the wisdom to turn to that inner power which is God in our lives, by which we are able to meet and overcome all the difficulties of life on earth. Through Jesus Christ, our Lord. Amen.*

> **DAY 30**

Why art thou cast down, O my soul? and why art thou disquieted within me? hope thou in God: for I shall yet praise him, who is the health of my countenance, and my God.

PSALM 42:11

Hope and expectation are two dynamic words that can change your life. Write these words in gigantic letters across the sky of your life, as you sometimes see sky writing advertisements against the heavens. Deeply embed these until they become a motivational part of your whole being. Do this and your life will be good, very good, no matter how much pain or difficulty you experience.

The Bible, which is the wisest document ever known in human existence, which defies the ravages of time and change because it contains the truth that cannot be changed or invalidated, says in Psalm 42:11: "Why am I discouraged? Why am I restless? I trust you! And I will praise you again because you help me, and you are my God." What a text! There is power in it.

LIFE LIFTER: *As an old hymn says: "Change and decay in all I see. O Thou who changest not, abide with me." The years pass, changes follow one after the other, and we sadly say, "Things are not as they were." But one thing never changes, because it is truth. So, let us cleave to that which never fades, never withers—the word of God that stands forever.*

MAY

*According to all that the Lord commanded
Moses, so the children of Israel made all the
work. And Moses did look upon all the work,
and, behold, they had done it as the Lord
had commanded, even so had they done it: and Moses
blessed them.*   EXODUS 39:42–43

I remember sitting on the porch with my mother and
saying, "Mother, I want to amount to something. I'm
going to make money and come back with enough to
buy and sell some of these people around here."

But my mother said, "Ambition, Norman, is good if
God controls it. But what I want you to be is a clean,
decent, honorable, upright Christian man with love in
your heart, serving God and His children, and I want
you so to live that when you finish your course of life,
I'll meet you somewhere in the eternities of our Lord."

That sounds sentimental. But this is the ideal that
Christian mothers have put into us—or rather that
they have fanned into flame because it was God
Himself who planted in us the instinct to be children
of God. So touch the hem of His garment that you
may be made perfectly whole.

PRAYER: *Our Heavenly Father, we the sons and
daughters of beloved mothers give You thanks for them.
We ask that we may touch the hem of Your garment. We pray
that we may have part in the bringing of Your Holy Kingdom
on earth. Through Jesus Christ, our Lord. Amen.*

DAY 2

And Moses and Aaron came in unto Pharaoh, and said unto him, Thus saith the Lord God of the Hebrews, How long wilt thou refuse to humble thyself before me? let my people go, that they may serve me.   EXODUS 10:3

A man told me about a business associate who once enclosed a card in one of his letters. On one side the card said, "Expect a miracle." And on the back, "God is on your side." He was about to throw it out, but the card intrigued him. He put it in his wallet.

Every time he opened his wallet, this card would fall out: "Expect a miracle." "God is on your side." The message began to seep into his consciousness. He began to send up little prayers. Then he started taking a new positive attitude toward the problems which had baffled and frustrated and defeated him. And finally he went around expecting a miracle.

You get what you expect. Life is full of all kinds of disappointments and sorrows. But it is also full of wonders. And if you expect wonderful things, wonderful things will happen. When God is on your side you can expect a miracle.

> **LIFE LIFTER:** *You may have tried all your life long to rid yourself of your weaknesses without success. But it can be done in no time at all by Christ. He will do for you what you cannot do for yourself. Ask Him to change you— and mean it.*

| DAY 3 |

For thou hast made him a little lower than the angels, and hast crowned him with glory and honor.
PSALM 8:5

Listen to what the psalmist says: "You made us a little lower than you yourself, and you have crowned us with glory and honor. You let us rule everything your hands have made. And you put all of it under our power." Does this mean dominion over other people? Not at all. It means dominion over your weaknesses, your fears, your sins; dominion over your grief, your frustration, your disappointment, your sadness. Are you that way? Or are you a pushover for everything that comes along? Are you a weakling, a victim of everything and everybody?

"Lord, give me a high opinion of myself." You can pray that prayer, because you are, if you will allow yourself to be, a wonderful person. You are a wonderful person by realizing the best that is within you.

LIFE LIFTER: *In maintaining high spirit, it is important to cultivate the attitude of spiritual surrender. Place yourself, your interests, hopes and purposes completely in God's hands. If we surrender ourselves to the direction of God, being guided by His mighty hand, He will exalt us—help us attain our purposes and rise above all defeats. God cares for you, so turn all your worries over to Him. This is a supreme Life Lifter.*

DAY 4

For with thee is the fountain of life: in thy light shall we see light.   PSALM 36:9

"The life-giving fountain belongs to you." What a picture! An upsurging, sparkling fountain. And out of that fountain comes great goodness. Yet we are very painfully aware that not everyone comes to that source of goodness. "Morality in America is not crumbling; it has crumbled," claims one magazine.

Well, now, I don't know whether I am willing to accept that appraisal, but people who believe in God and in Jesus Christ and in the Ten Commandments and in the moral standards of our civilization should rise up and do something about it. Churches must attack current problems through spiritually oriented programs aimed at changing the lives of people.

For it is also true—thanks be to God—that there are thousands upon thousands of people who know that life is good and want what is good. The pity is that too often the churches fail to tell them that through the power and the grace of Jesus Christ they can have life that is good and wonderful and ever new.

PRAYER: *Our Heavenly Father, we ask Your blessing for all Your people. Give to each a deep confidence, a deep powerful philosophy of life, a deep and abiding sense of peace and control, so that all may rise above the vicissitudes of human existence and live constantly on victorious levels. Through Jesus Christ, our Lord. Amen.*

| DAY 5 |

And Jacob awaked out of his sleep, and he said, Surely the Lord is in this place; and I knew it not. GENESIS 28:16

The Lord does speak to people. And there is such a thing as an inward ear with which you hear His voice. Where you really hear is deep in your soul. And Stanley Jones heard. The Lord said to him, "I want you to do a job for Me in India. You can't do it the way you are, breaking down all the time. Will you give Me your worries, your anxieties? If you will, I'll give you such health as you never dreamed of." "Lord" said Jones, "I'll close that bargain right away." I heard Dr. Jones say twenty years after this event, "Since that night I never had another breakdown. I had not only physical health, but I had mental and spiritual health as well. I seemed to have tapped new life for body, mind and spirit. And I had done nothing but take it!"

I tell you, friends, what can be done for a human being seems so incredible that the person who hasn't the eye or the ear of faith can hardly understand it. So let God help you. He will help you and He will do it soon.

LIFE LIFTER: *A physician told me that a large percent of patients did not need medicine; they needed God. Tolstoy said, "To know God is to live." Show me a man who really knows God and I will show you a happy, enthusiastic and vital man.*

DAY
6

So David and all the house of Israel brought up the ark of the Lord with shouting, and with the sound of the trumpet. II SAMUEL 6:15

I have always maintained that it is an objective of Jesus that people shall live happy lives. Of course, the word "happiness" is sometimes used in a very superficial sense. Maybe the word "joy" is better, for it suggests something deeper. The Gospel never promises that a Christian shall be free from the difficulties of this world. But Jesus says that those who do what He asks will find happiness. He wants people to live joyously.

I realize that the minute I make that statement I am bound to be criticized by the small, supercilious, sophisticated, group of articulate preachers who seem to think that nobody should be happy. I don't know what they want for humanity unless they want everybody to be miserable. In some circles there seems to be a notion that a person cannot be a true Christian unless he goes around with a sour look on his face. This is a distortion of what Jesus taught. It is a carryover of a mistaken notion that it is a sin to enjoy life.

LIFE LIFTER: *In Titus 3:1–2 are listed just a few things that put happiness in your heart: Do good, help people and bring blessings into their lives. Become an island of peace in a world of turmoil. Do the simple, honest Christian things. Life will be good, and you will love it.*

DAY 7

And we desire that every one of you do show the same diligence to the full assurance of hope unto the end.　　　　HEBREWS 6:11

One day I was on a Boeing 707, and the pilot came back and sat down beside me for a few minutes. I happened to look out the window and saw something I didn't understand. I said, "Captain, out there along the wing, there are blades set at intervals. What are those things?"

"Those are vortex generators," he replied. "When we have a smooth flow of air, these big planes don't steer as perfectly as they do when there is slight turbulence. The flow of air swirling around those blades gives us enough turbulence for perfect performance."

If you had nothing but absolutely smooth flight conditions on the voyage of life, you wouldn't attain the objective for which you are designed. So the Lord has put vortex generators into human existence in order that we may grow strong and learn to steer our course and arrive at the destination He has set for us. These vortex generators seem very big sometimes and we feel defeated by them. But a person is lifted above defeat by getting hold of the hope we have in Christ.

PRAYER: *Our Heavenly Father, help us to rise above trifling with Christianity or using it only in a diluted, formal way. Help us to pray the kind of prayers that have depth, the kind of prayers that release the power. For this we give thanks, through Jesus Christ, our Lord. Amen.*

DAY 8

What shall we then say to these things? If God be for us, who can be against us?

ROMANS 8:31

This morning while having breakfast, I listened by radio to a Baptist minister who was preaching a sermon on the end of the world. It was the kind of preaching I used to hear when I was a boy—very powerful. It is a sad thing that Christianity is seldom preached that way today, and many people look upon it as a kind of country club adjunct to a respectable life.

We all have problems and difficulties and sometimes these seem overwhelming. But the Bible says, "If God is on our side, can anyone be against us?" No matter what problems or difficulties you may have you can conquer them and, not only that, be more than a conqueror through Jesus Christ who loved you so much that He died on the cross for your salvation.

That is what Christianity teaches. Some people take it and run with it and have a tremendous time in their lives. Others stay bogged down and defeated. It is startling what vast differences there are between people. And the force that makes the biggest difference is a powerful faith.

PRAYER: *Our Heavenly Father, help us to know that as we take You into our hearts and our lives we shall win more than a victory. For this glorious fact, we give You thanks, through Jesus Christ, our Lord. Amen.*

DAY 9

Thou shalt not have in thy bag divers weights, a great and a small: Thou shalt not have in thine house divers measures, a great and a small. DEUTERONOMY 25:13–14

The Bible is a straightforward, honest book. It does not guarantee freedom from pain, sorrow, trouble, difficulty and heartache, but it does promise inner happiness and good days. So to have better ways to better days, keep all this in the background of your mind.

One suggestion for realizing better days is to live honestly. How many people live with absolute honesty? Have you ever been completely honest with yourself? Have you ever told yourself the whole truth about yourself? Have you ever faced yourself, not as you think you are, but as you really are? How long has it been since you made an appraisal of your strengths and your weaknesses? Do you know whether you are deteriorating or whether you are growing? Are you a better, more confident, more knowledgeable person now than you were ten years ago—or are you a worse person now than you were ten years ago? Honesty is the first principle for having better ways to better days.

LIFE LIFTER: *To live successfully, one must develop the deft and skillful touch that makes things turn out right. If you let God's Word seep from your conscious to your subconscious mind, it will correct the error pattern within you and gradually endow you with wisdom.*

| DAY **10** | *But the high places were not removed: nevertheless Asa's heart was perfect with the Lord all his days.*   I KINGS 15:14 |

Faith is an acceptance of spiritual truth, a belief in yourself as a child of God. I think everybody, once every day, ought to draw himself up and say, "I am a child of God." And when you believe that, then you begin to release powers within your mind, your soul, that can lift you above your defeats. If you just stay at your earthly level then when you look up at these great big defeating problems, they will overwhelm you.

But as a child of God you are much taller than you are of yourself. You have an extension in you and with this extension by the power of faith you can overcome any difficulty in this world. The problems of life are infinitesimal in comparison with the extension powers that are in you as a child of God. There are your problems; they seem very big to you. But you yourself are much bigger than you think. I've seen it happen again and again: God comes into a man's mind, into his thought, and the inspiration produces an explosion and the man rises above his difficulty.

LIFE LIFTER: *If, over a long period of time, a person habitually fears something, there is a tendency for that fear to become a reality. But if you hold the faith thought, the positive thought, you will create about yourself an atmosphere propitious to success, health and well-being.*

| DAY 11 | *Saviors shall come up on mount Zion to judge the mount of Esau; and the kingdom shall be the Lord's.* OBADIAH 21 |

People practice various kinds of religion. They observe a formal kind, which means carrying out precepts and following the proper forms. They practice a doctrinal religion, which is acknowledging certain truths and creeds. Unfortunately, that is as far as most people ever get.

Then there are those who find a lifesaving, life-changing religion. They come upon a power, and it helps them to overcome pain, weakness, sorrow, frustrations, and defeats. It gives them a sparkle in their eyes and a glow on their face and elasticity in their step. It changes them so they love everybody. Their whole life flows out to bless humankind. This is vital Christianity, religion in depth.

LIFE LIFTER: *The proud and puffed up will have a hard time, for even God resists them. But he who humbly depends upon God will receive a vast strength. Get close to God and God will be very near to you. Cleanse yourself of evil and get your thinking straight. Humbly admit your faults, ask God for strength and He will lift you up. Humbly follow Him and your life will be good, very good.*

<table>
<tr><td>DAY
12</td><td>*And he took and sent messes unto them from before him: but Benjamin's mess was five times so much as any of theirs. And they drank, and were merry with him.*</td></tr>
</table>

GENESIS 43:34

Do you know the meaning of the word abundance? I didn't, until I looked it up one time. And I was thrilled. The derivation of the word abundance goes back to the Latin verb *undare,* which means "to rise up in waves." Isn't that great? Life rises up in waves. Have you got any waves of life? Or are you living on little dribbles? Almighty God is a generous God. He never meant that we should dribble through life. He intended us to live in abundance.

Of all handicaps that hold people back from being successful in their living and from overcoming weakness and having strength, the worst is a lack of love. There is no wisdom like that of the Bible, which tells us not to be angry with people and not to hate them, but love them, not to be irritable with people, but love and serve them. If you so live, life will flow back to you in great waves.

LIFE LIFTER: *Our spirits rise when we learn how to receive the abundance of good things God wants to give us. Practice receiving. Believe that you have been given. Then feel your spirits lift as you realize that God's blessings are actually showered upon us.*

<table>
<tr><td>

DAY

13

</td><td>

Ye have heard that it was said by them of old time, Thou shalt not kill; and whosoever shall kill shall be in danger of the judgment….

MATTHEW 5:21

</td></tr>
</table>

One day I was reading the fifth chapter of Matthew. I've read that chapter hundreds of times. But this time I had a revelation about it. It is a blueprint for happiness. The descriptions of what you must do to be happy go on through the whole chapter. And it says not only to love your friends, but also love your enemies and pray for those who mistreat you. Then the great sermon rises to a climax where it says, "You must always act like your Father in heaven."

You may say, "That is unattainable. That is too hard."

That is why Jesus is Jesus. He put it high, because He believed that there was something great in human beings. He tried to get us to see that if you have what it takes to rise to this challenge, you will find happiness in a way you cannot find it anywhere else. If you are courageous enough to take it, your life will be great.

PRAYER: *Our Heavenly Father, deliver us from our everlasting indecisiveness. We want, yet we don't want. We dream, yet we don't dream. We reach, yet we don't reach. Help us to say "By the grace of God I will do it." Then, we know, everything will start marvelously changing. Through Jesus Christ, our Lord. Amen.*

DAY 14

Then Eli answered and said, Go in peace: and the God of Israel grant thee thy petition that thou hast asked of him. And she said, Let thine handmaid find grace in thy sight. So the woman went her way, and did eat, and her countenance was no more sad.
                                                              I SAMUEL 1:17–18

You can judge the depth of a person's Christianity by how big a person it makes of him. The person who has it in depth becomes a strong character, becomes a victorious person. And one thing such a person characteristically has is a recognition of the fact that in difficulty there is a potential good. That is basic in the Christian philosophy of life. The philosophy known as optimism is related to it.

True optimism is the belief that the goods of life outweigh the evils and that always behind a difficulty there is an inherent good. When faced with difficulties the optimist does not say, "Isn't this awful?" but says to the Lord, "Lord, You've given me a difficulty, but I know there must be good in it and I will seek to find that good."

LIFE LIFTER: *Let God's words sink deeply into your consciousness, and the experience of God's protection will be yours. How your spirit will rise as the sublime truth grips you that nothing in this world can hurt you. His amazing kindness surrounds you always. You go through life with a high-hearted spirit. God watches over you.*

DAY 15	*When the scorner is punished, the simple is made wise: and when the wise is instructed, he receiveth knowledge.* PROVERBS 21:11

A mixed-up, defeated man started coming to Marble Collegiate Church and one day he found Someone here, that Someone who can change any individual. This is a letter that he wrote me.

Dear Dr. Peale:

As you well know, alcohol was not the only problem I had six years ago. I was one of the most negative people anybody ever met. I was one of the most super-critical, impatient, cocky individuals that you could imagine. Now, please don't think that I have overcome all these things. I haven't. At times I become discouraged with my progress. Gradually, by trying to follow the teachings of Jesus, I am learning to control myself and be less critical. It is like being released from a prison. I never dreamed life could be so wonderful.

Do as this man did and you will say to yourself with gladness in your heart, "How good God is."

PRAYER: *Our Heavenly Father, we are grateful that we have a Savior who can save us from stress and tension. May our hearts and minds be filled with the healing touch of Your everlasting peace. Through Jesus Christ, our Lord. Amen.*

| DAY **16** | *For thus saith the Lord God, the Holy One of Israel; In returning and rest shall ye be saved; in quietness and in confidence shall be your strength: and ye would not.* ISAIAH 30:15 |

Dwell on this tremendous thought from Isaiah: "I will make you strong if you quietly trust me." One of the basic ingredients of the Christian religion is strength.

Those who built Christianity knew how the onslaughts of circumstance, difficulty, pain, sorrow, opposition and resentment can break a human being down. But the prophets and apostles and, most of all, Jesus Himself built into the structure of our faith a power that can make us men and women who handle life majestically. Your job and mine is to handle life. If you don't handle life, it will handle you. So the issue is who handles what. You are created in the image of God. Go home and look in the mirror and tell yourself that through Him this strength can be yours.

LIFE LIFTER: *One thing the believer can always count on is the love of God as demonstrated in Christ. So great and so constant and unvarying is this love of God, which we find in Christ, that nothing of any sort, no matter how formidable, can separate you from it. Tuck this tremendous promise close up against your heart, insert it deeply into your mind, and never forget it. Keep close to Christ and His loving protection and help will follow you all the days of your life.*

<table>
<tr><td>DAY
17</td><td>Then he said unto them, Go your way, eat the fat, and drink the sweet, and send portions unto them for whom nothing is prepared: for this day is holy unto our Lord: neither be ye</td></tr>
</table>

sorry; for the joy of the Lord is your strength.

NEHEMIAH 8:10

God's Kingdom radiates with love and health and happiness and goodness. Our God is so completely outgoing, so overwhelmingly generous, that He wants to give you every good thing. If this is God's good pleasure, why don't we experience everything that is good and beneficial? Perhaps one reason is that we block the flow of good by the miserable negative attitudes we develop toward life, toward other people, and even toward God.

How can one overcome failure that comes from negative attitudes? One way, and a very important one, is to practice seeing everything as developing rather than as deteriorating. See only good as coming to you. Practice visualizing it. Practice being conscious of it. Really see it coming to you and practice thanking God for it. There is a law whereby in so doing you actually attract it to yourself.

> **LIFE LIFTER:** *When unsatisfied longings well up within you, affirm that you receive from Jesus the ultimate in soul satisfaction. A deep inner peace will gradually grow upon you.*

DAY
18

A new heart also will I give you, and a new spirit will I put within you: and I will take away the stony heart out of your flesh, and I will give you an heart of flesh.

EZEKIEL 36:26

A friend of mine has always impressed me with his vivacity, his sense of delight in life, his eagerness. I asked him once how he managed this, and he said, "I pass expectancy thoughts through my mind every morning." What a technique!

Another vibrant friend explains his secret for living joyously and without boredom this way. "Every morning I read the Bible, spend ten minutes in quiet meditation and close by saying, 'O Lord, thank You so much for the eventful day You are going to give me.' And I do have one eventful day after another, days filled with joy and excitement."

How is your heart? Everyone needs a new heart at times, for the old one tends to get tired. How is your spirit? Everyone needs a new spirit at times, for the old spirit often becomes weary. If you haven't got a heart like that, or a spirit of that sort, let God give it to you.

PRAYER: *Our Heavenly Father, we ask You to bless everybody today. Let that light, which You commanded to shine out of darkness, come into our minds to change us with new faith and new heart. Through Jesus Christ, our Lord. Amen.*

DAY 19

For he is not a God of the dead, but of the living: for all live unto him.　　LUKE 20:38

How much of Christianity do you want? Are you content to have merely a set of ethics? Or would you like to be deeply stirred and released? James Russell Lowell in his poem, "The Cathedral," wrote:

"I, that still pray at morning and at eve…
Thrice in my life perhaps have truly prayed,
Thrice, stirred below my conscious self, have felt
That perfect disenthralment which is God."

There is a power that can lift us above ourselves, give us victory over all our weaknesses, fill our minds with courage and make us count in the day and age in which we live, can make us flaming tongues of fire to live with power. And only a few people reach for it. The others are content with something halfway alive. But a human being is meant to be a tremendous person.

One way to start becoming such a person is to say, "By the grace and power of the Lord Jesus Christ, I'm going to find interest in life; I'm going to put interest into my living. By the grace and power of the Lord Jesus Christ, I'm going to live with delight and excitement; I'm going to live with enthusiasm."

LIFE LIFTER: *Size up your problem, do all you can about it, and affirm, "Things that are impossible with humans are possible with God." The outcome may not be what you now desire. But it will be what God wants it to be.*

| DAY **20** | *And the Lord shall smite Egypt: he shall smite and heal it: and they shall return even to the Lord, and he shall be entreated of them, and shall heal them.* ISAIAH 19:22 |

Arriving by train to speak at a rally in Pennsylvania, I headed for a cab. A somber man was sitting in the front seat with the driver, and a woman was in one corner of the back seat. I got in and took the other corner. Then along came another woman with a suitcase and a couple of paper bags. I moved over and she got in. Then she took us all into her love. She asked, "How are you all today?" I said I felt fine.

The man in front turned around and asked, "What makes you so happy?"

"Jesus makes me happy," the woman replied. "I used to be the most miserable woman in Pennsylvania. But I found Jesus and He resurrected me." And by the time she got out, she had made us all happy.

If you are feeling weak, tired, sick, defeated, unhappy—you can be made new. And once this resurrection by Jesus Christ takes hold, you will becomes strong. Resurrection makes strong people.

PRAYER: *Our Heavenly Father, we pray that every child of Yours may learn to live in harmony with Your law, Your law that makes for freedom and health and self-control. So may we live with quiet power. For this we give You thanks. Through Jesus Christ, our Lord. Amen.*

<table>
<tr><td>

DAY
21

</td><td>

And he that sat upon the throne said, Behold,
I make all things new. And he said unto me,
Write: for these words are true and faithful.
REVELATION 21:5

</td></tr>
</table>

The New Testament begins with a star and a song and it marches up to a cross and another song, the song of the redeemed. It is a tremendous story. Toward the end of the Bible, in Revelation 21:5, we find these glorious words: "I am making everything new." It doesn't matter how much you have failed, how you have messed things up, how many defeats you have experienced.

But how are you going to keep this newness, this freshness, this wonder in it? There is one big fact which I think you ought to have in mind as you approach the future, and it is that life will give back to you just exactly what you give to life. That is the deal. That is the way life is. So if you want to know what the future is going to mean to you, you have to decide what you are going to mean to it. Life is very fair. It pays in the same coin. It is scrupulously honest. It gives to you what you give to it.

> **LIFE LIFTER:** *The greatest experience is spiritual experience. You get it by completely surrendering yourself to God and experiencing His presence. Although no one can permanently live in such exalted emotional heights, the power stays with you so that when you get up against situations that used to be difficult, it keeps you going.*

<table>
<tr><td>DAY
22</td><td>*Therefore if any man be in Christ, he is a new creature: old things are passed away; behold, all things are become new.*</td></tr>
</table>

II CORINTHIANS 5:17

A few years ago a Rotarian came to the New York club laboring under terrible sorrow. His son Steve had fallen into trouble; he had driven a stolen car over several state lines and was in jail in New York. The father had come to the Rotary Club for comfort and assistance.

The club turned the problem over to two laymen. They got in touch with me and explained that they'd been appointed a committee to handle this case, and asked if I would help. They said, "We want Jesus Christ on this committee too, because only He can help this father and this boy." Later they came to my study and we prayed together, putting Steve and his father in the hands of Jesus. And Jesus, the alive Christ, took charge.

We went to the judge in the case and the boy was paroled to us. A few years later Steve became a pastor. Moreover, his seminary sent him to other seminaries to testify to the students what can happen to an individual who meets the living Christ.

PRAYER: *Our Heavenly Father, if today we are defeated or weakened by anything that may have entered our lives, help us to know that if we expect great things of You, great things will come. Through Jesus Christ, our Lord. Amen.*

<table>
<tr><td>

DAY

23

</td><td>

But as for you, ye thought evil against me; but God meant it unto good, to bring to pass, as it is this day, to save much people alive.

GENESIS 50:20

</td></tr>
</table>

My friend Richard Prentice Ettinger, who founded the Prentice-Hall publishing company, was present at a breakfast I attended. He'd had throat cancer and had a little tube in his throat but spoke distinctly and well. That morning we had a wonderful conversation. In the course of it he said, "You know my theory that whatever happens, happens for the best? When I got cancer I thought, 'Oh, oh! How is this going to be for the best?' The cancer took twenty pounds off me. The doctors said afterward that the weight had been affecting my heart. Because the excess weight is gone, I will live ten years longer. Whatever happens, happens for the best."

One of the greatest things that ever happened for the best in my life was to know an undefeatable man like Richard Prentice Ettinger who demonstrated in the most difficult circumstances that if you do your best and you put your best in the hands of God, you can make things happen for the best.

LIFE LIFTER: *As you develop the thought that any adversity can actually be turned to your advantage, you then have an immense mental asset going for you. Make a list of your friends and determine who is the most positive thinker among and then deliberately cultivate his society.*

| DAY **24** | *Therefore is the name of it called Babel; because the Lord did there confound the language of all the earth: and from thence did the Lord scatter them abroad upon the face of* |

all the earth.

GENESIS 11:9

Quietness is a profoundly creative element. Who was the tallest character who ever rose up from among the American people? Well, in my book it was Abraham Lincoln. Now Lincoln in his early years was fortunate enough to live in the virgin forests of the Middle West. As a distinguished writer on Lincoln once observed, "In the making of him, the element of silence was immense." Great trees that seemed to scrape the sky were his companions, the silence of the forest whispered its wisdom to him, and later in the days of crisis he was sustained because he had within him quietness from which he drew confidence.

We're too noisy; we're too hectic, we're too disturbed; we're too confused. We have noise all the time. Consequently, we have noise inside. So we lose our confidence. Then we lose our strength. Remember: "I will make you strong if you quietly trust me."

LIFE LIFTER: *Feed your mind with thoughts that cause it to be peaceful. To have a mind full of peace, merely fill it full of peace. Go to sleep using the conscious thought that whatever you may be called upon to handle the next day, God and you will be able to do it together.*

DAY 25

Light is sown for the righteous, and gladness for the upright in heart.   PSALM 97:11

Sir Arnold Lunn was an authority on the geography of Switzerland. He traveled over practically every valley, every mountain and wrote about them with the fervor of a poet. In the summer of 1940, when the German army was marching into France, Lunn was summoned to England. At Berne he looked at the mountains and wondered whether he would be back.

The war ceased. Lunn arrived at Berne in the late afternoon. The sky was overcast, the mountains invisible. Suddenly the clouds parted and there they stood. The light of the sun upon them seemed to say that there are certain things in life which no cloud, no war, no hate, no force can destroy. This was for Arnold Lunn a spiritual experience, reassuring him that no matter how much suffering exists, God remains.

So I would say that there are two pillars upon which happiness rests. One is moral decency, mastery over self. The other is the knowledge of the love of God and of His presence at all times, come what may.

PRAYER: *Our Heavenly Father, it seems that to have peace of mind we must somehow reach back to a different condition. So far back—and—up must we reach that we hear the voice of Jesus saying, "My peace I give to you." For this we give You thanks. Through Jesus Christ, our Lord. Amen.*

| DAY **26** | *That he would grant you, according to the riches of his glory, to be strengthened with might by his Spirit in the inner man....* |

EPHESIANS 3;16

It is not necessary to be victimized by depression. There is a sure cure for depressive feelings. I think the Bible defines it pretty clearly in Ephesians 3.16. The answer is to ask God's help and allow the Spirit to make you a strong follower.

We find great subtlety and significance in those words. What your life is on the outside depends on what you are on the inside. The outer world is but a reflection of the inner world. And what Jesus Christ does for people who are smart enough to get near to Him is this: He strengthens them by His Spirit so that they drive the shadows off. They rise above depression, they experience the sure cure for depressed feelings. I have personally seen this miracle take place in the lives of so many people that I confess I am filled with a boundless enthusiasm for what a person's life can become if he or she experiences this wonderful gift.

LIFE LIFTER: *Bread and water are symbols of the deepest longing of mind and soul. Until that hunger and thirst are satisfied there can be no deep peace or joy. When we surrender and truly accept Him by faith as Lord then mind and soul hunger and thirst will be deeply and perpetually satisfied. Jesus Christ satisfies.*

<table>
<tr>
<td>

DAY

27

</td>
<td>

Thou wilt show me the path of life: in thy presence is fulness of joy; at thy right hand there are pleasures for evermore. PSALM 16:11

</td>
</tr>
</table>

If we believe in the Holy Bible, we ought to realize that no matter how many difficulties we face, through Jesus Christ we find release from, and victory over, all depressing things and have wondrous joy.

"Oh," you say, "but you're overly enthusiastic. You are unrealistic." What am I supposed to be? Am I supposed to tell you that you might as well go around in dark gloom, shedding tears all the time, hopeless, negative? I'll never do that, because I don't believe it. Jesus came so that we might have a joyful and abundant life.

"Oh," you say, "life is hard. You don't know the gloom that fills my mind." But I do. And don't think I haven't had plenty of it myself. But we should remember that we are children of God, and that God has built what you might call "altitude" into us. That means that we are not meant to be denizens of the dark overcast, the cloud blanket, because above it—always above it and touching it and exercising the power to pierce it—is the powerful joy of Almighty God.

PRAYER: *Our Heavenly Father, we thank You for making us what we are. We put ourselves back into Your hands and ask You to bring us forth in newness of power and joy and greatness. Through Jesus Christ, our Lord. Amen.*

<table>
<tr><td>DAY
28</td><td>*Let every soul be subject unto the higher powers. For there is no power but of God: the powers that be are ordained of God.*</td></tr>
</table>

ROMANS 13:1

The Bible says the only power in this world is of God. And the earthly powers that be are ordained by God. We are created by this wondrous power. Are you living on the great flow of it? Or on a mere trickle?

"Well," you say, "how can God's power be released?" One way you can release it is by getting a higher opinion of yourself. It is my conviction that most human beings have a much lower opinion of themselves than the facts justify. If you see a person who seems to have an extraordinary opinion of himself, it may be that he is just overcompensating. Actually he may be throwing his weight around to give the impression that he amounts to quite a lot, while inside he feels he amounts to nothing. Most people underestimate themselves. And if you underestimate yourself, you will be underestimated by others. Your achievements in life agree with your own appraisal of your capacities.

PRAYER: *Our Heavenly Father, we ask Your blessing upon every person that this message reaches. Help each to become by Your grace the great person dormant in him or her, so that we may live effectively and joyously all our days. Through Jesus Christ, our Lord. Amen.*

<table>
<tr><td>DAY
29</td><td>*Create in me a clean heart, O God; and renew
a right spirit within me.*   PSALM 51:10</td></tr>
</table>

There is a verse in Psalm 51 that says, "Create pure thoughts in me and make me faithful again." But can you get a new heart when you are old and tired and worn and weak and sick and discouraged? Of course you can. I'm not referring to the physical organ known as the heart. When we ask God for a new heart, what we are asking is for a new inner motivation, a new depth of feeling, new basic attitudes. Such heart transplants never fail.

When you come to the point where you commit your life to Jesus Christ and stop trying to run it yourself, you will experience the most amazing, dramatic, fascinating, and exciting changes. There are people who knew that they needed a new heart, but couldn't get it themselves. They turned to the Lord Jesus Christ as their Savior, and He saved them from themselves.

PRAYER: *Our Heavenly Father, we want to reexamine our lives. Keep us stirred up, Lord. Keep us agitated. Make us think. Make us seek new ways to live better lives. And for giving us the desire for this, we give You thanks. Through Jesus Christ, our Lord. Amen.*

| DAY **30** | *So Saul died for his transgression which he committed against the Lord, even against the word of the Lord, which he kept not...* |

I CHRONICLES 10:13

Leo Tolstoy went through his whole calendar of sins trying to make life good. But it was dust and ashes. He knew he had to find the secret of life. He went out into the country where he met peasants and said to them, "My friends, you must teach me your secret."

They said, "When you stay in contact with God then joy is continuous. But if you get away from God then you get away from the life force. Return to God. Return to His Son, and you will find good days."

Tolstoy wrestled with himself, because there were some things he didn't want to let go. Then one day he gave it all up; he accepted Christ and gave himself to God. He wrote later that he had no sooner done this than joyous waves of life seemed to surge through him.

You can make your days good. But in the deeper sense of the word they are made good by God. I like that picture of Tolstoy—joyous waves of life surging in and out of him.

PRAYER: *Our Heavenly Father, we give You thanks that we can be recipients of Divine truth and gain victory over life itself. Grant, O Lord, that the error that is within us may be driven out by taking into our minds that mind which was in Christ Jesus, our Lord. Amen.*

<table>
<tr><td>DAY
31</td><td>*But the Lord is with me as a mighty terrible one: therefore my persecutors shall stumble, and they shall not prevail: they shall be greatly ashamed; for they shall not prosper: their*</td></tr>
</table>

everlasting confusion shall never be forgotten.

JEREMIAH 20:11

An analysis was made of the experience of 2000 American soldiers in World War II who were taken prisoner by the Nazis. All had been in concentration camps where they were brainwashed, beaten, starved, and treated with indignity. Many died; others became physical wrecks; others were emotionally maimed.

But a small group of men emerged unhurt mentally, spiritually, and physically. These men had decided that they wouldn't let the terrible circumstances destroy them. They kept their spirits up by telling one another about how wonderful life was going to be when they got back to the United States. They described the girls they were going to marry and their plans for the futures of their children. In other words, they practiced hope. And they were saved by hope. Hope is one of the great blessings offered to us by Jesus Christ. Put on the helmet of hope and change your thought processes.

LIFE LIFTER: *It isn't you who will remove big mountains of trouble from your path. It is rather your great faith— the kind that comes by deep desire and earnest prayer—that changes impossibles into wonderful possibles.*

JUNE

<table>
<tr><td>DAY
1</td><td>For he that will love life, and see good days, let him refrain his tongue from evil, and his lips that they speak no guile: Let him eschew evil, and do good; let him seek peace, and ensue it.</td></tr>
</table>

I PETER 3:10–11

So how do you find good days? It is very simple. If you want to be happy, if you want to have good days, just skip the evil and go for the good. It is just that open and shut. Sit down with yourself and ask, *What is my worst weakness?* Don't ask your spouse what your chief weakness is. He or she will probably name a half dozen. Just ask yourself, *What is my chief fault?* When you find it, then study it. Maybe it is the thing that has been holding you back from better days. But, once having isolated it, once having faced it honestly, you can decide what you are going to do about it, with the help of the Lord Jesus Christ. A person who is honest with himself, has isolated his chief fault and taken it to God, can do something about it. And, when a real fault is out of your way, what glorious better days you can have!

LIFE LIFTER: *The way to happiness: keep your heart free from hate, your mind from worry. Live simply, expect little, give much. Fill your life with love. Scatter sunshine. Forget self, think of others. Do as you would be done by. Try this for a week and you will be surprised.*

| DAY 2 |

And a letter unto Asaph the keeper of the king's forest, that he may give me timber to make beams for the gates of the palace which appertained to the house, and for the wall of the city, and for the house that I shall enter into. And the king granted me, according to the good hand of my God upon me.   NEHEMIAH 2:8

Getting acquainted with Jesus Christ means that you get to know His mind, that you develop the ability to think, that you are at peace. Then, out of inner peace comes intelligent understanding, and, as a result, good will come to you. I'm impressed with the power of the Bible to say something great in a highly understandable manner. The Bible knows how to communicate.

Knowing this, you can find an answer to your problems. The answer may be what you desire and want, what you have hoped for. And if this should be the case, I rejoice with you; that is wonderful. On the other hand, the answer may not be what you want. But if it has been hammered out with God, it is the right answer. There is no one who has a problem for which there is not an answer through the wisdom and the guidance of God.

LIFE LIFTER: *The strain and burden of life may make you tired. Perhaps you are carrying life too heavily. It is our minds, not our muscles, that become overtired. Turn to Jesus, He will give you rest.*

| DAY 3 | *These things have I spoken unto you, that my joy might remain in you, and that your joy might be full.* JOHN 15:11 |

Christianity is one of the most joyful religions in all the history of the world. In fact, it may not be claiming too much to say that it is the most joyful religious faith that has ever been developed. This, I know, runs counter to a rather general conception of Christianity. It has been portrayed—for altogether too long, I believe—as a dour, ultraserious, sad way of thought.

Now it is true that Jesus Christ was a Man of Sorrows and afflicted with grief. The true Christian is sensitive to the pain and the sorrow and the injustice in our world and tries always to do something about it. But there is built into Christianity, in its very essence, an upbeat, victorious presence that can lift a person above every valley in human life. It is never flippant; it is always concerned; but always there is in it inherent joy.

LIFE LIFTER: *Joy has healing value, whereas gloom is sickening. This is why Jesus so emphatically tells us to rejoice. Learn to live the joy way. Take a hopeful and optimistic attitude. Think happy thoughts, say happy things and put joy into people's lives. The more you do this, the more surely you will keep your own spirit high.*

> **DAY 4**

And he said, O Lord God of my master Abraham, I pray thee, send me good speed this day, and show kindness unto my master Abraham.
GENESIS 24:12

Friends, Christianity was established on this earth two thousand years ago by the wisest Man who ever entered into human affairs. He knew the relationship between human beings and the divine. He knew the working of the human mind. He understood full well the handling of a problem. And one of the great things that He taught us was to let God help us. This may seem to you an overly simple theme. But how often we try to do the whole thing ourselves! We tug and we pull and we strain over our problems, trying to handle them with a strength we haven't got. We were not meant to proceed in this manner. We were meant to understand that the illimitable power of God is at our disposal, and that if we will yield ourselves to Him wholeheartedly, God will let His power flow to our aid.

LIFE LIFTER: *Most people live on the surface. They miss the most astonishing things. People go to church, but the Gospel never penetrates their inner consciousness. That is because they do not listen with all their faculties. But if you listen as though life depended upon letting it sink into the mind by a deep and powerful penetration, then it falls like a healing potency. Every spiritual disease is killed, and that person lives with new health and strength.*

DAY 5

And the sight of the glory of the Lord was like devouring fire on the top of the mount in the eyes of the children of Israel.   EXODUS 24:17

While vacationing in Switzerland, a troubled young man visited me. We went to a little cafe in Interlaken. There is a meadow in the heart of the town, and towering over this meadow is the great mountain, the Jungfrau (Young Wife). Like a coy young wife, she often throws a veil of clouds over her face. That morning, however, the veil had been cast aside and there she was, in all of her white, sparkling, radiant glory. We sat at the cafe. The boy gazed at the mountain and said, "That's the way I want to be: clean, like that!"

"You can be," I said, "if you will bring Jesus Christ into your life."

"Oh," he exclaimed, "thank God! That's what I wanted to hear you say!" Apparently, no one else had said that to him. He leaned over the table where we were having coffee and, at my urging, gave his heart to Jesus Christ. "Go up there among the mountains where it is clean and talk with God," I said. That boy now knows that not only is there real good in life, but where to find it.

PRAYER: *Our Heavenly Father, in the midst of life we face difficulties, trials, defeats. But we have with us One who gives us power for overcoming difficulty and defeat—the Lord Jesus Christ, in whose name we offer this prayer. Amen.*

| DAY **6** | *Is there not an appointed time to man upon earth? are not his days also like the days of hireling?* JOB 7:1 |

If you have no confidence, if you're defeated, if you're being beat down, if you're troubled by fear, diffidence, apprehension, weakness, then come to where the power is, where the confidence is to be found: in your faith, in the Savior. It is good that we should call Him Savior, because that is what He does. He saves you from your defeats and gives you confidence with which you can handle life with mastery, satisfaction, and happiness. You can have confidence. You must have confidence if you are going to live well. Never let anything get you down, no matter how difficult, how black, how hard it is, how hopeless it may seem, how utterly depressed you may become. Whatever the quality and the character of the circumstances involved, never let anything get you down. Always there is help and hope for you.

PRAYER: *Our Heavenly Father, we ask Your blessing upon all who receive this message. Grant that into our weakness may come Your strength, that into our ineffective lives may come Your incredible power, that into our dissatisfaction may come Your inexpressible delight. This we pray through Jesus Christ, our Lord. Amen.*

DAY 7

Peter therefore was kept in prison: but prayer was made without ceasing of the church unto God for him.   ACTS 12:5

When faced with a difficult problem—whether it be a health problem, a money problem, a domestic problem or whatever—walk around it prayerfully. Now that phrase is not my own—I only wish it were. It was given to me by one of the greatest Christians I ever knew. He used to say, "Let's lay the problem out there on the table, boys, and walk around it prayerfully." And he would tell us there is no problem in this world that doesn't have a soft spot somewhere. "Walk around it prayerfully," he would say, " poke at it until you find the soft spot."

"Well," you say, "that may be all right, but you don't know my problem. My problem is a hard one." I know. Sure, your problem is a hard one. Just walk around it a little more—prayerfully—and you'll get your answer.

PRAYER: *Our Heavenly Father, we thank You for the wonderfulness of Jesus Christ and for all the incredible things that can happen in human experience when we get out of the realm of the material and deeply into the area of the spiritual. Help us to put our lives and whatever is bothering us into the hands of the One who can really give us the power to change, to overcome, to grow and to be. Through Jesus Christ, our Lord. Amen.*

| DAY 8 | *For he that soweth to his flesh shall of the flesh reap corruption; but he that soweth to the Spirit shall of the Spirit reap life everlasting.* GALATIANS 6:8 |

God gives us life, and this life continually recreates itself if we stay in harmony with Him. For He not only creates, He re-creates. But if you abandon Him, if you cut Him off, if you stop the practice of devotion, if you cease to cultivate your spiritual understanding, then disabilities creep in, and you begin to deteriorate.

The next question is: How can we recover our identification with God so that we become vital and well? Important in this are the thought patterns we constantly employ, the attitudes by which we live, the pictures of ourselves that we form in our consciousness. There is a great life force that should work for health in us through God, and we must release it. To release it we must believe in it, and we must cooperate with it. That may be done by affirmation: I hereby affirm that I have within me the life given to me by God and that it is in charge of me, it is encompassing me. It is directing my life.

> LIFE LIFTER: *A spiritually darkened mind is a breeding ground for terrifying fears. Flood the darkness with light and fears scurry away. Fill the mind with light, and fears are driven off. Fears develop when one feels weak. But the Lord transmits strength. Result? You are afraid of nothing.*

<table>
<tr><td>

DAY

9

</td><td>

*And said unto them, Hear me, ye Levites;
sanctify now yourselves, and sanctify the
house of the Lord God of your fathers, and
carry forth the filthiness out of the holy place.*

II CHRONICLES 29:5

</td></tr>
</table>

Knowing yourself and getting yourself healed can be a long, hard process if you try to do it by yourself, but the mysterious power of Jesus Christ is such that He comes into the life of anyone who will permit Him to do so and transforms it utterly, releasing the person.

As we go along through life, our minds get clouded so that they do not function in a clear, clean-cut manner. Nervous apprehension or ill will or some sinfulness or vindictiveness creeps in, or you take yourself too seriously or you live with yourself too much so that your mind gets confused.

There are behaviors and ways of thought that are not compatible with real happiness. Most of the frustration in our lives is self-imposed. And Jesus Christ offers us release from it, calling us to know the truth, so that the truth may sweep the dust from our minds and we may be free.

PRAYER: *Our Heavenly Father, we thank You that though we may by nature be weak, yet we are at the same time strong through Jesus Christ, who gives us of His grace and makes perfect His strength in our weakness. For this we give thanks through Jesus Christ, our Lord. Amen.*

<table>
<tr><td>

DAY

10
</td><td>

And he believed in the Lord; and he counted it to him for righteousness.   GENESIS 15:6
</td></tr>
</table>

You want to live a successful, meaningful existence. How much do you want that? Well, the Bible tells us that things will happen to us according to our faith.

You may say, "That's okay; I go for that and I believe it; but it is awfully hard to have that kind of faith." That's right. It is. Because faith has to be practiced. Some people have a greater capacity to believe than others, and it is part of the job of a therapist or counselor to help an ill or disturbed person to develop his capacity to believe. When such a person gets to the point where he can truly believe, where he can trust faith, he can get well. Faith will heal.

Faith may seem to be an unsubstantial thing to put your feet down on, and you may be inclined to think that the wise ways of the world are better. But there is nothing in the world wiser than what you get from the instrument panel. If you learn to have faith in faith and believe in it, it will see you through.

PRAYER: *Our Heavenly Father, we are ever amazed by the marvelous things that You can do with a human being who will yield himself to You. We would commit ourselves utterly to You and take authority and fight the good fight and keep the faith until we finish the course. Through Jesus Christ, our Lord. Amen.*

DAY 11

Thus saith the Lord God; Let it suffice you, O princes of Israel: remove violence and spoil, and execute judgment and justice, take away your exactions from my people, saith the Lord God.

EZEKIEL 45:9

I never steer away from the pathos of human life. Everyone needs help of one kind or another. Take, for example, a man who has been hounded by fear all his life—does he need help? Is it pointless to help him? Or consider a couple whose marriage is about to break up. They need a lot of help. Is it irrelevant to help them? One might say they are just two individuals out of the billions on this planet. But are we concerned now only with masses? Don't we see the pain on a human face? Have we no compassion for heavily burdened human hearts? What has come over us, that helping the individual should seem trite and insignificant?

A church alive in Jesus Christ helps both the masses and the hurting individual. Both missions deserve your dedication. We must help the world and we must also help individuals, the poor souls who live in it.

PRAYER: *Our Heavenly Father, help us to be thankful for this day and every day, and to treat each one as a precious gem to be filled to the full with meaning and love and human service. Through Jesus Christ, our Lord. Amen.*

<table>
<tr><td>DAY
12</td><td>*Then said he, Unto what is the kingdom of God like? and whereunto shall I resemble it? It is like a grain of mustard seed, which a man took, and cast into his garden; and it grew,*</td></tr>
</table>

and waxed a great tree; and the fowls of the air lodged in the branches of it. LUKE 13:18–19

A young man I knew wanted to be a social worker but he did not have enough education to qualify. He worked nights driving a rickety truck. One Sunday, he turned on the radio. A voice was saying, "Believe in the potential you possess, and yield to the One Who has the infinite skills to bring your potential into action."

He wasn't too impressed, but he took to listening to that program every week. Finally one night he said, "Okay, Lord, if this is true, please help me." He described his goal and said, "I can't do it without You."

Soon he began to work days, and went to school at night. Not long ago, he wrote a letter telling me: "I am now a social worker, and I am having the time of my life helping people. I will never quit. I will believe."

Now what do you call that? A miracle of real faith! Jesus doesn't say you have to have a lot of faith; just a little real faith. Quite an offer, isn't it?

LIFE LIFTER: *Pray that your mountainous difficulty shall be removed and, as you pray, believe that it is being done then and now. Have no doubt in your heart, but believe that God is removing it for you now.*

DAY 13

One law and one manner shall be for you, and for the stranger that sojourneth with you.
NUMBERS 15:16

All of us are concerned today that there be found a constructive American and Christian solution to the problem of race relationships. This has burst violently upon the people of this land who surprisingly seem rather ill prepared to meet it. When you break this problem down into its basic component parts it is a human problem. It will take more than new laws to bring about brotherhood, respect and understanding between people of different races in this country.

Here is an area where we should turn once again to the practical problem-solving power of Christianity, which teaches that all human relationships can be brought to a higher level where people live in mutual respect, understanding and esteem. This is the great message of the New Testament. It is the only ground upon which the great social question of race relations will ever be resolved, now and for the future.

PRAYER: *Our Heavenly Father, we thank You for this wonderful fellowship with these dear and beloved people. We live in the midst of controversy, but grant, Lord, that we may love one another and love all men. Help us to transmit the Gospel by word and by example so that the church and the Kingdom will be stronger to serve mankind. Through Jesus Christ, our Lord. Amen.*

DAY
14

And I will make thy seed as the dust of the earth: so that if a man can number the dust of the earth, then shall thy seed also be numbered.
GENESIS 13:16

Health and prosperity may be yours. I realize that you may regard this as an extravagant assertion—a big order, so to speak: But please remember that I do not make this assertion on my own authority. I have this on the authority of the wisest Book ever written. The Bible isn't as fearful of promising big things as some of the more timid, halfhearted preachers of the Gospel. The Bible makes superlative promises, because its promises are inspired by a loving and omnipotent God.

But the Bible is also subtle. And it points out that the blessings of health and prosperity are not easily given or easily received. Parenthetically, I want to say that by prosperity the Bible does not mean merely material affluence, but it means to enter abundantly into the blessings of God's grace. And it tells us that health and prosperity come to us when our soul is in harmony with God.

LIFE LIFTER: *Prayer can heal the sick. I have seen this demonstrated many times. People who have been given up on by doctors have been raised up when someone has put them unreservedly into the hands of the Great Physician. There is tremendous power in the prayer of faith as applied in cases of illness.*

DAY 15

Ye are blessed of the Lord which made heaven and earth.

PSALM 115:15

My wife taught me one of the greatest truths in the world, that God is always with you. And I can guarantee to you what she guaranteed to me: If you put your problems in His hands and trust Him, He will guide you and bless you and take care of you till the day you die. And He won't stop there. He will take care of you the rest of the way.

"Well," you may say, "that is sensible; that is logical, but I never felt any closeness to God." I'm sorry to hear anyone say that. Are you going to live all your life and never feel the presence of God? Haven't you had some high moments spiritually when you felt lifted out of yourself, lifted to a higher level? At some time in your life, you should feel deeply the presence of God. Then, even though there be times when you feel that He is far away from you, you know He is with you, and then nothing can overcome you.

LIFE LIFTER: *The greatest fact of all is that God is with us. We are not alone. He will never leave nor forsake us but will protect, guide and comfort us at any time, anywhere. When the going is hard and you feel insecure and maybe fearful, just say this wonderful promise and remind yourself that He is always with you—always.*

DAY 16

And when he was in affliction, he besought the Lord his God, and humbled himself greatly before the God of his fathers.

II CHRONICLES 33:12

One part of learning to live successfully under pressure is to analyze our lives and honestly face any of our attitudes that would be a cause of pressure. What most often breaks people down is an impairment of the mental processes by negative thoughts and feelings, or the weight of sin upon their souls. Fear, hate and resentment give rise to tensions that become continuous, preventing adequate relaxation between peaks of activity. Eventually, they so impair a person's resiliency that the daily pressures get him down.

If you are so fortunate as never to have had a crisis, you can count on one thing—you will have a crisis sooner or later. And it will take all your faith, all your strength, all your thought, everything you've got, to meet it. But remember this: In any crisis, you have a big God you can turn to in order to find the answer that answers.

> PRAYER: *Our Father in Heaven, bless this simple message, which we have given earnestly and sincerely. Grant that it may touch the lives of people who are a problem to themselves and to others, that they may find a solution through Jesus Christ, Savior of mankind, in whose name we pray. Amen.*

<table>
<tr><td>DAY
17</td><td>*And the Lord said, If ye had faith as a grain of mustard seed, ye might say unto this sycamine tree, Be thou plucked up by the root, and be thou planted in the sea; and it should obey you.*</td></tr>
</table>

LUKE 17:6

Mary B. Crowe rose from humble circumstances to become one of the most successful insurance agents in the United States. At the age of twelve, Mary was left in charge at home. She got the meals for a family of ten, cleaned the house, did the laundry, and went to school.

Later, after she became the first college graduate in the history of her family, she decided she wanted to be a life insurance agent. At that time the idea of women selling life insurance was practically unheard of. She asked to see a manager about selling insurance, and he did his best to discourage her. Long after he had retired, that agency manager was present at a luncheon in honor of Mary Crowe's twenty-fifth anniversary.

If you remember His everlasting presence and look to Him for help, nothing will be so hard that you cannot think it through and see it through. So you need never let anything, anything, ever get you down, you wonderful person, you immortal child of God.

PRAYER: *Our Heavenly Father, we give You thanks for the principles laid down by Jesus Christ our Lord. Help us to be wise enough to follow them that we may attain what we want from life. Through Jesus Christ, our Lord. Amen.*

DAY **18**	*And hast made us unto our God kings and priests: and we shall reign on the earth.*

REVELATION 5:10

Christianity not only outlines procedures and a methodology for solving problems, but provides the "go-power" that gets solutions into working order. You name the problem—and practical Christianity has an answer for it. A problem can be pesky, difficult and complicated, but there is an answer. This applies to individual and social problems alike.

Years ago, Marble Collegiate Church began the practice of recognizing no difference whatsoever between the races. Neither have we ever had any regard for differences in economic or social status. To think that the church of Almighty God should receive some persons differently from others because of differences in economic condition, social position, or color is a blasphemy. And if this church has spiritual power it is because we have tried to follow the teachings of Jesus, who said: "I am giving you a new command. You must love each other, just as I have loved you" (John 13:34). This sounds very idealistic, but is utterly practical.

PRAYER: *Our Heavenly Father, You created us all and we are grateful for that. You put something of Yourself in us and thus we are more than mere humans. Help us to keep looking to Jesus and to grow in understanding and strength. Through Jesus Christ, our Lord. Amen.*

DAY 19

Now thanks be unto God, which always causeth us to triumph in Christ, and maketh manifest the savour of his knowledge by us in every place.   II CORINTHIANS 2:14

If you want enthusiasm, a good place to look for it is in the Bible; the Bible is packed full of enthusiasm. What does it talk about? In 2 Corinthians 2:14, we read these marvelous words: "I am grateful that God always makes it possible for Christ to lead us to victory." If you really surrender your life to Jesus Christ and follow Him— alive, vital Jesus Christ who has the answers that really answer—you will have enthusiasm. He will keep enthusiasm going for you so that you can overcome your defeats, so that you can make a real contribution to humanity.

If you are constantly in the company of negative people, you will take on a negative mind—your mental reactions will be negative. So you have to practice enthusiasm. You do that by thinking it, by believing it, by praying it, by talking it, until enthusiasm becomes part of your better nature.

LIFE LIFTER: *So long as we are in unbroken contact with God, the life force continues strong within us. Love God, obey His voice, cling to Him. Then He will truly be your life all the length of your days. The basic method for constantly getting more out of life is simply to have more life within you.*

<table>
<tr><td>

DAY

20
</td><td>

As every man hath received the gift, even so minister the same one to another, as good stewards of the manifold grace of God.

I PETER 4:10
</td></tr>
</table>

I spent several days with Leslie Carver, a reticent man, visiting camps for Palestinian refugees. We talked about everything. But if I touched on religion, he'd say, "I lost myself and found myself in Jerusalem." One day, we met an old man in the cellar of a bombed-out building. Carver sat down, took the man's hand and chatted with him in Arabic. When Carver stood up, I saw wondrous love written on the old man's face.

When we came out of the cellar, I saw the Garden of Gethsemane straight ahead of us. I said: "You found a Man in that Garden, and He put love in your heart. You love the people because you love Jesus Christ."

He just answered, almost gruffly, "Didn't I tell you I lost myself and found myself in Jerusalem?" I returned home and about six weeks later I received a letter that said Leslie Carver had died in an accident while "on one of his usual errands of love."

That is the way to get excited about life. Lose yourself, for in so doing you find yourself.

> PRAYER: *Our Heavenly Father, we thank You for what we are and for what You are. Help us to face trouble and to struggle through it, both individually and collectively, to bring about the higher good. Amen.*

<table>
<tr><td>

DAY
21

</td><td>

Therefore we are buried with him by baptism into death: that like as Christ was raised up from the dead by the glory of the Father, even so we also should walk in newness of life.

</td></tr>
</table>

ROMANS 6:4

Paul told the Romans that we are raised to new life. Life should never grow dull or flat to us. It should never lose its luster. So if you want enthusiasm that never runs down, then run (don't walk) to a nearby church. Because wherever the Gospel is believed in and preached, people learn to walk in newness of life.

What a wonderful concept this is—newness of life! It means a renewal of the soul. God built enthusiasm into us when we were created. You should never let it run down. But if it has run down, it can be rejuvenated, it can be reactivated, it can be built up again, it can be enhanced with a powerful new upthrust. And when this happens, this thing that we call rebirth, then a person becomes perpetually enthusiastic and excited. In rebirth, a person comes alive. It is where he comes up out of death and decadence into life and vitality.

PRAYER: *Our Heavenly Father, we give You thanks for the newness with which Christianity is filled, sparkling like the dew with freshness, light, and power. Grant that we may walk in newness of life and come out of darkness into Your marvelous light. Through Jesus Christ, our Lord. Amen.*

DAY 22

The meek will he guide in judgment: and the meek will he teach his way.   PSALM 25:9

After a speaking engagement in Florida, my hosts assigned a Navy captain to fly me home. En route, the captain told me that there was a heavy overcast at New York. "As a matter of fact," he said, "we'll have to go in on instruments." We went down, down, down. And finally, I saw the lights of the runway and we came right up to the ramp. It was a beautiful landing.

The captain said, "The primary ingredient for a good landing is faith. I have to have faith in these instruments. If I didn't I might think, 'Well, maybe this instrument isn't exactly right so I'll make this adjustment.' And that could have tragic consequences."

Your religious education is your instrument panel for safe navigation through the long flight of the years. When clouds gather, storms develop, and trouble looms, if you lose faith in your instruments, you can be lost. But if you have faith in the teachings of the Bible, in prayer, in the church, in goodness, love and hope, your instruments will bring you through.

PRAYER: *Our Heavenly Father, help us to stand up to life and let it know we are not afraid, remembering that we have Someone with us; we have a power going for us. And for this we give You thanks through Jesus Christ, our Lord. Amen.*

DAY 23

And thou, Ezra, after the wisdom of thy God, that is in thine hand, set magistrates and judges, which may judge all the people that are beyond the river, all such as know the laws of thy God; and teach ye them that know them not.

EZRA 7:25

My friend built a house in Topanga Canyon—a beautiful place in an attractive, wild setting. I was in Los Angeles when a fire swept through the canyon and destroyed 565 houses. My friend's house was among the ruined buildings. I telephoned and said, "I'm sorry that your house burned down."

"Why, what are you worrying about me for?" he said. "Sure it burned. But my wife and kids are safe."

"Did you save anything from the house?" I asked.

"Nothing but my philosophy and my faith," he said, "But that's all I need. I'm going to build again. Don't worry about me until I get into some real trouble."

That is the kind of talk I like to hear: Nothing left but "my philosophy and my faith!" If you'll start digging into the Christian faith and applying its principles you will be able to meet and handle victoriously the tough situations of life.

> **PRAYER:** *Our Heavenly Father, we thank You for all the potential You have built into us. Grant that we may grow upon it, forget our failures, and build a great new life, a great new world. Through Jesus Christ, our Lord. Amen.*

| DAY **24** | *And David reigned over all Israel; and David executed judgment and justice unto all his people.*   II SAMUEL 8:15 |

A young man was sitting next to me on a plane. It was so dark that the lights had to be turned on. But we took off with clockwork precision and in seconds we were above the overcast and into the clear afternoon sky.

I was in the window seat. Suddenly, I felt a boy leaning over to see this marvelous sight. He exclaimed, "Did you ever see anything like it? To come out of darkness into this glorious light—isn't it something? Don't tell me God isn't in His heaven!"

I looked at the young man's face. It was the great, full face of someone who loved life and loved the world. And he poured out to me his hopes, his dreams, his ideals and objectives. All of them had to do with human justice and making the world a better place. He had meaning packed into his life.

There are people everywhere who pack meaning into their lives because they pack something else into their lives: faith and goodness and love and hope and fellowship, and every other good thing.

PRAYER: *Our Heavenly Father, help us to know that Jesus walks the highways and the thronging streets of our world. Help us accept Him and to follow after Him to remake this world according to Your will. Through Jesus Christ, our Lord. Amen.*

| DAY **25** | *He hath made his wonderful works to be remembered: the Lord is gracious and full of compassion.* PSALM 111:4 |

I once met a man known as Brother Andrew. Hearing that people in Communist lands wanted the Word of God, he went to the missionary society in Amsterdam and asked them to send him to Eastern Europe. They said, "No, it's too dangerous."

"Will you pray for me if I go on my own?" he asked. He fixed up a car so it could conceal a supply of Bibles, and he crossed the border with them. Finally, he was caught. But the border agents knew how valuable the Bibles were; they confiscated them and sold them for high prices. This didn't bother Brother Andrew, because at least his Bibles were getting into circulation. He returned to that border seven more times to get the agents to sell more Bibles.

Sitting and talking with this dedicated man, I asked him, "Why do you do this?" He looked at me and answered, " I do it because the Lord set me free, and the only thing that can set these people free is the Word of God."

PRAYER: *Our Heavenly Father, we thank You for the blessing of knowing that we were created to be free. Help us to put ourselves in Your hands and never again weakly settle for supposed limitations. Through Jesus Christ, our Lord. Amen.*

DAY 26

Ye shall not fear them: for the Lord your God he shall fight for you. DEUTERONOMY 3:22

We are either destroyed or made whole by the kind of thoughts we think. You can cancel out a fear thought or an apprehension thought with a faith thought. Don't be afraid—just believe. If you have been victimized by the fear of some sinister thing that might happen down the road, just believe and healing will start. If you believe strongly enough, you can drive any apprehensive fear out of your mind. So the number one antidote for fear is to fill your mind full of God.

This may seem to you to be a strange expression. How can you get your mind full of God? Well, you read about God, you think about God, you talk to God, you try to serve God, you try to live God's way. After a while, your mind gets full of God. And when your mind is full of God it cannot have anything negative in it. It can't have prejudice, it can't have hate, it can't have resentment, it can't have impurities of any kind. It is holy, wholesome and good.

PRAYER: *Our Heavenly Father, in our hearts we want to be what You want us to be. But we are held by these other things which prevent. Help us to be through with them, that by the grace and the power of Jesus Christ we may henceforth "walk in newness of life." Amen.*

DAY
27

For the Lord our God, he it is that brought us up and our fathers out of the land of Egypt, from the house of bondage, and which did those great signs in our sight, and preserved us in all the way wherein we went, and among all the people through whom we passed.... JOSHUA 24:17

I was invited to a gathering to honor the mothers who had lost sons in the war. I went with the understanding that I was to give an invocation. But when I picked up the program I saw that I was on the program to make a speech! I was aghast. I had no confidence.

General Theodore Roosevelt, Jr. was sitting next to me. He said, "Each of those mothers has lost the idol of her heart. Can't you get up and tell them that God loves them and their country loves them and at some time, somewhere, in the mercy of God they will meet their sons again? Forget about yourself, son. Put yourself in the hands of God and do the best you can."

To this day I love that man, for he taught me a tremendous principle: Love other people, do the best you can, and put your faith in God. This is the secret of confidence and security in an insecure world.

PRAYER: *Our Heavenly Father, we pray for everyone, that whatever their difficulties, their hardships and problems, they will know the great, wonderful fact that with God all things are possible. For this we give You thanks, through Jesus Christ, our Lord. Amen.*

DAY **28**	*Although my house be not so with God; yet he hath made with me an everlasting covenant, ordered in all things, and sure: for this is all my salvation, and all my desire, although he*

make it not to grow. II SAMUEL 23:5

Almighty God put you and me in a hard, tough universe. Oh, He filled it with sunshine and babbling brooks and beautiful forests and misty valleys filled with eternal peace. He sprinkled the heavens with illimitable stars. He gave us dawning and sunset, lovely eyes to look into, dear friends to cling to. He gave us all that.

But He wanted to grow His human creatures, so He also made it hard. He knew it would get so hard that His creatures would want to quit the hard highway, abandon the upper climb, so He gave them support. He said, "I'll send Jesus to them and call His name Emmanuel, which means they will never be alone, that God is with them always." Jesus Himself said, "I will be with you always, even until the end of the world" (Matthew 28:20). So, you children of God, thank God for that truth, because He is with us and nothing in this world can overwhelm us. You can be strong.

> PRAYER: *Our heavenly Father, we thank You that in this hard and difficult world, we have the presence of the Strongest One, who will see us through this life and into the next life where we shall have peace and joy everlasting. Through Jesus Christ, our Lord. Amen.*

DAY 29

And we know that all things work together for good to them that love God, to them who are the called according to his purpose.

ROMANS 8:28

Romans 8:28 is a tremendous text. It means that everything that happens in your life—harsh, painful, hard though it be—combines with all the rest of your experience for your good, if your life is dedicated to God. This is one of the deepest philosophies ever declared. We are to take all things—what we think is good and what we think is bad—and draw them all together into a symphony of creativity and make it work for good. And that's the way it is, if we are in harmony with God's will and mindful of His love. So I submit that this is the secret of having a bright future in this chaotic world. If enough people were to take hold of this idea and live attuned to it, moving out from the churches into the world outside, we could make all things work together for good in the world, too.

LIFE LIFTER: *We read in the Bible of the marvelous things Jesus did for people, and wistfully we ask, "Why can't that happen to me?" It can. Jesus Christ has the same power to change human lives now as when He walked the shores of Galilee. Anything He ever did for anyone, He can do for you. It all depends upon how completely you surrender yourself to Him, and how sincerely you believe.*

DAY 30

Let us hear the conclusion of the whole matter: Fear God, and keep his commandments: for this is the whole duty of man.

ECCLESIASTES 12:13

What kind of people are happy people? In reply to this question some would say that the mood of unhappiness today is very high. A distinguished writer declared in a magazine article that unhappiness is the commonest thing there is. And T.S. Eliot, the famous British poet and literary critic, once asked plaintively, "Where is the life we have lost in living?"

A great many writers, perhaps because they themselves have lost the secret of happiness, dwell on the prevalence of unhappiness. But I believe there are untold numbers of people who have discovered a precious secret, the secret of how to have happiness in depth. And, as a matter of fact, unless there is depth in happiness, it isn't genuine. It is spurious and of little value. Apparently, many people are discovering this. They are finding out how to live in this confused and bewildering world while at the same time having peace within their hearts and a deep happiness within their natures.

LIFE LIFTER: *To ask in Jesus' name means complete unselfishness and sacrificial spirit. The great secret is to ask for that which He wants us to ask for. And it shall be granted overwhelmingly.*

JULY

<table>
<tr><td>DAY
1</td><td>*And the Lord said unto Joshua, Stretch out the spear that is in thy hand toward Ai; for I will give it into thine hand. And Joshua stretched out the spear that he had in his*</td></tr>
</table>

hand toward the city.   JOSHUA 8:18

It is really unworthy of a Christian to say, "Well, I guess I've had it. It's too much for me. I can't handle it anymore. I will just accept defeat." You say, "Look at all the difficulties." I am looking at them. Our forefathers made a new world. Were our forefathers any greater than we are? We, too, can make a new world if we think we can and if we have the same quality of faith as they had. No, we don't need to be defeated by anything. Never accept defeat.

If you feel defeated and you think, "I'm tired and weary and I've had it," that is exactly how it will be. You can count on it for sure. You will be what you accept in your mind. But if, on the contrary, when the going gets hard and difficult, you think, "I won't accept this—I will continue to think victory and not defeat," then what happens is that all the resources of your nature flow toward effecting a victory situation and circumventing a defeat condition.

> **PRAYER:** *Our Heavenly Father, help us to become wise and to remember that Jesus offers that which will work. Help us to get on His team and give ourselves to build a great new day. Through Jesus Christ, our Lord. Amen.*

DAY 2

And Jabez called on the God of Israel, saying, Oh that thou wouldest bless me indeed, and enlarge my coast, and that thine hand might be with me, and that thou wouldest keep me from evil, that it may not grieve me! And God granted him that which he requested. I CHRONICLES 4:10

Carl Erskine, the great pitcher for the Brooklyn Dodgers, once told me, "The simplest and greatest truth that I have ever learned in my whole life is this: Whatever the problem, whatever the challenge, difficulty, hardship, pain or suffering—you need never have confidence knocked out of your heart if you believe and remember that God is with you and if you submit your life into His hands."

I know that sounds simple. The greatest things in this world are simple. Christianity is not a religion of complexity. It is taking the complex and inscrutable and making it so simple that a child can understand. Just put your life in God's hands; do the best you can, trust it to Him and you will have the blessing of confidence. It does not come easy. It requires practice. But when you get it then you have the secret of peace and confidence.

> **LIFE LIFTER:** *When difficulties come, receive them as a sign of God's deep favor. And remember if we are wounded He binds up and heals. God loves us like that; it is a love greater than anything we will ever know.*

DAY
3

...Thou shalt have no inheritance in their land, neither shalt thou have any part among them: I am thy part and thine inheritance among the children of Israel. NUMBERS 18:20

A company was building a bridge and discovered a sunken ship in the channel where they had to put down some footings. They had to get it out of the way. A young crewman suggested a solution. He said to the foreman, "Sir, if I were you, I would send down a diver to work chains underneath the hulk and attach the chains to flat boats on either side. Let the tide float it out." The foreman saw the reasonableness in the suggestion and adopted it, and presently the ocean tide came surging into the harbor. The shoulders of the sea got under those flat boats and lifted the hulk free.

Now haven't you seen people wearing themselves out, trying to lift a great weight, when through surrender to God they could get the mighty shoulders of God under it? Let God help you. The power of God will flow to your aid if you give yourself to Him, commit yourself to Him, and have faith in Him.

LIFE LIFTER: *Knowledgeable persons recognize the validity of spiritual principles as verifiable scientific procedure. They know that power operates through the mind as surely as it moves through wires, and that faith produces results. Why be defeated when you are free to draw upon a Higher Power that can do everything for you?*

DAY 4

For the children of Israel walked in all the sins of Jeroboam which he did; they departed not from them.　　　II KINGS 17:22

The problem of preserving our country is acute. We do not realize how easily a civilization can decay. I have been to Byblos, at the Eastern end of the Mediterranean Sea, where you can see at a glance the excavated traces of seven successive civilizations (thanks to the skill with which the excavations there have been performed): Egyptian, Persian, Greek, Roman, and others—all mighty civilizations. If at the height of any of those civilizations a preacher had stood in a pulpit and said, "This civilization can die," he would have been laughed at. But they all did die, and their cities were covered over by dirt and sand and a few crumbling monuments. That is all that is left of them. This mighty civilization of ours likewise has within it the seeds of death. All human beings have within them the seeds of death. You have them, I have them. It is necessary to counteract these seeds of death with those of life. Our civilization can die, or our civilization can live.

PRAYER: *Our Heavenly Father, we thank You for the memory of all those who laid the foundations of this land. We ask Your blessings upon the generation yet unborn who shall take this nation and shall establish the kingdom of God on this earth. Through Jesus Christ, our Lord. Amen.*

DAY 5

And showing mercy unto thousands of them that love me and keep my commandments.
DEUTERONOMY 5:10

If people will love the dear Lord and love others and love this beautiful world, they will overcome fear. A great factor in overcoming fear is to get a sound mind. Think of all the tangled ideas to which we have been subjected and from which we may never have escaped—quirks, notions, ghosts, shadows in the mind—affecting our attitudes toward ourselves and toward the world. A sound, clean, wholesome mind is a mental machine in which there is no sand—finely lubricated and working with precision.

When you have a mind like that, then you have a mental engine that delivers power. Difficulties start with obsessive things that you pick up over the years: prejudices, hates, notions, fears, tensions, opinions of yourself that are incorrect. When you begin to know God, when you learn to love Jesus, then you begin to see yourself as you really are, not as you had thought you were. You cast out defeat elements.

PRAYER: *Our Heavenly Father, speak in Your own language to each of us, we pray You, that we may enter into our inheritance as children of God. Bless us, Your people, with good things, with good health and above all with the salvation of our souls now and through eternity. Through Jesus Christ, our Lord. Amen.*

DAY 6

By humility and the fear of the Lord are riches, and honour, and life. PROVERBS 22:4

A popular local television host invited me to his studio for an interview. When I met him, I was rather startled. He was abnormally short, his hands were disproportionately large with stubby fingers. He had an unimaginative face, but when he began to talk, his countenance became animated; his eyes flashed with depths of understanding. There was a tremendous charm about the man.

Before we went on the air he told me, "I was a defeated person. I was self-conscious and resentful. I think you can understand why: you have only to look at me. However, some instinct kept telling me that being bitter would only make things worse.

"In my unhappiness I began to read the Bible. Gradually a big idea dawned upon me: changed thinking changes everything. So I resolved that I would learn to think spiritually about my handicap. And as I did so, everything changed for me."

Then I knew why his television program was so popular. Even when he talked about ordinary things, he gave people something special.

LIFE LIFTER: *God's promises mean that no matter what happens, nothing can separate you from His love and protection. Dwell on this mentally until it becomes an unshakable fact.*

<table>
<tr><td>
DAY

7
</td><td>
But I must die in this land, I must not go over Jordan: but ye shall go over, and possess that good land. Take heed unto yourselves, lest ye forget the covenant of the Lord your God,
</td></tr>
</table>

which he made with you, and make you a graven image, or the likeness of any thing, which the Lord thy God hath forbidden thee. For the Lord thy God is a consuming fire, even a jealous God.   DEUTERONOMY 4:22–24

Now just what does the process of praying do to you that relieves you of worry? One thing it does is release and activate your built-in strength. Every one of us has more strength by far than he ever dreamed of. Have you ever used all your strength? ALL of it? No, you have never used one-half your strength, nor have I. I'll go further and say that I doubt that any of us has ever used one-tenth of his strength. We have tremendous reservoirs of power that we could call into action if we wanted to. I don't know but that the greatest achievement in life is to know how to continually break out from yourself the strength that is there. You pray the strength out, you believe it out, you practice it out. And then the worry fades away. It is amazing the strength that people have—that you have—that I have.

LIFE LIFTER: *If power isn't coming through, find the block and remove it. Always poke around a problem, looking for its soft spot, for nearly every problem has one. Then break the problem open and find the solution.*

<table>
<tr><td>DAY
8</td><td>*And as he lay and slept under a juniper tree,
behold, then an angel touched him, and said
unto him, Arise and eat.*   I KINGS 19:5</td></tr>
</table>

I had a friend who managed a hotel in Florida and was one of the happiest men I ever saw. He had a very interesting way of starting the day. The first thing he did in the morning was go down to the ocean and take a dip. No matter what the weather was, he did this every morning. And just before plunging in he would offer this prayer: "O God, as I breathe into me this fresh morning air, so I breathe in Your Holy Spirit. Come fill me with Your holiness, fill me with Your peace, fill me with Your kindness, Your purity and wisdom. Fill me with Your joy. And O, God, fill me with Yourself." Then he would plunge into the sea and come out feeling alive to his fingertips, a song on his lips, vital and vibrant for the day. That was how he began his daily practice of happiness. And his joyous personality was impressive evidence that by practice we can be happy people notwithstanding difficulties and adversities. So don't continue practicing old unhappiness. Practice happiness.

LIFE LIFTER: *Don't write off the importance of hard work, the guts to keep at it, a definite goal and the ability to have fun in the process. If there's no fun in it, something's wrong with all you're doing. Always maintain hopefulness, especially when the going is hard.*

> **DAY 9**
>
> *So God created man in his own image, in the image of God created he him; male and female created he them.* GENESIS 1:27

What is the highest form of God's creation? Human nature—with its weaknesses but with its strength; with its defeat but with its victory; with its sins but with its goodness; with its illimitable possibility under God. What, then, would you like to be? You name it, and by God's grace you can be it.

You may say, "That is going too far. That is promising too much." But, mark you, I have not said you can attain this through your own strength, because you cannot. You are weak. You are of the world, earthly. But you are also of heaven, heavenly. And through God's grace, you can realize your highest dreams.

As a boy and as a girl you had long, long thoughts of what you might be. Have you now become so old and tired and cynical that you have forgotten these dreams of your youth; these high expectations of yourself? Never lose them no matter what you lose. Lose your stock certificates, lose your property, but don't lose your dreams. For this urge to be someone, to be something, was put into you by Almighty God.

PRAYER: *Our Heavenly Father, our lives are in Your hands. Help us live so that not only do we have strength and joy ourselves, but we may help others and build Your kingdom on earth. Through Jesus Christ, our Lord. Amen.*

DAY 10

In that day it shall be said to Jerusalem, Fear thou not: and to Zion, Let not thine hands be slack. The Lord thy God in the midst of thee is mighty; he will save, he will rejoice over thee with joy; he will rest in his love, he will joy over thee with singing.
ZEPHANIAH 3:16–17

If you are discouraged, I have news for you—good news. There is a way to end discouragement. And the word itself gives the clue. "Discouragement" is formed by putting the prefix *dis-* before the word *courage*. In effect, you have a "discounting" of courage. Therefore, the way to end discouragement is to remove the prefix and to lay under your life a solid foundation of courage. Winston Churchill expresses it well. He says, "Success is never final. Failure is never fatal. It's courage that counts."

It is a pity that the Christian religion is presented as a genial philosophy, but with no power in it. Few speak of the tremendous power that Jesus Christ can let loose in a human being, power that can change even the cyclical rise and all of your mental and emotional life so that you become a controlled human being, not the victim of your moods, but the master of them.

PRAYER: *Our Heavenly Father, we pray that every human being may discover this priceless secret of courage and self-control, that his life may be rich and full and honest and whole. Through Jesus Christ, our Lord. Amen.*

DAY 11	*Turn thou us unto thee, O Lord, and we shall be turned; renew our days as of old.*
	LAMENTATIONS 5:21

Some people must be revised in order that they may have a new life every morning. If you become a revised, new person, your tomorrows will be altogether different. I'd like to relate to you a letter that illustrates this point. It is from a woman who lives in Columbia, Missouri. She says: "I never knew before the effective use of faith. Now I find myself practicing my beliefs and, as a result, I have a cheerful outlook. I have been able to make new friends out of old enemies. I finally learned and accepted the fact that no one was against me but myself. I have come out of my shell at long last. I cannot adequately describe the happiness I now feel, instead of the self-pity and self-hate that once was me."

This woman walked away from her yesterdays. She applied the principle that by personal revision with God's help you can become a new person. It is a simple formula. It takes discipline, it takes effort, but you can work it if you really want it, and thus be able to start life new every morning.

LIFE LIFTER: *You can become free of worry by practicing the opposite and stronger habit of faith. With all the strength and perseverance you can command, start practicing faith. Affirm that God's blessings are being given, and spend most of your prayers giving thanks.*

DAY 12

Give, and it shall be given unto you; good measure, pressed down, and shaken together, and running over, shall men give into your bosom. For with the same measure that ye mete withal it shall be measured to you again.

LUKE 6:38

Belief is the key to a transformed life. Hear the words of the Gospel of Luke, chapter 6, verse 38: "If you give to others, you will be given a full amount in return." Now the question is: Do we believe that? Do you believe that if you do so it will work?

The first thing is to believe in faith and trust it. The second thing is to go out and practice faith. Actually, there isn't much of a distinction between believing in faith and practicing it, because if you truly do believe, you practice it. For the person who learns the techniques of faith and practices them, nothing is too good to be true. If you are sick you believe that God with the doctor will heal you; if you are weak you believe you will become strong; if you have a great opportunity you believe that you can handle it. You trust and you do the best you can. Whatever the situation is, you believe in and practice faith.

LIFE LIFTER: *Successful and happy living is built into you by God who created you. Visualize God, who created you, as constantly re-creating you in every element of being. With God, life can always be vital, always dynamic.*

DAY
13

The fear of the Lord is the beginning of wisdom: and the knowledge of the Holy is understanding.   PROVERBS 9:10

You can find amazing truth all caught up in one verse from the Bible: "Respect and obey the Lord! This is the beginning of wisdom. To have understanding, you must know the Holy God" (Proverbs 9:10). Any person who needs a change within himself or within his life can have this take place by changing his mind. But this cannot be a superficial mental change; it must be one in depth. Such a change can be extremely effective.

Are you perhaps facing a hard situation? Are you involved in some unsatisfactory personal relationship? Is there some other kind of trouble in your life? We could hardly enumerate all the problems a human being has to deal with. But there is a great answer to them all—and it is this: they can all be changed, and you can be changed—everything for the better— through the magic of a positive mental attitude.

PRAYER: *Our Heavenly Father, when You created this universe, You permitted problems to come to us. We assume that You did so for a purpose. Help us therefore to know that out of the handling of problems comes wisdom by Your help and guidance. If we determine to handle a problem right, we will get a right and a proper answer. For this we give You thanks. Through Jesus Christ, our Lord. Amen.*

<table>
<tr><td>DAY
14</td><td>*And they were helped against them, and the Hagarites were delivered into their hand, and all that were with them: for they cried to God in the battle, and he was entreated of them;*</td></tr>
</table>

because they put their trust in him.

I CHRONICLES 5:20

We are given instruments of faith and silence and meditation and prayer and unselfishness and love. And if we believe in these instruments and always trust them, we can come in through any overcast to a safe landing. I don't mean to make this sound too easy. It isn't easy. But neither do I mean to make it sound impossible, for it is possible. Simply apply to each problem in life the love and the faith and the unselfishness and the spiritual perceptiveness which Jesus Christ gives to those who identify their lives with Him.

PRAYER: *Our Heavenly Father, we thank You for this wondrous, sparkling, vital gift called Christianity. We know that Jesus Christ came to set us free from ourselves, and that we, in losing ourselves, may find life exciting, thrilling, wonderful, good. For this we give thanks. Amen.*

DAY
15

It came even to pass, as the trumpeters and singers were as one, to make one sound to be heard in praising and thanking the Lord; and when they lifted up their voice with the trumpets and cymbals and instruments of music, and praised the Lord, saying, For he is good; for his mercy endureth for ever: that then the house was filled with a cloud, even the house of the Lord. II CHRONICLES 5:13

One day after a speech I gave in Chicago, a young woman in a waitress's uniform rushed up to me and told me her amazing story.

"I have a little boy. When he was five years old, he got sick. The doctor prepared me for the worst. I felt my whole world would go to pieces if I lost my boy. Then a neighbor gave me one of your sermons to read. And in that sermon you said, 'If you have a loved one who is ill or about whom you are worried, give the loved one to God.' So I prayed and I put my boy in God's hands. And He let me keep my boy. And now God and I are raising him together."

And so we separated. And I went my way refreshed by yet another wonderful drama of human life rising to high places even out of humble circumstances.

LIFE LIFTER: *Always remember that God has built potential strength into you. Commit this statement to memory and say it now and then: "I asked the Lord for help, and he saved me from all my fears" (Psalm 34:4).*

DAY 16

John answered, saying unto them all, I indeed baptize you with water; but one mightier than I cometh, the latchet of whose shoes I am not worthy to unloose: he shall baptize you with the Holy Ghost and with fire.

LUKE 3:16

A church in the South periodically holds what they call a "thought-burning" service. They bring urns before the altar and light fires in them. Each person in the congregation is given paper on which he is to write the thoughts he wants to be rid of—then, one by one, the congregants file down the aisle, drop their thoughts into the urn, and watch them curl up into ashes. I can well imagine the service ending with the hymn, "Praise God, From Whom All Blessings Flow."

Well, you don't need an urn to burn your regrets and hates and failures. You can set fire to them in your mind through the cleansing power of the Holy Spirit. Forget past failures. When you have failed, ask God to show you how to do the thing better the next time, and then go back at it and give it all you've got.

LIFE LIFTER: *Don't waste mental energy brooding over past events or worrying about the future. Live a day at a time and do a job at a time. Go to sleep using the conscious thought and affirmation that whatever you may be called upon to handle the next day, God and you will be able to do together. Do not spurn God's help, for He has broad shoulders, strong arms, and wonderful ideas.*

DAY 17

And the men of Kirjath-jearim came, and fetched up the ark of the Lord, and brought it into the house of Abinadab in the hill, and sanctified Eleazar his son to keep the ark of the Lord.

I SAMUEL 7:1

Sometime ago, after giving a speech I returned to my hotel where the desk clerk informed me, "A woman has been waiting for you, and she has two of the noisiest children I've ever seen." The minute she saw me, she rushed over. "I just prayed and asked the Lord to help me," she said. "I want to tell you my problem."

Now I've heard a mess of problems in my life, but this was really something. "Well," I said, "let's pray and let us turn all these problems over to Jesus." I prayed as best I could, and at the end she and her children said in unison, "Hear our prayer, blessed Jesus."

Later the woman wrote to me: "Driving home that night, my heart was full of peace and my mind was full of cleanness. I knew that Jesus had answered my prayer and given me victory over everything. It hasn't been easy, but the victory of that moment has held."

PRAYER: *Our Heavenly Father, we ask You to bless all Your wonderful people today. You know the conflicts and difficulties faced by everyone. By Your grace, we know we can be master over everything, if we will receive this mastery and use it in Your holy name. Through Jesus Christ, our Lord. Amen.*

> **DAY 18**
>
> *And ye shall know that I am the Lord, when I have wrought with you for my name's sake, not according to your wicked ways, nor according to your corrupt doings, O ye house of Israel, saith the Lord God.* EZEKIEL 20:44

Look at a tough situation this way: "Well, it does present difficulties. I'm not going to be flippant about it. I know I have a problem here. But God is with me. I have a few friends. And Jesus Christ is helping me. Other people have solved problems like this. So I'm going to pour what confidence I've got right on this difficulty."

I hope those who read this meditation will start thinking about God, Who gives abundantly above all we ask or even think. This is a big promise, isn't it? He gives us abundance, according to what we ask, more than we ask, above what we can ask, and more than we can even think. That is what He wants to give us all. But whether we receive or take it depends on the power that is working within us. The essence of the matter is the way we think. What goes on in the mind determines everything.

PRAYER: *Our Heavenly Father, we thank You that amidst conflict and confusion there is clear and simple truth; that Jesus Christ is the way, the truth. Help us to follow Him always, knowing that as we do, we have truth and the truth gives inevitably the right answers to our problems. We thank You. Through our Lord, Jesus Christ. Amen.*

DAY
19

*And I will dwell among the children of Israel,
and will be their God.*   EXODUS 29:45

Once when I was sitting in a hotel coffee shop
having an early breakfast alone, a man came in, and
with a cheerful good morning to the cashier at the door
and to the waiters, he came walking through the place,
saw me and apparently knew me, for he pulled up a
chair, asking, "May I sit down with you?" Before I could
say yes or no, there he was. He shook out his napkin and
exclaimed, "Boy, this is going to be another great day!"

I was astonished to hear this kind of conversation so
early in the morning. "I gather you've had many good
days," I said.

"Oh, yes," he assured me. "I learned that if I pass a
series of expectancy thoughts through my mind every
morning, God will bring my great expectations to
pass. He can bring the good out. Therefore I just go
along with Him, passing expectancy thoughts through
my mind."

May I ask you, my reader, a question? What kind of
expectation thoughts have you in your mind right now?

LIFE LIFTER: *Contact with God establishes within us
a flow of the same type of energy that re-creates the
world and that renews springtime every year. Simply practice
thinking about God. This will make your mind spiritually
receptive. At least ten times every day affirm, "I expect the
best and with God's help will attain the best."*

| DAY 20 | *And be not conformed to this world: but be ye transformed by the renewing of your mind, that ye may prove what is that good, and acceptable, and perfect, will of God.* |

ROMANS 12:2

Sometime ago, I met with a group of doctors and one of them asked me, "How many times a year do you discuss the problem of stress and tension from the pulpit?"

"About once a year," I replied.

He pulled a prescription pad from his pocket, wrote something on it, and pushed it across the table to me. "This is a prescription I give to patients after I have done everything I can do for them medically."

On the pad he had written: "Romans 12:2: Let God change the way you think." And lest you think this particular physician is odd, I assure you that his professional standing is extremely high.

I believe that the Bible has the answer to every personal and social problem. And I believe that by using such a great treatment as Romans 12:2, you can cure yourself of being victimized by pressure.

PRAYER: *Our Heavenly Father, we ask Your blessing and we pray that each of us may feel his heart emptied now of fear and filled full of You, in whose presence there can be no apprehension. Help us to know that we need not be afraid. Through Jesus Christ, our Lord. Amen.*

| DAY **21** | *Cast thy bread upon the waters: for thou shalt find it after many days.* ECCLESIASTES 11:1 |

The more you give, the more you shall receive. I saw an example of this at a luncheon for businessmen. The speakers were mostly in their forties, I would say, except for one man who was obviously older than all the rest. I sat down beside him and asked, "Are you head of one of these businesses here?"

"Sure am," he answered. "Why? Don't I look like I could handle it?"

I said, "I just heard you are eighty years old."

"Well," he demanded, "what's wrong with being eighty years old? It isn't how long you've been around; it's what you've done while you've been around. Don't think that just because I have a game leg I can't handle the business. You don't run a business with your leg; you run it with your head."

Naturally, the man had found this zest where it really comes from. Through the teachings of the Lord Jesus Christ, who says He has come that we might have life and have it more abundantly. That is what He offers us. Take it!

PRAYER: *Our Heavenly Father, we thank You for what You are able to do for human lives. You would give us life, vibrant life, life full of excitement, of enthusiasm that will never run down. Help us to believe in it with all our hearts. Through Jesus Christ, our Lord. Amen.*

DAY

22

Behold, a son shall be born to thee, who shall be a man of rest; and I will give him rest from all his enemies round about: for his name shall be Solomon, and I will give peace and quietness unto Israel in his days. I CHRONICLES 22:9

I had a chat with an old friend who had been his state's attorney general. Some years ago, this man had said to me, "If I don't find a way to reduce the tension in my life, I'm going to die." I discussed the problem with him and advised him to have a quiet time every day for communing with God and the Lord Jesus Christ. Later I saw him and he was quiet, calm, composed, stronger physically than he was when he was ten years younger. He told me this was due to the beneficial effect of practicing creative silence.

You are a child of God. God never meant you to be victimized by pressure. He meant you to live in an effective, powerful manner. But that is only possible when you keep Him at the center of your life and in your own thinking. He will keep you in perfect peace if you keep your mind on Him.

> **LIFE LIFTER:** *To drop tension from your life, practice getting tranquility by passing peaceful words and thoughts through your mind daily and nightly. They have a healing quality. Remember that you will never be spiritually blessed until you forgive. Goodwill cannot flow toward you unless it flows from you.*

DAY 23

For he doth not afflict willingly nor grieve the children of men.   LAMENTATIONS 3:33

When he was thirty-one, Ludwig van Beethoven wrote of the "disastrous affliction," the growing deafness, that had befallen him. "I was soon compelled to keep apart, to live a life of loneliness," he wrote. "How could I possibly admit an inferiority in the one sense that should have been more acute in me than in others? I almost reached the point of putting an end to my life. Only art, it was, that held me back. It seemed impossible to depart this world until I had brought forth all the things I felt inspired to create. And so I went on living this miserable life. O God, You Who lookest into the depths of my soul, You understandest me, You knowest that the love of mankind and the desire to do good live with me!"

Beethoven overcame that discouragement. He lived for another twenty-five years, the years of his greatest creativity. Such is the struggle that people have with black moods, and such are the victories of great faith. With the help of God, out of our discouragement and struggle, we may bring messages to bless mankind.

PRAYER: *Our Heavenly Father, for too long we have let ourselves be hampered, hobbled and tripped up by our weakness. Motivate us so that the divine power, which You have planted within us, may rise out of weakness into strength. Through Jesus Christ, our Lord. Amen.*

DAY 24

I will lift up mine eyes unto the hills, from whence cometh my help. PSALM 121:1

Dr. Robert Schuller grew up in Iowa, and he tells an awe-inspiring story about a tornado. One afternoon Bob and his father heard a rumbling like many freight trains. The sky grew dark. Then out from the dark clouds bulged an enormous funnel.

Seconds later, the whole family was in the car racing down the road. They stopped and watched the tornado hit with elemental force. In ten minutes, it was gone. They saw the whole terrible sight; not one building was still standing—their house had vanished. Mr. Schuller told his wife and son to wait where they were and got out of the car. He went poking in the ruins and brought back a battered motto that had hung in the kitchen. It said, "Keep looking to Jesus."

Some people would have lost their faith. But Mr. Schuller rebuilt. He replaced the lost livestock and buildings and equipment. A few years later, farm prices rose sharply. Before long, the mortgage was paid off! He died the prosperous owner of a thriving farm.

LIFE LIFTER: *People become quite remarkable when they start thinking that they can do things. Develop a tremendous faith in God and that will give you a humble yet realistic faith in yourself. Picture yourself as the kind of person you wish to be, affirm that you are that, then practice being it.*

DAY
25

And, behold, the glory of the God of Israel was there, according to the vision that I saw in the plain.　　　EZEKIEL 8:4

A man from Elmira, New York, came to see me in my office. He put his head in his hands and said, "Everything is lost. It's hopeless."

"Well," I said. "I'd like to explore this. Let me ask you a few questions. Your wife has left you, of course? And no doubt your children are all in jail?"

"What do you mean?" he retorted. "My wife loves me. Of course she hasn't left me. My kids are good kids. Of course they're not in jail."

"Well," I reminded him, "you told me everything was lost." We went on through a few more things like that. Then I said, "Look at the things you've got left! Plus God. Brother, you're in! What do you mean, you want to blow your brains out? All you need to do is blow your faith up." He found new courage and went home to straighten up his life.

If you are disheartened about anything today, forget it. Blow your faith up. Look to the Lord Jesus Christ. Let Him get into you and change your thinking.

PRAYER: *Our Heavenly Father, we thank You for the greatness of the Christian faith. Help us so to incorporate it into our lives that, having a big God, we shall in turn become big people, strong people who carry out great exploits. Through Jesus Christ, our Lord. Amen.*

<table>
<tr><td>

DAY
26

</td><td>

And Jesus said unto them, I am the bread of life: he that cometh to me shall never hunger; and he that believeth on me shall never thirst.
JOHN 6:35

</td></tr>
</table>

We are given the gift of life. Now that is a wonderful thing. But the strange thing is that, having the gift of life, we apparently do not know how to use it. We mess it up. We limit it. We even desecrate it, though it is so extraordinarily valuable to us. Many people, no matter how long they may have lived, have never yet grasped the secret of how to handle it. And that is a tragedy.

What then is the secret? In the sixth chapter of John's Gospel are these enormous words: "I am the bread that gives life." (That is, "I put substance into life.") "No one who comes to Me will ever be hungry." What a thought! And it goes on to say, "No one who has faith in Me will ever be thirsty."

Do you ever get hungry? Not the hunger for food, but the hunger for something else, something deep? If you accept Him as the bread of life you will never be hungry. And what goes for hunger goes for thirst.

LIFE LIFTER: *You can have complete confidence in the Lord and in His promises. He will always hear you. And God does always answer sincere prayer. He answers in three ways: (1) Yes, (2) No, (3) Wait awhile. And every answer, whatever it may be, is for our good as long as we are in His will.*

DAY 27

And Solomon the son of David was strengthened in his kingdom, and the Lord his God was with him, and magnified him exceedingly.   II CHRONICLES 1:1

Be someone! And what is that supposed to mean? Nowadays everyone wants to be a big shot. What is a big shot? I've heard a big shot defined as a little shot who keeps on shooting. But there are a great many phonies among big shots, as well as a great many fine people.

In any case, to be a big shot or a celebrity is not a goal worthy of a real person. I would say a real person wants to be his or her best self. That is, a real person wants to realize all the potential inside. He or she wants to bring into focus every God-given talent. Such a person wants to attain the best results, not for himself, but for the world and for God. To be someone in that true sense is the highest realization of one's self as a child of God.

We need a reassessment of values. The end and aim of life is to be an organized, integrated, dedicated, useful, outgoing, loving, helpful individual worthy of the approval of God.

PRAYER: *Our Heavenly Father, we are grateful that simple truths are profound truths, teaching us that to be happy we must choose happiness, that we must love, and that Jesus in the heart is the way of highest happiness. Through Jesus Christ, our Lord. Amen.*

DAY 28

Art thou better than populous No, that was situate among the rivers, that had the waters round about it, whose rampart was the sea, and her wall was from the sea? NAHUM 3:8

Once I had the great honor of speaking to the troops in Vietnam. At one place where I was to speak, I noticed a detachment of men on a hilltop about half a mile away. I asked, "Who are those men out there, General?"

"That's your security," said the general.

I sat there thinking it over and looking at those boys. And I said, "General, I don't feel right about all this security. Those boys—what is their security?"

"Their security," he replied, "is their training, their arms, and Almighty God."

"Well," I said, "I don't have the training or the arms, but I'll put my trust in God." And I thought, "Do I really mean that? Am I ready to go into the dangers of human existence with calmness and peacefulness in my heart, knowing that in life or in death He will take care of me?" I turned to the general and quoted I Peter 5:7, "God cares for you, so turn all your worries over to Him." This is the only real security.

PRAYER: *Our Heavenly Father, we know that because Christ lived we shall live also, and that those who have gone on before us will be waiting when we cross the river into eternal morning. Help us so to live that immortality may be in our souls. Through Jesus Christ, our Lord. Amen.*

DAY 29

Go and proclaim these words toward the north, and say, Return, thou backsliding Israel, saith the Lord; and I will not cause mine anger to fall upon you: for I am merciful, saith the Lord, and I will not keep anger for ever. JEREMIAH 3:12

Daniel Negris was a musical genius. As a young man he began smoking marijuana, then he tried heroin, and soon became addicted. He lost job after job. He realized he needed help, but he didn't know where to turn.

Each time Daniel went on a tour his mother put a Bible in his suitcase. He never read it; but one night, in deep despair, he took out the Bible and idly flipped through the pages until he saw these words: "If you are tired from carrying heavy burdens, come to Me and I will give you rest." Trembling, he fell to his knees and prayed, "Lord, forgive me and take away my burden." Immediately he felt cleansed of sin and guilt, and was overwhelmed by God's love. And he said, "I never touched drugs again. My recovery has been total."

Who did that for him? The One who is able to put power into anyone. Turn to Jesus. Take the power He gives. Your life will become so wonderful that you will thank God all the time for the miracle of it.

LIFE LIFTER: *No difficulty is impregnable. Never think you "haven't a prayer." You do have a prayer to carry you through. Remember that while the doctor treats you, God heals you.*

DAY 30

And David said to Solomon his son, Be strong and of good courage, and do it: fear not, nor be dismayed, for the Lord God, even my God, will be with thee; he will not fail thee, nor forsake thee, until thou hast finished all the work for the service of the house of the Lord. I CHRONICLES 28:20

An old friend of mine was a salesman. When I first knew him, he was one of the most depressed, defeated, negative individuals I've ever known. He was a lovable fellow but was getting nowhere fast. God had endowed him with a tremendous personality, but it was soft and flabby and had no force behind it. As I got to know him better, I saw that he was afraid. He was afraid of people, of economic conditions, of himself. He tried to cover up this fear with ingratiating sociability. But he didn't get any orders, and even I know that is what you have to do to be a successful salesman. At length, he talked with me about this problem and I prayed with him. All I ever did was to lead him to Christ. But that was enough because he went on from there to be successful as a person and successful as a salesman.

LIFE LIFTER: *Be sure to see yourself rightly, for we tend to become as we see ourselves. So see yourself confidently. Drop the idea that you are Atlas carrying the world on your shoulders. The world would go on even without you. Don't take yourself so seriously. Trust God and live a day at a time.*

DAY
31

And one cried unto another, and said, Holy, holy, holy, is the Lord of hosts: the whole earth is full of his glory.   ISAIAH 6:3

Modern science sets up a roadblock of questioning. Even some poetry teaches us that this whole visible universe is but a reflection of vaster realms beyond. The beauty and the loveliness and the charm and the love and the joy of this world are but tokens of that greater world of immortality. Sensitive people become aware of it. For example, Wordsworth at Tintern Abbey wrote, "I have felt a presence that disturbs me with the joy of elevated thoughts."

What is this sublime ecstasy that even amid commonplace things sometimes surges through the human heart and suffuses the whole world with glory? This could very well be a reflection of immortality, that greater, lovelier world intertwined with and superimposed upon this world.

LIFE LIFTER: *Become a positive thinker. No matter how dark things seem to be or actually are, raise your sights and see the possibilities. They're always there. The more you lose yourself in something bigger than yourself, the more energy you will have. Remember that the most powerful motivation is spiritual motivation. So expose yourself to the spiritual. One of the greatest techniques of human well-being is surrendering yourself to the recuperative power of God.*

AUGUST

<table>
<tr><td>DAY
1</td><td>*Cast thy burden upon the Lord, and he shall sustain thee: he shall never suffer the righteous to be moved.*   PSALM 55:22</td></tr>
</table>

"Our Lord, we belong to you," says Psalm 55. "We tell you what worries us, and you won't let us fall." That is the first thing to remember in dealing with the toughest problems. The second thing is to equate the toughness that is within you with the toughness of the problem. Almighty God knew what He was doing when He created you and me. He built toughness into us. It has been built into the soul and the mind. You are tough. And you have a Savior who is the toughest man who ever lived. He is the kindly, gentle Jesus, but do you think Christianity would have endured for two thousand years if He were just a gentle man? Not on your life. Jesus Christ is tough in His faith, in His insights, in His strength and in His wisdom. If you accept Him, you get Jesus Christ built into you and nothing can overwhelm you. So when you have a tough problem on the outside, say to yourself, "I equate with this outer toughness an inner toughness, the toughness of my faith and strength."

PRAYER: *Our Heavenly Father, we give You thanks for the usable techniques of Christianity, which give us victory over difficulties. In this tense age we need self-control for thinking our problems through. Help us let Your peace rule in our hearts. Through Jesus Christ, our Lord. Amen.*

| DAY 2 | *Although affliction cometh not forth of the dust, neither doth trouble spring out of the ground; Yet man is born unto trouble, as the sparks fly upward.*   JOB 5:6–7 |

It is written in the book of Job that "suffering...[is] all part of life, like sparks shooting skyward." We cannot escape from problems, but we are called to struggle with problems and overcome them. So we may as well learn to handle problems. How do you go about doing that? Well, there is a great text in the Gospel of John that says, "The Spirit will show you what is true" (John 14:17). The Christian religion is built upon perception, upon insight, upon understanding, upon wisdom. And there is a wisdom about problems. One of the basic elements of this wisdom is the profound philosophy that sees a problem as a part of the creative process of testing and growth.

If we didn't have problems, we'd have to invent them, because our directional facility would be lost without problems. Problems help to steer a course through the years.

PRAYER: *Our Father, we thank You that there is within us much more power and strength and greatness than we have yet allowed to come into action. Forgive us for living the hard way. Grant that by identifying ourselves with You, we may let the life in us flow out in satisfying power and effectiveness. Through Jesus Christ, our Lord. Amen.*

| DAY
3 | *And God remembered Noah, and every living thing, and all the cattle that was with him in the ark: and God made a wind to pass over the earth, and the waters assuaged.* |

GENESIS 8:1

Never give in! You don't need to, for the Lord God will help you. Follow the stick-it-out-and-never-give-up principle. And keep in mind another idea: the keep-God-in-it principle. No one can be strong, vital and heroic without the presence of God. This is a big, overwhelming world and we are small. It is like the prayer the Normandy fishermen offer when they go out on the deep to fish. Before they cast off their little boats they pray, "O Lord, take care of us. The sea is so vast. We are so small." And He does and He will.

I tell you, from the bottom of my heart: The secret of meeting life victoriously is how close you are to God, how deeply and sincerely you receive Jesus Christ into your life. And I guarantee to you that if you give your life to God, if you commit your life to Christ, until this becomes your consuming passion, you will have an immunity—not from difficulty, but from defeat. And that is all we can ask.

PRAYER: *Our Heavenly Father, the problems of life are with us and sometimes we grow frightened and bewildered. But, thanks to You, we have Jesus with us. For this we give You thanks. Through Jesus Christ, our Lord. Amen.*

DAY
4

Six days shalt thou labor, and do all thy work.
EXODUS 20:9

You can relax the soul by filling your mind with great words from the Scriptures about God. Say them to yourself and let them sink deeply into your mind. Let me suggest several texts: "The Lord gives perfect peace to those whose faith is firm" (Isaiah 26:3); "If you are tired from carrying heavy burdens, come to me and I will give you rest" (Matthew 11:28); "I give you peace, the kind of peace that only I can give. It isn't like the peace that this world can give. So don't be worried or afraid" (John 14:27).

In order to be an effective person, able to live and participate and lead, you need emotional control, serenity of mind and what the Quakers call "peace at the center." You need the steadiness and sustaining power that can be yours only if you learn the relaxed approach to problems. So, develop inner peace. And the way of doing this is open to us all.

LIFE LIFTER: *The relaxed person is the powerful person. Practice word therapy—serenity, civility, patience, equanimity. Say those powerful, mind-healing words over to yourself every day. Let them recondition your stressful attitudes. Faith power in the mind, like adrenaline in the body, can release amazing power within you in crisis.*

DAY
5

And of some have compassion, making a difference.   JUDE 22

A famous man of letters said that when God wants to make a point with His children, He plants His argument in our instincts and suggests that, in deep feelings that cannot be put into words, the greatest truths of life are communicated.

I personally had my doubts in my younger days. He who never has to fight a doubt is not a thinker. I sometimes receive letters from parents who are troubled by their children's doubts. A mother will write, for example, that she is worried about her son because he questions everything—he doubts. And I will advise her, "Thank God for your son's questioning. It means that he is alive, that he thinks. You cannot hand faith down in packaged form, like an heirloom to your children. They must find it and develop it for themselves."

When you have to struggle to develop faith, the faith you discover is really your own. It will be a stronger faith if it has had to overcome the pain and struggle of doubt. I can only tell you now that I haven't the slightest doubt about immortality.

PRAYER: *Our Heavenly Father, we thank You for Yourself. Help us all, we pray, to overcome frustration and turmoil through the peace of Christ in our hearts. And for this we give You thanks. Through Jesus Christ, our Lord. Amen.*

<table>
<tr><td>

DAY

6

</td><td>

And it came to pass in the fortieth year, in the eleventh month, on the first day of the month, that Moses spake unto the children of Israel, according unto all that the Lord had given

</td></tr>
</table>

him in commandment unto them.

DEUTERONOMY 1:3

One time I was to speak at a luncheon for a group of professional people. The presiding officer was a doctor. He looked out at the group and said to me, "If I could reduce the tension and strain under which these people live, I would reduce my caseload. I can't remove those things. But," said he, "there is one Doctor who can." He then quoted from the 119th Psalm, 165th verse: "You give peace of mind to all who love your law."

Now what is His law? The laws of nature are a part of it. When Almighty God created us He knew we could never live as He intended without influences of serenity and beauty and healing peace surrounding us, so in order that our souls might grow great and strong, He set us in a world of great loveliness governed by natural laws. Love God's law; then you will have within you great peace.

LIFE LIFTER: *The attitude you take toward problems and difficulties is far and away the most important factor in controlling and mastering them. People who are really efficient seem to do things easily, with a minimum of effort. In so doing, they release maximum power.*

<table>
<tr><td>DAY
7</td><td>*Surely the Lord God will do nothing , but he revealeth his secret unto his servants the prophets.*   AMOS 3:7</td></tr>
</table>

When you go to church, or when you are in deep prayer, there is Someone with you far greater than any person, Someone who knows you through and through. He tells you that you are greater than you think—that these conflicts, these obsessions in the mind pale to the blessings He gives. He tells you to let the troubles go. He tells you that you can have a sound mind. So let your fears go.

The Lord Jesus came and taught and died on the cross—for what reason? To save us. Save us from what? To save us from sin, to save us from our weak defeated selves, to save us from our notions, our obsessions, our prejudices, our hates, our fears: to cleanse us in our minds. That is the great secret. For God has not given you a spirit of fear. You got it yourself, and you can let it go yourself, with His help. Right now, today, you can begin. Depending on the depth of your faith, you can complete the process whereby you shed all your fear and anxiety.

LIFE LIFTER: *Take charge of your thoughts instead of allowing them to control you. To help reduce tension, practice the peace of God, which surpasses all understanding. Then note the quiet power that wells up within you. Realize you are greater than you've ever considered yourself to be.*

DAY
8

Am I a God at hand, saith the Lord, and not a God afar off? Can any hide himself in secret places that I shall not see him? saith the Lord. Do not I fill heaven and earth? saith the Lord.
JEREMIAH 23:23–24

In Switzerland, my wife Ruth and I went up to a high valley six thousand feet above sea level, surrounded by the Bernini Peaks. We lingered for only five minutes. But those five minutes will forever remain in memory. All around us stretched a pristine world, golden sunshine, snow gleaming like myriads of diamonds, and a blue sky above. I was so overwhelmed that I didn't even tell Ruth how I felt. But that night I said to her, "I have today spent five minutes in immortality."

If mountains can be that beautiful, so can a human being. This is the greatest form of immortality known to us in this life—not the splendor in nature, but spiritual radiance manifesting in man. Strange thing about us: we have evil in us as well as good in us; we have high desires and we have low desires. But Almighty God can change people and bring forth the immortality that is within them.

PRAYER: *Our Heavenly Father, we thank You for reminding us that we are Your children, with something great in us equal to the stars that can be released as we learn to love You and Jesus Christ. We thank You for the wondrous excitement of living. Through Jesus Christ, our Lord. Amen.*

<table>
<tr><td>

DAY

9

</td><td>

Acquaint now thyself with him, and be at peace: thereby good shall come unto thee.

JOB 22:21

</td></tr>
</table>

Consider today a Scripture passage so wise that it contains the answers, or the method for obtaining the answers, to your problems. It is Job 22:21: "Surrender to God All-Powerful! You will find peace and prosperity."

I realize that embracing problems isn't a popular notion. We often encounter an insipid notion that the best thing we could do for people is to free them from all their problems so that they never again have any pain, any difficulty, any hardship, any struggle. Well, no proper-thinking person would adhere to such an idea as that. Almighty God has made problems an inherent part of the universe—but why? What is He trying to do? What is it all about? He wants to grow strong people: people who tussle with difficulty and grow tough in their minds and in their spirits, the kind of people on whom a great world can be built.

LIFE LIFTER: *Cushion the painful effects of hard blows by keeping enthusiasm going strong, even if doing so requires struggle. The Bible knows the score, the facts of life, so much better than any cynic. The tough-minded optimist views any problem as a challenge to his intelligence, ingenuity, and faith. He keeps on thinking, praying, and believing. He knows there is a solution and so he finally finds it.*

<table>
<tr><td>DAY
10</td><td>*And while he yet talked with them, behold, the messenger came down unto him: and he said, Behold, this evil is of the Lord; what should I wait for the Lord any longer?*   II KINGS 6:33</td></tr>
</table>

These are exciting times! A lot of people grump and whine and keep reminding you that this world is full of trouble. Well, years ago in Syracuse, New York, I knew a preacher by the name of David Keppel, an Irishman from Belfast. He was almost ninety. I was in my thirties then. One day I was telling him what a terrible state I thought the world was in. "In Ireland we have a saying," he explained, "when there is trouble on earth it means there is movement in heaven. The more trouble on earth, the more movement in heaven." Which is a way of saying that the Kingdom of God is going to come down out of heaven to replace your trouble in this world.

Who ever lived through more exciting times than these? We see more equality of status among races and expanded opportunities than our ancestors dreamed of fifty years ago. Wonderful things are happening today.

PRAYER: *Our Heavenly Father, You meant that our spirits should be alive and vital, gloriously enthusiastic. Give us today, dear Lord, this burst of new life and light and power. And may we transmit it, a marvelous blessing, to others. Through Jesus Christ, our Lord. Amen.*

DAY 11

He delivereth the poor in his affliction, and openeth their ears in oppression. JOB 36:15

What is the remedy when you're upset? I find it in the book of Job: "Hard times and trouble are God's way of getting our attention! And at this very moment, God deeply desires to lead you from trouble."

Now what does that mean? It means that when you accept God's direction and build it into your life, no one can make you inwardly troubled. It doesn't make any difference how many people around you are trying to make trouble; they can only trouble you as you allow them to do so. When you have a deep inner quietness, the trouble others try to make for you, or the trouble you think they try to make for you, is absorbed and has no power over you.

And when you have deep inner quietness, receiving it from God, then trouble that you've been causing yourself fades away. It is lost in the depth of His quietness. So when you're upset, draw upon God for quietness and receive it. Then you will have control, orderliness, and a sound philosophy for life.

LIFE LIFTER: *Saturate your thoughts with peaceful experiences, peaceful words and ideas, and ultimately you will have a storehouse of peace-producing experiences to which you may turn for refreshment and renewal of your spirit. Learn to let God run your life. You'll like the results better than your own self-management.*

<table>
<tr><td>DAY
12</td><td>*Behold, God is my salvation; I will trust, and not be afraid: for the Lord Jehovah is my strength and my song; he also is become my salvation.*
ISAIAH 12:2</td></tr>
</table>

Commit yourself. By committing yourself, I mean to commit yourself to God. You are a child of God. God made you. God gave you birth. You are His. When your life on earth is ended, God will take you to Himself. You are God's all the way—unless by an act of will you turn away from Him, which would be the most dangerous thing you ever did in your life, because then the power goes. So put yourself in God's hands, trust Him, believe in Him, don't doubt Him, stay with Him—and He will give you the power to do anything with yourself. But your belief has to be belief in depth, no mere surface belief. It has to go down deep. To get the kind of power I am talking about, you must really believe.

LIFE LIFTER: *The world in which you live is not primarily determined by outward conditions and circumstances, but by thoughts that habitually occupy your mind. Two great forces operate in the mind: fear and faith. Fear is very powerful, but faith is more powerful. Commit the following statement to memory and say it now and then: "I asked the Lord for help, and he saved me from all my fears" (Psalm 34:4).*

| DAY **13** | *Heaviness in the heart of man maketh it stoop: but a good word maketh it glad.*
PROVERBS 12:25 |

I was impressed by something I read about John Masefield, the poet. He used to perform what he called "the practice of the getting of tranquility." Each night he sat in a chair and repeated to himself, "This body is a sacred thing. It is the temple of the soul. God created it for my use. God is putting His quietness upon my body." Then he put his hand on his heart and said, "The hand of God is in this hand and I put this hand on my heart. Let not my heart be troubled. I believe in God." By this time his body would be quiet, free from the quivering tensions of the day.

Next he would say, "I hereby empty my mind of all jealousy. I hereby empty my mind of all resentment. I hereby empty every impure and evil thought out of my mind. I drain my mind." And then: "I now fill my mind with goodness and with love and with forgiveness and with hope."

With practice, Masefield gained inner peace and achieved victory over tension.

LIFE LIFTER: *The power to change your life comes in seven magic words: "I can do all things through God." With all the strength and perseverance you can command, start practicing faith. Put your trust in God and just go calmly on your way.*

DAY 14

For by fire and by his sword will the Lord plead with all flesh: and the slain of the Lord shall be many. ISAIAH 66:16

I met a lady who said to me, "I heard your wife make a speech at the church I belong to—and she said something I will always remember." The woman explained that she had been struggling in prayer for something she wanted and God wasn't answering her prayers. Mrs. Peale in that speech remarked that there are three ways God answers prayer: yes, wait awhile, and no. "And when she said that," the woman told me, "I knew I had my answer. It was no. But I hadn't wanted to take a 'no' answer."

"Maybe that 'no' answer is going to lead you to some great experience," I said. "Later, on some bright day, you will realize, 'If He had not said no, this wonderful thing I now have would not have come to me.'"

The attitude that really leads to life in all its fullness is that of a child walking with Him, loving Him, trusting Him, seeking to serve Him. Prayer in this attitude can change your life wonderfully.

PRAYER: *Our Heavenly Father, help us to believe. Break through our doubts and our resistances. Help us to have the simplicity of mind that goes with uninhibited thinking and to give all we've got to life, knowing that the surge of life returned to us will be terrific. And for this we give You thanks. Through Jesus Christ, our Lord. Amen.*

| DAY 15 |

The Lord is good, a stronghold in the day of trouble; and he knoweth them that trust in him.

NAHUM 1:7

I wish to give you a statement that is worth serious pondering. It is from the prophet Nahum, who said, "The Lord is good. He protects those who trust him in times of trouble." This statement says three things. First, God is good. Second, He protects. You can depend upon Him, no matter what comes. Third, He knows intimately and personally everyone who trusts Him.

Everyone at one time or another has been faced with an unsatisfactory situation. The first thing you must recognize is that some unsatisfactory situations cannot be changed; some you just must live with. But the power of God is so great there is not much need to dwell unduly upon this, and it is mentioned merely because one should acknowledge the fact.

The Roman philosopher-king Marcus Aurelius once said, "Adapt thyself to the things among which thy lot has been cast." Men say these things because they recognize the so-called inevitable difficulties in life. Well, that is heroic indeed. But life would be bleak if all you could do about it was to endure it.

PRAYER: *Our Heavenly Father, we give You thanks for Your goodness. We know that by the power You put into us, we can have the blessing of a life as never before. For this we give You thanks. Through Jesus Christ, our Lord. Amen.*

DAY
16

The Lord is my strength and my shield; my heart trusted in him, and I am helped: therefore my heart greatly rejoiceth; and with my song will I praise him.   PSALM 28:7

Psalm 28:7 declares, "You are my strong shield, and I trust You completely." That is a tremendous affirmation. I don't know how you begin each day, but here is a suggestion. Instead of rising in the morning and telling yourself, or your wife or your husband, all the difficulties and emergencies you have to face, forget all that and just stand and stretch yourself tall and say, "The Lord is my strong shield." Start the day like that often enough and you will develop composure, confidence, greatness of spirit, understanding, perceptiveness, clear thinking, and the right answers. That is the secret. "The Lord is my strong shield."

LIFE LIFTER: *Get the spiritual experience that really changes things; the in-depth type that brings you alive and keeps you alive every day all the way. The greatest power available to a human being is in-depth faith, the force by which you can move mountains of difficulty. Live by faith that will never let you down.*

DAY 17

So Israel rebelled against the house of David unto this day.   I KINGS 12:19

Do you get in your own way? Everyone should honestly face this question. You can be your most difficult obstacle. To live effectively, you must solve this problem.

Sometime ago, I spoke at a convention in Atlantic City. At the end of this meeting, I saw a man whom I have known since we were youngsters. He frequently used to be in my prayers, because he'd become a heavy drinker. After the meeting he said to me, "I finally got wise to myself. I sure got all fouled up. I messed up years of my life. But that's all gone by now. I finally got wise."

"How did it happen?" I asked.

"I went back to the church where I grew up," he told me, "and I found the Lord and He changed my life."

This man is now one of the most devoted lay workers for the church in his community. But every time he sees me, he says again, "What a pity to have wasted all those years! It took a breakdown to get me to where I didn't go on messing myself up anymore." That is rather uncultured language, but it describes plainly what happens when you get in your own way.

LIFE LIFTER: *The cure of frustration is the belief that God will help you obtain your heart's desire. Trust in God with all your heart, and you will be able to keep on working in health and happiness for long years to come.*

| DAY **18** | *That the house of Israel may go no more astray from me, neither be polluted any more with all their transgressions; but that they may be my people, and I may be their God,* |

saith the Lord God.
 EZEKIEL 14:11

I read an article by a doctor about an experience he had had. He was at home when the telephone rang. A man's voice said, "Will you please come to my house? My wife is having hysterics." So the doctor drove to this couples' beautiful country home and listened as the wife poured out all her troubles and implored him for something to "hold on to." At that moment, the husband came in with three glasses of whiskey, and said to his wife, "This will help your hysterics," and said to the doctor, "This will help you, too." Well, the doctor put the glass on the floor and said, "This whiskey is nothing to hold on to. Why don't you turn to God?" He sat and talked to them about God and Jesus Christ. When he left, the hysteria was gone, peace was beginning to come.

When you put yourself into the hands of Jesus Christ, He calms your agitation and upsetness. You become quiet and are able to handle your problems confidently and intelligently.

LIFE LIFTER: *"He promised you perfect peace and rest, but you refused to listen" (Isaiah 28:12). Say these words slowly, emphasizing their quiet melody. At the same time conceive of peace, rest, and renewal as coming to you.*

<table>
<tr><td>DAY
19</td><td>*And he died in a good old age, full of days, riches, and honour: and Solomon his son reigned in his stead.*   I CHRONICLES 29:28</td></tr>
</table>

A businessman arrived late at a meeting at our church. He announced, "I am tense because I was late. I am going to relax the tension in me. In fact, I am going to practice my technique for overcoming tension."

"How are you going to do that?" I asked.

"I am going to think about Jesus." He added, "And I am going to relax my body. I have a rather peculiar practice. I imagine that my body is a big burlap bag of potatoes. Mentally, I take a pair of scissors and cut the end of the bag. All the potatoes roll out, and I am the bag that remains. Now I ask you, is anything more relaxed than an empty burlap bag? I can just feel my whole body falling into complete relaxation."

There was humor on the man's face, but also dead seriousness. "I want to live a long life," he said. "I feel I have a contribution to make to my country and my God, and I want to be healthy for the long pull. And in order to do it I must practice relaxation of body, mind, and soul."

LIFE LIFTER: *Realize that you can, of yourself, do much to make yourself a healthy, vital and alive individual. Never think or talk "lack," for in so doing you are decreeing lack. Always you can go higher, for within yourself you are greater than you think.*

<table>
<tr><td>

DAY

20

</td><td>

Behold, I will bring it health and cure, and I will cure them, and will reveal unto them the abundance of peace and truth.

JEREMIAH 33:6

</td></tr>
</table>

Power always comes from a calm center. Did you ever see a tornado tearing the sky? I have. It is a sight, believe me! It has astounding force. It can lift up a house and deposit it a mile away. It can take a great board and drive it like a nail through a wall. The poet Edwin Markham said, "At the heart of the cyclone tearing the sky...is a place of central calm." That is to say, a cyclone derives its power from a calm center.

The human being also derives power from a calm center. We have to learn how to get rid of tension, how to live relaxed. And to do that, acquaint yourself with Jesus and be at peace. I will go so far as to guarantee that if you will commit your life to Jesus Christ, if you will accept God as the guide of your life, and really live this out, you will have no further problems with tension or stress that you can't handle.

LIFE LIFTER: *You'll always get an idea if you think and don't panic. Quiet your mind so that inspirations may rise from its depths. An inflow of new thoughts can remake you regardless of any difficulty you may now face, and I repeat—any difficulty.*

<table>
<tr><td>

DAY

21

</td><td>

What is it then? I will pray with the spirit, and I will pray with the understanding also: I will sing with the spirit, and I will sing with the understanding also.

</td></tr>
</table>

I CORINTHIANS 14:15

I made a list of some of the most enthusiastic human beings I have known. And by analyzing these people, I came up with three essential attributes they all seem to have in one degree or another.

First: These enthusiastic people were very much alive. They were interested in things, concerned, eager. They were sensitive to events and to people and to conditions, they were thrilled by the world, they were excited.

Second: They participated. They gave their whole selves to life. They threw themselves into things.

Third: They all had a deep spiritual motivation that freed them from inhibitions frustrating the free flow of their personality.

Focus mentally and spiritually upon all that is right about life. Because life is mighty good. A lifetime on this wonderful earth doesn't last long either. It is here today and gone tomorrow. So love it while you can. And you'll be full of enthusiasm.

LIFE LIFTER: *You will get results in proportion to the faith that you have and use. Tackle life with abandon. Go all out, hold nothing back. Believe that you are bigger than your difficulties, for you are, indeed.*

DAY 22

He that is not with me is against me; and he that gathereth not with me scattereth abroad.

MATTHEW 12:30

The call comes to each of us individually. Are we going to give our lives to Him, or are we going to give our lives to something else? That is the issue.

We had better be with Him. We will never be truly happy unless we are. We will never find abiding peace unless we are.

Betray Him and you betray yourself. Betray His call to discipleship and you betray your own future. And if a society continues to reject Him, it brings woe upon itself.

But human beings have goodness; human beings have God in them. When they see the truth, they respond and they respond gloriously. When we identify with Him, we cease to betray ourselves and our society ceases to betray itself. In new faith, we lay the groundwork for a new and glorious fulfillment of the greatest ideals and principles ever known. So let's come alive. Let's go forth as redeemed people to redeem the life of our time.

PRAYER: *Our Heavenly Father, help us to face whatever difficulty comes to us and not be afraid. For You are with us and in Your strength we are infinitely strong. And in Your strength we can overcome anything—anything. For this we give thanks. Through Jesus Christ, our Lord. Amen.*

<table>
<tr><td>DAY
23</td><td>*Then the fire of the Lord fell, and consumed the burnt sacrifice, and the wood, and the stones, and the dust, and licked up the water that was in the trench.* I KINGS 18:38</td></tr>
</table>

Christianity has often been made out to be a soft kind of thing, something pleasant and nice. But Christianity is the toughest religion ever formulated in the history of the world. What is its symbol? Its symbol is a cross. Not one of those chaste gold crosses that hangs around a lady's neck, but a tough crossbeam of wood—splintery and hard. That is the symbol of Christianity.

This may sound oratorical and poetic, but it isn't. It is practical through and through. It is what we must do now as a nation, for this country will have to get back to a strong belief in the authority of government under God and have an enormous spiritual buildup if it is going to survive the confusions of our time. It is also what we need as individuals. Christianity is a tremendous religion, for it makes tremendous people who, when the going is not-so-good, know what to do. They just draw nearer to God and keep on keeping on—and victory comes.

PRAYER: *Our Heavenly Father, help us to know that there is value in the difficulties of life and that by the power of Christ working upon the inner person we may have the vitality and strength to rise from darkness into light. Through Jesus Christ, our Lord. Amen.*

<table>
<tr><td>

DAY

24

</td><td>

But I would have you without carefulness. He that is unmarried careth for the things that belong to the Lord, how he may please the Lord.   I CORINTHIANS 7:32

</td></tr>
</table>

The other day I was sitting in a luncheon meeting with some business people, and I got to talking about a problem with the man sitting next to me. "Norman," he said, "don't ever let a problem worry you."

"What do you do, Bob, about a problem?" I asked.

"I do everything I can think of; I give it all I have. Then I put it in God's hands and leave it there. Sometimes, I come up to a fine line where it looks like I'm going to be defeated, but if I put the problem in God's hands, He takes care of it."

In other words, he was telling me what I am now telling you. Before our meeting was over, the problem was solved in a beautiful way. And as we parted, Bob handed me this note: "Norman, do you see what happens when you let God take care of things? He moves people a lot better than we earthly guys." Who says that Christianity isn't practical? It is the most practical philosophy of human life ever formulated.

PRAYER: *Our Heavenly Father, You have given us laws for living; and if we practice them in cooperation with Jesus Christ, such power can come that no difficulty can cause the worst to come to us—but only the best. For this we give thanks. Through Jesus Christ, our Lord. Amen.*

DAY 25

For unto us a child is born, unto us a son is given: and the government shall be upon his shoulder: and his name shall be called Wonderful, Counsellor, The mighty God, The everlasting Father, The Prince of Peace. ISAIAH 9:6

There is a great passage in Isaiah that tells us: "His names will be wonderful Advisor and Mighty God, Eternal Father and Prince of Peace." So that is part of the good news. There will come a time when Rachel will not be crying for her children. There will come a time when our own children will not be broken, there will be no maimed bodies in the earth. There will come the time foreseen in Tennyson's vision of which he wrote: "Til the war drum throbbed no longer and the battle flags were furled/In the Parliament of Man, the Federation of the world…" It will come, I do believe.

Then there is this other great promise, this other part of the good news. "I came so that everyone would have life, and have it in its fullest" (John 10:10). That who might have life? All of us. Everybody wants life in its fullest, and there is no one who can offer it to you save Jesus.

LIFE LIFTER: *Those great hopes and dreams and ideals of yours are not dead, if you let God breathe into them the breath of fresh life. Practice hope. As hopefulness becomes a habit, you can achieve a permanently happy spirit.*

DAY
26

The thief cometh not, but for to steal, and to kill, and to destroy: I am come that they might have life, and that they might have it more abundantly.
                                                    JOHN 10:10

While in France one glorious Sunday at the Palace of Versailles, I watched as the marvelous fountains were turned on. The water burst forth with a gush and a roar and an upthrust as though reaching for the sun, dancing and singing. In the same way, when you get God in your life, you get so excited that you can hardly endure it. It makes life good.

"I came so that everyone would have life, and have it in its fullest," says that marvelous passage in the tenth chapter of John. You see, Christianity is designed to produce not glum, sour, growling, griping people; but happy people, lilting people, victorious people, enthusiastic people. All this takes into account the pain and problems in the world. Despite problems, and even out of them, God brings to people a consciousness and plan of victory.

> **LIFE LIFTER:** *As you go through life, do not practice subtraction; but instead add up your blessings, opportunities, possibilities. In so doing you will be relaxed, outgoing, and successful. The more you venture to live greatly, the more you will find within you what it takes to get on top of things and stay there. Pray big; God will grant big things if you ask for them and are big enough to receive them.*

| DAY **27** | *And being made perfect, he became the author of eternal salvation unto all them that obey him.* HEBREWS 5:9 |

I came across a passage from Washington Irving's *Sketch Book*. "Little minds," he says. "are tamed and subjugated by misfortune, but great minds rise above it." What a picturesque phrase! "Little minds are tamed and subjugated by misfortune." But great minds—humanity touched by the glory of God—rise above misfortune. Never accept defeat.

We have cultivated in recent years a "soft" philosophy, namely, that it is the right and privilege of everyone to be pampered and shielded from the harsh, cruel vicissitudes of human existence. It is true that in the name of Christ we are to bear one another's burdens and so fulfill His gospel. And it is our duty to care for those less fortunate than we, and those who suffer without opportunity; social awareness, social love, social service are part of living as Christ taught. But they are not supposed to minimize the fact that a human being should stand in regal, persistent strength and face life heroically in the name of Christ.

> **PRAYER:** *Our Heavenly Father, we thank You for the joy and the victory of the Christian religion. Help us to remember the truth that we can draw upon the inner strength which comes from You to stand up to our difficulties and calmly overcome them. Through Jesus Christ, our Lord. Amen.*

| DAY **28** | *And he hath put a new song in my mouth, even praise unto our God: many shall see it, and fear, and shall trust in the Lord.*   PSALM 40:3 |

I stopped for lunch with a friend whom I've known for many years. This man is really one of the most inspirational men I have ever known. I greeted him by saying, "I just met a man who told me it was impossible to be happy anymore."

"No happiness?" he asked. Then he reached in his pocket and pulled out a card. This is what it said:

TAKE TIME TO LAUGH: It is the music of the soul.

TAKE TIME TO PLAY: It is the source of perpetual youth.

TAKE TIME TO PRAY: It is the greatest power on earth.

TAKE TIME TO LOVE AND BE LOVED: It is a God-given privilege.

TAKE TIME TO BE FRIENDLY: It is the road to happiness.

TAKE TIME TO GIVE: It is too short a day to be selfish.

I was impressed by this but said to my friend: "There is one thing left out. I'd like to add it, if you don't mind." TAKE TIME FOR GOD: It is the way to life.

And it is, too.

LIFE LIFTER: *The chief struggle in gaining mental peace is revamping your thinking to the relaxed attitude of acceptance of God's gift of peace. In every circumstance, always look for the good that's surely present there.*

<table>
<tr><td>DAY
29</td><td>*And to stand every morning to thank and
praise the Lord, and likewise at even.*
I CHRONICLES 23:30</td></tr>
</table>

Our forefathers grew great and sturdy and strong because they drew strength from the sky and the hills and the streams, the forces and the wonders of nature. Enthusiastic people are those who live in relationship with nature and with God. So activate your mind and let it flow out and become a part of the world. Thrill to the world, thrill to people. Heed the Bible, which tells us we should walk in newness of life. That is a powerful idea. We're not supposed to be old, dead, dull, desultory. He who embraces the Gospel walks in newness of life. Life is new every morning and fresh every evening. Anyone who tells you that the Bible is a dull book hasn't read it, for the Bible positively glows with excitement and enthusiasm. It is the Book of Life. Be renewed not merely on the surface of your mind, but in the deeper spirit that activates your thoughts. Love life and life will love you back.

LIFE LIFTER: *Follow a steady program of renewing and revitalizing your positive attitudes. Never allow your reactions to become dull or insipid. Keep them new, fresh, vital. To keep the magic of enthusiasm working for you, have an eye for the charm and romance of living, and practice aliveness.*

DAY 30

And say thou unto the people, Sanctify yourselves against to morrow, and ye shall eat flesh: for ye have wept in the ears of the Lord, saying, Who shall give us flesh to eat? for it was well with us in Egypt: therefore the Lord will give you flesh, and ye shall eat.

NUMBERS 11:18

I believe that everything that is good and worthwhile in this world can be found in Jesus Christ. If you want mental life, you will find it in Him, for He has the clearest mind that ever entered into human history. If you feel your health is deteriorating, that you're growing old, that you are low in energy, vitality and strength, I earnestly urge you to give yourself to Him, for through Him you can experience a renewal, a rejuvenation, a rebirth in the body. Even if it be God's will that you suffer from some malfunctioning or malady or disease, you can find through Jesus Christ strength, vitality and power in your soul that will lift you above all of the defeats and vicissitudes of this life. So, I earnestly lay before you the claims of Jesus Christ upon you. I know that if you commit yourself to Him and surrender yourself to Him you will be fully alive and every day of your life can be a good day.

LIFE LIFTER: *Every day spend some unhurried moments in thinking energy, thinking vitality, actually "seeing" the life force at work in you. Your energy and vitality will continue on and on.*

DAY 31

O that ye would altogether hold your peace! and it should be your wisdom. JOB 13:5

We can reduce the pressure in our lives by the practice of creative silence. Most of us today have no idea how to practice creative silence. But it's a great art, which we all should learn. Rabindranath Tagore, the great Indian poet, said, "Every day wash your soul in silence." What a good thought that is! If you want to master pressure, I would urge you to yield yourself everyday to the silence of God. If we encouraged our young people in this practice, they would develop into more efficient men and women. So I offer the suggestion that in every schoolroom in the land once, every day, there be a brief silent period. Just plain non-sectarian silence. I would hope, of course, that some child in this silent period just might start thinking about God. Every family should have a quiet time every day. Every one in business—or in any place of work—could well have a quiet time each day in his office. Just shut the door, push the papers aside, and be silent. A person communing with the silence will hear right things in it and find new peace.

PRAYER: *Our Heavenly Father, You know us better than we know ourselves. We long to draw near to You. Enter our lives, we pray, and use us and fill us with the spirit that brings victory, peace and power. Through Jesus Christ, our Lord. Amen.*

SEPTEMBER

<table>
<tr>
<td>DAY
1</td>
<td>Therefore, behold, I will allure her, and bring her into the wilderness, and speak comfortably unto her. And I will give her her vineyards from thence, and the valley of Achor for a door</td>
</tr>
</table>

of hope: and she shall sing there, as in the days of her youth, and as in the day when she came up out of the land of Egypt.

HOSEA 2:14–15

The Christian faith is a tremendous thing. It's the greatest force in your life, and it's your hope for life here and life beyond. It can do anything with you that you will admit that it can. Faith can take the limitations from you and set you free from fear.

If you have a fear that you don't seem to be able to handle, bring it to Jesus and apply His techniques for overcoming it. Say to yourself, "I now determine I will be rid of this problem." That is the first step. You determine to get rid of it. Then surrender the problem to Jesus Christ absolutely and believe that you will be relieved of your fear. Finally, start living the Christlike life to the best of your ability.

LIFE LIFTER: *If you feel afraid, you can make yourself courageous by acting courageous. If you are feeling unhappy, by deliberately acting happy you can induce happy feelings. If you have lost confidence in your ability to win, make a list, not of the factors that are against you, but of those that are for you. Know for a fact that with God's help you take what you have to take courageously and victoriously.*

<table>
<tr><td>DAY
2</td><td>It is vain for you to rise up early, to sit up late,
to eat the bread of sorrows: for so he giveth his
beloved sleep.
PSALM 127:2</td></tr>
</table>

I rather like the idea of taking a new thought pattern to change your condition in the way you'd take medicine to heal you. And how can you take faith, when that is the medicine you need? You can take it either through the eye or through the ear. For example, suppose you read the Bible. The printed words are reflected as an image on the retina of the eye. This is transmitted to the mind where it conveys an idea and the idea affects the diseased area of the mind with its healing potency. That is why you should read the Bible.

The other way you can take faith is through the ear. Suppose you come to church. You hear the reading of the Bible, you hear the great music, you hear the sermon, you hear the prayers. All these make impacts on the eardrum. And these travel to the mind by a process that I do not pretend to understand, and reach the diseased area where the fears are. And if you do this sufficiently and earnestly, you can be healed of your fears, your apprehensions and your anxieties by the strong message of faith.

LIFE LIFTER: *Faith power works wonders. Those four words are packed with dynamic and creative force. Set your goal. Hold that goal in consciousness. Keep that image always before you and your goal will materialize.*

| DAY 3 |

Arise, cry out in the night: in the beginning of the watches pour out thine heart like water before the face of the Lord: lift up thy hands toward him for the life of thy young children, that faint for hunger in the top of every street.

LAMENTATIONS 2:19

A man wrote telling how he had come through a crisis. "My left hand," he said, "was caught in a rotary mower turning at full speed. I clutched my left hand as blood poured through the cotton work glove. I won't even try to recount what happened from that moment on. I got depressed. Life turned flat."

Then he read an inspirational article by W. Clement Stone on how to draw on your faith when the going gets tough. "That was the turning point for me," he declares. "I said, 'Take me over, Lord. Bring what You want out of this.' And when I said that, I began to feel a sense of peace and, finally, power."

What is your difficulty? How painful is it? There is no difficulty that is as big as you are, if you ask and accept the help of Jesus Christ. Jesus Christ is bigger than any sin, any failure, any difficulty. If you put your life in His hands, you grow along with Him.

LIFE LIFTER: *You can make your life what you want it to be through belief in God and in yourself. Start and end every day, and in between times too, by thanking God for everything.*

<table>
<tr><td>DAY
4</td><td>*The Lord God of gods, the Lord God of gods, he knoweth, and Israel he shall know; if it be in rebellion, or if in transgression against the Lord, (save us not this day).*   JOSHUA 22:22</td></tr>
</table>

We want to live in peace with our fellowman and I am sure one of the great signs of the times is the ecumenical spirit which brings Catholic, Protestant and Jew together in closer fellowship. But I'm also sure that the followers of the Jewish religion want to preserve the great tenets of Abraham, Isaac and Jacob, and that the Catholics want to preserve the great traditions of their faith. And so do we Protestants want to preserve the great heritage we have from Martin Luther, Calvin, Wesley, Zwingli and those heroes of the Reformation who went to the stake for their faith.

We are too quick to compromise our convictions. We give in too easily to being timorous, afraid, apathetic, indolent. We don't fight. If you believe something—I tell you as a minister of Jesus Christ—if you believe something, stand up and fight for it no matter what happens to you. And if we live like that we will never grow old; life will seem good; and we will have enthusiasm all our days.

LIFE LIFTER: *Be sure to see yourself rightly, for we tend to become as we see ourselves. So see yourself confidently. Follow a steady program of renewing and revitalizing your positive attitudes. Keep them new, fresh, vital.*

<table>
<tr><td>DAY
5</td><td>*All that found them have devoured them: and their adversaries said, We offend not, because they have sinned against the Lord, the habitation of justice, even the Lord, the hope of their fathers.*</td></tr>
</table>

All that found them have devoured them: and their adversaries said, We offend not, because they have sinned against the Lord, the habitation of justice, even the Lord, the hope of their fathers.

JEREMIAH 50:7

A friend of mine once felt that he was completely defeated. Then one day, walking gloomily along a street in Pittsburgh, he turned a corner where, though he did not yet realize it, destiny awaited him.

On a church's high iron fence was a big bulletin board with a Scripture quotation posted on it. The text there seemed to reach out and grip my friend as he passed. It said: "If God is on our side, can anyone be against us?" (Romans 8:31).

He went to his hotel and picked up the Bible. He read and read and read, finding that his whole being was being refreshed. And in that hotel room he finally prayed, "Dear Lord, I dedicate my life to You."

In the days that followed, the same old problems were there, but they didn't defeat him anymore, for now he had an inner assurance, an uplift of thought. He had discovered in a flashing moment how to change his defeats into victories.

PRAYER: *Our Heavenly Father, touch each of us, we pray, with deep and serious thought. Help us to commit ourselves to keeping the faith, until we finish the course. Through Jesus Christ, our Lord. Amen.*

<table>
<tr><td>

DAY

6

</td><td>

O thou that art named the house of Jacob, is the Spirit of the Lord straitened? are these his doings? do not my words do good to him that walketh uprightly?　　MICAH 2:7

</td></tr>
</table>

Thanks-givers are blessing receivers. I believe it is a law of human life that there's a correlation between inner attitudes and outer manifestations. That is to say, what we are within ourselves, we tend to have or create outside us. For example, if your mind is full of hate and resentment and ill will and grudges, you can be sure that you will manifest these things in the life outside your inner soul. We act out what we think. If you're filled with fear, anxiety, worry, and apprehension, you manifest these attitudes so that your life becomes one of fear and anxiety.

By the same token, if in our minds we entertain thanksgiving, we manifest blessings. The more thankfulness a person cultivates, the more he will open to himself the power flow, the vast wealth of heaven. Blessings will pour out upon him.

LIFE LIFTER: *When most people say they are being "realistic" they delude themselves; they are simply being negative. You must feed your mind even as you feed your body, and to make your mind healthy you must feed it nourishing, wholesome thoughts. Ease or difficulty in your work depends upon HOW you think about it. If you believe it is hard, it is hard. Think it is easy, and it is easy.*

| DAY 7 | *Shadrach, Meshach, and Abednego, answered and said to the king, O Nebuchadnezzar, we are not careful to answer thee in this matter.*
DANIEL 3:16 |

You can't be a commander of life unless you learn the great art of keeping your head in any crisis. And how is that done? "So let the peace that comes from Christ control your thoughts" (Colossians 3:15). The secret of attaining self-control is the application of practical spiritual principles. The Bible is filled with techniques that are so simple that anyone can understand them. And these, when believed in and applied, will in due course give victory over any lack of self-control or lack of calmness.

Here are the steps. When confronted with a big problem, think. Apply all of your mental powers to it. Second, pray about it, to get God's guidance, because you will never come out right as long as you think wrong. Third, do all you can do about it. Fourth, put it in the hands of God. Let Him take over and trust Him for guidance and for the outcome. These four principles constitute a basic scientific spiritual formula that will work for the great or the simple.

> **PRAYER:** *Our Heavenly Father, You know the difficulties and problems of each one of us. Help us to be able to keep the faith always and to overcome all resistance, pain, difficulty and failure. In His holy name. Amen.*

<table>
<tr><td>DAY
8</td><td>That if thou shalt confess with thy mouth the Lord Jesus, and shalt believe in thine heart that God hath raised him from the dead, thou shalt be saved.   ROMANS 10:9</td></tr>
</table>

With God's help, I preached the same sermon in the pulpit every Sunday for thirty years. It has had a little variation but it is the same theme, namely: If an individual will surrender his life to Jesus Christ, accept Him as Lord and Savior, and condition his life according to His will, he will have the precious secret of life. I believe that today even more so than in the days gone by. I believe there is no human problem, no human weakness, no human frustration that cannot be solved, overcome, and a victory attained if a person will build his life around Jesus Christ and live by His principles. To me it is just that simple.

> **LIFE LIFTER:** *We may live victoriously, not because we have any power within ourselves, but because when we give ourselves to God, He gives Himself to us. This is the great key to humble self-confidence. The unconquered and unconquerable of this world are those who hold ever fresh in their hearts an abiding faith in God and in their own destiny. Don't waste mental energy brooding over past events or worrying about the future. Live a day at a time and do a job at a time. Practice creative anticipation, the power of positive expectation. Have confidence that you can draw the best, not the worst, to yourself.*

<table>
<tr><td>

DAY

9

</td><td>

And Jesus said unto them, Because of your unbelief: for verily I say unto you, If ye have faith as a grain of mustard seed, ye shall say unto this mountain, Remove hence to yonder

</td></tr>
</table>

place; and it shall remove: and nothing shall be impossible unto you. Howbeit this kind goeth not out but by prayer and fasting.   MATTHEW 17:20–21

Let God's Spirit strengthen your inner spirit. Draw upon your own unused strength. How is that done? First—and I know I am claiming a lot when I make this statement, but I wouldn't make it unless I believed it— we must realize that nothing is impossible. Jesus says in Matthew 17:20–21, "Everything (is) possible for you." It doesn't mean you are going to get everything you want. But it does mean you can move out of the area of the impossible into the realm of the possible.

The human being is endowed with a tremendous capacity to grow and to outgrow. All life is growth. The minute a baby is born it begins to grow. The minute you put a seed in the ground it begins to grow. Unless you grow you die. And the secret of growth is to outgrow. The person who has a conscious desire to outgrow can do so by drawing upon his own unused strength.

> **LIFE LIFTER:** *Let the challenge of your aspirations rouse your slumbering and often unused powers into action. Go out today with the thought that an inner light is shining out of you. Prayerize, visualize, energize, actualize.*

DAY 10

What time I am afraid, I will trust in thee.
PSALM 56:3

Life tends to frighten people, for it can be pretty ferocious sometimes, pretty mean. But while fear is pervasive, a Christian, if he is really a Christian, shouldn't ever be frightened of anything. (I speak now of abnormal fear, not of normal caution.) If a person is truly living a Christian life, he should not be afraid of anything except God. And when we speak of having "the fear of God," we really mean living with great respect for God.

In Psalm 56, there is a passage that reads, "Even when I am afraid, I keep on trusting you." If you really believe this, really have it in your heart, you have a power against all difficulty. Life is just packed full of great, big difficulties, and sometimes you say to yourself, "Circumstances are too big for me. I can't handle them. I haven't got what it takes." Oh, yes, you have. There is no difficulty in this world that you can't handle. This I firmly believe, and this faith is justified by experience with many people.

LIFE LIFTER: *Go out of your way to talk optimistically about everything. You can if you think you can. Engrave those seven words deeply in consciousness. They are packed with power and with truth. Remember Edison's remark: "If we did all the things we are capable of doing we would literally astonish ourselves." Astonish yourself.*

DAY 11

And the Lord turned the captivity of Job, when he prayed for his friends: also the Lord gave Job twice as much as he had before. JOB 42:10

No good thing will be withheld from a person who lives a good life. Uprightness means honor, truthfulness, purity, decency—just general goodness. But sometimes we see instances that conflict with our understanding of goodness.

From the days of Job until now we have seen instances where the righteous suffer and bear heartache and pain, while the evil flourish like a tall tree. I've even had people tell me, "It never pays to be good." They contend that the smart ones get away with their wickedness, but that good people don't get any reward. An old farmer once told me, "God doesn't pay all His debts on the first of January." And he continued, "I've watched these evildoers over many years. They may get away with it for one year, five years, ten years, thirty years, maybe forty years. But I've lived a long life, and evil pays in its own coin in the end. Whereas those who are good do suffer, and there is no promise that they won't; but they come out on a higher value level." No good thing is withheld from those who are upright.

PRAYER: *Our Heavenly Father, we thank You for this marvelous state known as the happiness of the soul and of the mind. Help us to come upon the happiness that answers life's struggles. Through Jesus Christ, our Lord. Amen.*

DAY 12

Seek the Lord and his strength, seek his face continually. I CHRONICLES 16:11

A woman wrote to me saying, "My husband awoke one morning, drank several cups of coffee, and sat at the table looking so depressed that I couldn't help thinking to myself how very old and dejected he looked. Occasionally he emitted a giant sigh, followed by, 'I'm afraid I can't make a go of it. I'm afraid I'm licked.'"

She persuaded her husband to repeat affirmations after her. "He turned to me," she continues, "and said, 'I feel a little better already.' So off he went to work, repeating to himself, 'I go forth in the name of the Lord.' After a few days of this, his shoulders were thrown back and he was breathing deeply of the fresh morning air as he walked to his car. I thought, as I turned from the window, 'How alive he is now!'"

Certainly. God is life. This husband had put God out of his life. He was taking only shadows and fear into his life. But when he began to walk with God new faith cleared the quirks and shadows from his mind and canceled out his fear.

LIFE LIFTER: *No one has a problem for which there is not an answer through the wisdom and the guidance of God. Keep your mental and spiritual "contact points" cleaned so that God can operate through your mind.*

DAY 13

Thus saith the Lord, In an acceptable time have I heard thee, and in a day of salvation have I helped thee: and I will preserve thee, and give thee for a covenant of the people, to establish the earth, to cause to inherit the desolate heritages.

ISAIAH 49:8

George Romney, before he became governor of Michigan, was president of American Motors Corporation. At one point, the corporation was almost bankrupt. Everyone was lost in gloom, but Mr. Romney remained hopeful and enthusiastic. He kept telling his associates the situation would turn out all right. One of them asked him, "But, George, what's going to save the company?"

"God is going to save it," George said. "God always helps people who are trying to do the right thing."

So, to recapitulate: Don't get upset, remain calm. Think. And in the name of Jesus Christ, always do the right thing. God always helps people who are trying to do the right thing. The way to put these fundamentals into practice is to acquaint yourself with Him, so that you have His strength, so that you can be at peace, for then you can think, and then good will come.

LIFE LIFTER: *Deliberately conceive of God's advice as passing into your mind and that in due time you will "know" what that advice is. When you pray, ask the Lord to direct you. Then believe what He tells you. Do as He says.*

DAY 14

That the king said unto Nathan the prophet, See now, I dwell in a house of cedar, but the ark of God dwelleth within curtains.

II SAMUEL 7:2

A preacher friend of mine came to see me and started pacing the floor, saying, "I want to describe the church I hope to have some day." He pictured it all meticulously, specifically, to the smallest detail. He got me so excited that I leaped to my feet, exclaiming, "The church is already built! It is built in your mind. All you need to do now is finish the job." Ten years later, I dedicated his church and it was exactly what he had described to me ten years before.

What do you want to build out of your life? How high do you want to go? If you can only think to the rooftop, that is as far as you will go. But you can think your way without limit to the stars. What you are now is what you have been thinking for a long time. What you will be ten years from now depends on what you think from now on. If you want a great life in the future, think great thoughts.

PRAYER: *Our Heavenly Father, we would keep ourselves reminded of this truth. Deliver us from fastening bonds upon our own minds. Set us free, that the immense Godpower that You have planted in our minds and hearts and souls may find release and that we may really live as children of God. Through Jesus Christ, our Lord. Amen.*

DAY
15

But they that wait upon the Lord shall renew their strength; they shall mount up with wings as eagles; they shall run, and not be weary; and they shall walk, and not faint.

ISAIAH 40:31

A major-league baseball pitcher once pitched a game in Kansas City on an afternoon when the temperature was 105 degrees in the shade. Halfway through the game, he suddenly felt weak, listless, too washed out to continue.

But this ballplayer was a creative, practical Christian, so he walked around the pitcher's mound for a moment, repeating to himself a Scripture from the fortieth chapter of Isaiah: "But those who trust the Lord will find new strength. They will be strong like eagles soaring upward on wings; they will walk and run without getting tired."

He finished the game with energy to spare and reported that he never had a better time in his life with more feeling of mastery than in that game. This Christian discovered a great truth: the power of God is not only concerned with ethical precepts or with sociological and theological matters, but in a deep sense it has to do with the re-creation of the believer.

LIFE LIFTER: *If you want your situation to be different, perhaps the answer is to become different yourself. Tremendous things happen to the believer. So believe the answer will come. It will.*

DAY 16

And such as do wickedly against the covenant shall he corrupt by flatteries: but the people that do know their God shall be strong, and do exploits.
DANIEL 11:32

What is a weakness? A weakness is a deficiency in the personality. It is a defect. It is a disorganized area in a human being's nature. What is your policy toward your weaknesses? Or have you a policy? Do you just idly settle for a weakness? Perhaps you say, "Well, this is the way I am. I'm weak. There is nothing I can do but put up with myself like this and make the best of it." Is that your attitude?

One of the great reasons for studying the gospel and attending church is to help us overcome weaknesses and become strong. In the book of Daniel are these resounding, electrifying words: "Those who remain faithful will do everything possible." What a sentence! It is a masterpiece. The people that know their God shall be strong—and not only be strong; they will amount to something: They will do tremendous deeds. The ones who remain faithful will do everything possible.

LIFE LIFTER: *We become low-spirited when we give in to temptation. Such defeat dulls the spirit and reduces that keen sense of happiness one enjoys when in full control. The way to overcome temptation is to sincerely want God's help. Earnestly ask for it; believe you have it; act as God wants you to. This will make you happy and high-spirited.*

<table>
<tr>
<td>DAY
17</td>
<td>*Brethren, I count not myself to have apprehended: but this one thing I do, forgetting those things which are behind, and reaching forth unto those things which are before.*</td>
</tr>
</table>

PHILIPPIANS 3:13

One of the factors that contributes to mental health is the art of forgetting. Lest you think I rate forgetting too highly, I cite one of the great passages of the New Testament: "I forget what is behind, and I struggle for what is ahead" (Philippians 3:13). In other words, turn your back on past mistakes; put them out of your thoughts. The wisest Book ever written tells you to forget your failures and go ahead.

Well, you may say, I believe that; but how do you do it? It is difficult, you say, to put the memory of frustrations and disappointments out of your mind.

Whoever said it was easy? I am only saying it is necessary. If you carry on your mind all the failures and disappointments of the past, lugging them into the future, you'll have too great a weight upon you, and you'll be broken by it.

How then can you forget? My answer is: By will. By positive determination. By disciplining yourself.

PRAYER: *Our Heavenly Father, we thank You for letting Jesus Christ bring faith to this world, and love, and hope. Help us to keep faith, to keep hope, to keep love working for us. Through Jesus Christ, our Lord. Amen.*

DAY 18

But Daniel purposed in his heart that he would not defile himself with the portion of the king's meat, nor with the wine which he drank: therefore he requested of the prince of the eunuchs that he might not defile himself. DANIEL 1:8

I visited my old hometown and thought about my boyhood days. I remembered the time I'd been eating green apples, and I suffered for it. I called a doctor. He came and poked around at me and asked me what I had been doing. He gave me some peppermint and said, "You just take that and quit eating green apples. You will be all right." Then he put his hand on my head and said, "Son, I can cure your stomach. That is easy. But if you get bad thoughts in your mind, it will take a greater doctor than I am to cure you. So don't let bad or sick thoughts get in that head of yours."

How you think can even change the impact of sickness, physical deterioration, and aging. Christianity is life, friends. Jesus said, "I came so that everyone would have life" (John 10:10). And if you are going to have life, you have to cope with illness and deterioration and aging. And how you think has an important bearing on the aging process.

LIFE LIFTER: *Keep affirming that God's life force is flowing through you. Every day spend some time thinking energy, thinking vitality, "seeing" the life force at work in you. Your vitality will continue on and on.*

| DAY **19** | *But go thou thy way till the end be: for thou shalt rest, and stand in thy lot at the end of the days.* DANIEL 12:13 |

We live in an insecure world. Your body is no more secure than your ability to resist disease and infection. Accidents can happen to anyone at any time. This world is insecure. Yet you should never come to the point where you say, "Life is over for me, I am through. I can't do anything anymore, I haven't any confidence, I have no sense of security." Remember that the Lord is faithful; He will strengthen you and guard you against all evil. Don't live with too much caution.

It may seem strange that a man would stand in a pulpit and advocate throwing yourself into life, even at the risk of getting hurt. But I have observed that people who try to keep from getting hurt never amount to anything. Only those who throw themselves into risky circumstances—regardless of whether they may get hurt—become really great people. When you live daringly you do many stupid things, you often make a fool of yourself and people criticize you, and you may fail at one thing and another, but in the long run you will accomplish great things.

> PRAYER: *Our Heavenly Father, grant that we may have the resiliency that comes when Jesus Christ is in our lives. For this we give You thanks, through Jesus Christ, our Lord. Amen.*

> **DAY 20**
>
> *If any of you lack wisdom, let him ask of God, that giveth to all men liberally, and upbraideth not; and it shall be given him.*
>
> JAMES 1:5

All preaching should have practical applications, for Christianity is a way of life that really works—when it's lived properly. This includes how to make right decisions. In the long run, you determine what your life will be by your decisions. You can decide yourself into failure or into success, into mental turmoil or into mental peace, into unhappiness or into happiness.

A man remarked to me, "Let's face it: life goes the way the ball bounces." I don't go for any such idea as that at all. There is a deeper reality. We can control the bouncing of the ball of life's circumstances and outcomes as we learn the art of making right decisions.

And how do we learn it? I repeat: "If any of you need wisdom, you should ask God, and it will be given to you. Believe, really believe, that there is an answer for you and that God will give you the wisdom to find that answer. People who have become great people have been those who have discovered that God will guide them through the problems of their lives.

PRAYER: *Our Heavenly Father, we thank You that You are with us always, even until the end of the world. For this we give thanks, through Jesus Christ, our Lord. Amen.*

<table>
<tr><td>

DAY

21

</td><td>

Sow to yourselves in righteousness, reap in mercy; break up your fallow ground: for it is time to seek the Lord, till he come and rain righteousness upon you. HOSEA 10:12

</td></tr>
</table>

What depletes energy? Is it something in the physical being, some malfunctioning, some sickness? Are you tired because you are overworked? I doubt it. Energy is seldom depleted due to overwork alone. The factors resulting in our losing energy usually originate in our minds. We think tired, think depletion, think exhaustion, or we nurture hate thoughts, resentment thoughts, guilt thoughts, or prejudice thoughts. These habits siphon off our energy.

If you keep your thoughts alive, keep them clean, keep them healthy, and if you keep yourself in good physical condition, you can have abundant energy all your life. Almighty God, Who created you in the first place, Who gave you life, did not finish the creative process at that point. He not only creates; He re-creates. Through Him you can have new life, new vitality, new energy, every day of your life. In fact, you can possess energy that never runs down.

LIFE LIFTER: *Never bog down in a defeat psychology. Always, in the midst of defeat, keep looking for victory. Those who are fired with an enthusiastic idea and who allow it to take hold and dominate their thoughts find that new worlds open for them.*

| DAY **22** | *But God clave a hollow place that was in the jaw, and there came water thereout; and when he had drunk, his spirit came again, and he revived....* JUDGES 15:19 |

One day I was working on a sermon. The house was quiet—but I couldn't get the sermon outlined to save me. I finally said to my wife, "Let's take a walk."

The ground was covered with deep snow, so we put on our boots and went out. We had our dog Tonka with us. After walking a half mile, Tonka sat down, and Mrs. Peale and I stood beside him. We looked across the valley at the great snow-clad hills. There was not a sound to be heard save the gentle wind in the trees and the singing of the water in a nearby stream. Peace, quiet.

Presently I said, "Let's go back." And when we got back to the house I sat down and had the sermon outlined in about fifteen minutes. Something happened to my whole being when I let go and got out into the harmony and peace of nature where there is power. The secret is to live with relaxed power. When your attitude is easy-does-it, the power can come through.

LIFE LIFTER: *Practice a daily quiet time in which to listen intently for God's direction; listen more deeply than your own thoughts. Why be defeated when you are free to draw upon a Higher Power that can do everything for you?*

DAY 23

And it came to pass, when David had made an end of speaking these words unto Saul, that Saul said, Is this thy voice, my son David? And Saul lifted up his voice, and wept.

I SAMUEL 24:16

J.C. Penney told how he lived through the Great Depression when he had to face the hard fact that he had lost some forty million dollars. How would you feel if you lost forty million dollars? Well, J.C. Penney became terribly ill and put himself into a sanitarium.

One night, he got the notion that he was going to die. He wrote farewell notes to his family, made his peace with God, and fell into a troubled sleep. But when he opened his eyes and saw sunlight streaming into this room, he realized he had another day of life. He got out of bed, went down the hall and found a group of people singing, "God will take care of you."

As he sat listening, he felt two great loving arms go around him, and he knew that God loved him and would indeed take care of him. From that time on he was past being afraid, for he had found the love of God. He regained his health and set about rebuilding his great enterprise.

LIFE LIFTER: *Sincere meditation on God acts as a medication for the soul and body. Have great hopes and dare to go all out for them. Have great dreams and dare to live them. Have high expectations and believe in them.*

DAY 24

The keeper of the prison looked not to any thing that was under his hand; because the Lord was with him, and that which he did, the Lord made it to prosper. GENESIS 39:23

God makes you strong enough by His supportive presence. That is what He is: supportive. By His power He makes you strong enough to stand against anything.

Unfairness, injustice, hate, pain, sickness, weakness, infidelity—such are the enemies of human beings. Time and time again, a person falters under the onslaught of all this. Sometimes, after you have battled long and been thrown back many times and so many difficulties lie in your path, life throws the whole book at you, and you feel like giving up.

Have you ever felt like giving up? I have. I'd hate to tell you how many times I've felt like giving up. But do you know something? You must never give up, never. You must do like Paul: You must fight the good fight. You must finish the course. You must keep the faith. No, as a Christian you must never give up. As a human being you must never give up. And if you know this fact, this truth, that He whom they call Emmanuel is with you, you never will give up.

LIFE LIFTER: *Never let any mistake cause you to stop believing in yourself. Learn from it and go on. Stamp indelibly on your mind a picture of yourself as succeeding. Your mind will seek to develop this picture.*

<table>
<tr><td>DAY
25</td><td>*Laying up in store for themselves a good foundation against the time to come, that they may lay hold on eternal life.* I TIMOTHY 6:19</td></tr>
</table>

When you truly take hold of life, it is life indeed. Thousands of human beings have discovered this truth, some in dramatic ways, others in quiet, sudden insights. But there are millions more people everywhere trying to find life. Paul tells us where to find it. So help yourself to life. There is a generous supply for you. Take hold of life, which is life indeed.

When you get that life, you begin to develop a subtle insight; your mind gets sharpened. You get what is known as God's guidance and you develop perceptiveness. You are then able to handle the frustrations and difficulties of life and not let them throw you. You know then that you can take the mistakes and the sorrows and troubles and weave them into a pattern.

PRAYER: *Our Heavenly Father, we thank You for the power we may receive from You whereby we need not stand in awe of any difficulty, but shall know that we have through Jesus Christ the power to overcome it. Help us, Lord, to take this power, which is so freely offered to us, and live on a level we have never heretofore known. Through Jesus Christ, our Lord. Amen.*

DAY 26

Then David arose, and all the people that were with him, and they passed over Jordan: by the morning light there lacked not one of them that was not gone over Jordan.   II SAMUEL 17:22

Before a speech in San Francisco, a man approached me. "I came here tonight," he said, "because I believe in your philosophy that you never need to be defeated."

And he told me of his own experience. "Life just ganged up on me, and I felt I was completely through. Finally, I decided I couldn't live that way. So my wife and I started a little program. Every morning we read the Bible and we prayed. Out of this practice, I got some ideas. And these ideas helped me rebuild.

"I decided I would never accept defeat. Then I decided to start thinking creatively and spiritually. I stopped feeling sorry for myself. I got reacquainted with the God of the new start. Then I got God's directions on how to rebuild."

There was a full moon over San Francisco that night. It was fresh and clear and everything was bright and beautiful—but more beautiful than anything else was the look on the face of this man who had decided never to accept defeat.

LIFE LIFTER: *When you become convinced that you can make a comeback from any adversity, then all of your creative forces will come to your aid.*

| DAY 27 | *But, O Lord of hosts, that judgest righteously, that triest the reins and the heart, let me see thy vengeance on them: for unto thee have I revealed my cause.* JEREMIAH 11:20 |

I've heard it said so many times that "you've got to face the facts." Take a man about fifty-five years of age who loses his job and doesn't know where to get another one. A well-meaning friend says, "Jack, let's face it. When you're fifty-five, it's pretty tough to get another job. You might as well face the facts." Or consider a couple who got married and raised children but then began to grow apart, and some well-meaning person says, "Well, you might as well break up. You'll never get together again. You might as well face the facts."

But in each of these a wise friend should say, "Yes, this is tough. But be thankful we have a big God, and He will help you to straighten out that situation." The issue behind the problem is: How much are you willing to trust God? I tell you, friends, I honestly believe that if you trust Him completely, with all your heart, you'll never go wrong. Because He is rightness itself. There is no error in Him. And if you stay with Him, there will be no error in you.

PRAYER: *Our Father, we thank You for the greatness of our faith and the creative power which is inherent in it. Help us to commit ourselves to Him who can lift human lives into greatness. Through Jesus Christ, our Lord. Amen.*

| DAY 28 | *And it shall come to pass, if thou shalt hearken diligently unto the voice of the Lord thy God, to observe and to do all his commandments which I command thee this day, that the Lord thy God* |

will set thee on high above all nations of the earth.

DEUTERONOMY 28:1

A newspaper carried an item entitled, "There's a Fortune in Your Attic" that claimed there are several billion dollars in the form of unclaimed securities lying around in old trunks and elsewhere.

Now don't rush immediately to ransack old drawers, but if I may borrow the phrase, there is a fortune in the form of potential strength, power, joy, and peace in the attic called the human mind.

God who created you told you that He gave you dominion—not over any person but over the circumstances of life. So don't go on, defeated and crawling through life on your hands and knees. We need a new emphasis on the greatness of man. As Wordsworth says, "Trailing clouds of glory do we come from God, who is our home." Essentially, man is a tremendous being—a marvelous creature. That means you. It means me. Greatness!

PRAYER: *Our Heavenly Father, we thank You for Yourself and for Jesus Christ who leads us through the turbulent waters of this life and brings us out into peace. We give You thanks. Through Jesus Christ, our Lord. Amen.*

<table>
<tr>
<td>DAY
29</td>
<td>And they that know thy name will put their trust in thee: for thou, Lord, hast not forsaken them that seek thee.
PSALM 9:10</td>
</tr>
</table>

A missionary's wife in central China during World War II knew the Japanese were approaching her city. She was with her baby girl, two months old, and her son just over a year. Her husband had been taken to a hospital, himself ill. He was one hundred and fifteen miles away and would not be back for perhaps a month. The poor woman was filled with fear—alone, unprotected, in bitter January weather.

When morning came, she realized that she was without food for her children. She pulled off the calendar page. That day's verse stated simply: "Don't be afraid! I will take care of you and your children" (Genesis 50:21). There was a rap at the door. "We knew you would be hungry," said a longtime neighbor, "and you didn't know how to milk the goats. So I have milked your goats. Here is milk for your children."

Will you try to explain this away, handle it on an intellectual basis as just pure coincidence? But, when you come right down to it, what is coincidence? It is an act of God in the midst of time.

LIFE LIFTER: *For the next twenty-four hours, deliberately speak hopefully about everything, about your job, about your children's grades in school, about your health, and about your future.*

<table>
<tr>
<td>DAY
30</td>
<td>*And he said, Behold, I make a convenant:*
before all thy people I will do marvels, such as
have not been done in all the earth, nor in any
nation: and all the people among which thou</td>
</tr>
</table>

art shall see the work of the Lord: for it is a terrible thing
that I will do with thee. EXODUS 34:10

A woman wrote that she had become an alcoholic. One Sunday she saw herself in the mirror—not merely her outward form, but the defeated inner spirit. "I fell on my knees," she wrote, "and cried, 'O God, what a mess I have made of myself! Please, dear God, help me.'

"Then I got up and sat in a chair. The radio was on and a voice said, 'God will help you. Turn your life over to Jesus Christ. Your life will be different if you do.' It really got inside of me and I knelt down again and prayed, 'Dear Lord, I know the answer. I give You myself, I give You my problem. You take it.'"

This woman was cured instantly. She lost her desire to drink. Peace came to her, strength, cleanliness, hope, new life. What do you call such an occurrence? Well, you call it a miracle. It was a spiritual rehabilitation by a power that works when a person really takes it. Real faith works miracles.

LIFE LIFTER: *The word of God can make you clean of all guilt. How? The answer is by forgiveness from wrong thoughts and actions. The inner cleanness thus gained is an amazing source of high spirits.*

OCTOBER

But I will deliver thee in that day, saith the Lord: and thou shalt not be given into the hand of the men of whom thou art afraid.

JEREMIAH 39:17

As long as you live, no situation is hopeless. As long as you have life and God, so long as you have Christ and your own intelligence, why should any situation be hopeless? It is because you don't believe in yourself anymore, you don't really believe in God, nor in Jesus Christ. Actually, you don't believe in life itself. Start believing and get strength, such as is promised you, from God, who is good.

The statesman Mirabeau, whose clear thinking influenced the course of the French Revolution, once said, "Nothing is impossible to the man who can will." I believe that. What is will? It is the determination, the commitment, that you will do something. "Nothing is impossible to the man who can will." To have strong will, it must be backed up by faith. So strengthen that will of yours by strengthening your faith. God is good. He is a tower of strength. And He listens to you. So instead of regarding an unsatisfactory situation as hopeless, face it with a will. Then you can change it.

LIFE LIFTER: *Set yourself a goal that you've just got to reach. Then build under it the fire of anticipation and keep it burning. That goal will keep beckoning. These are the self-perpetuating motivators of enthusiasm.*

DAY 2

O Lord, to thee will I cry: for the fire hath devoured the pastures of the wilderness, and the flame hath burned all the trees of the field.
JOEL 1:19

Governor Charles Edison of New Jersey told me of the time when his father's laboratory at Menlo Park caught fire and burned down. The great inventor was sixty-seven years old, I believe. He stood there, his son told me, watching years of work go up in flames. "My heart ached for him," Charles Edison said. "He was no longer a young man. But then he spotted me and shouted, 'Charles, go find your mother. Bring her here. She'll never see anything like this as long as she lives!'"

And the next morning Thomas Edison remarked, "There is great value in disaster. All our mistakes are burned up. Thank God we can start anew." Great people do not allow the vicissitudes of life to defeat them. They have something within them that rises victoriously above the losses and disappointments. Whatever comes, life is good. And the thing that makes a person most aware of its goodness is to know God. Leo Tolstoy, one of the greatest men of letters who ever lived, said, "To know God is to live."

> **PRAYER:** *Our Heavenly Father, help us never to be discouraged nor overcome. Grant that we may enter into the life of our time with creative power to make it a better world. Through Jesus Christ, our Lord. Amen.*

DAY 3

Blessed is the man whom thou chastenest,
O Lord, and teachest him out of thy law.
PSALM 94:12

How can a person defeat the problem of tension and live with quiet power? Is there an answer? The answer is, "Our Lord, You bless everyone that You instruct and teach by using Your Law." That is from Psalm 94, verse 12. There is a law by which a person can be organized in his emotional life. It is as certain as the law that lifts the tides. It is not man's law, but God's law. Think God's way, live His way, and you will be freed from tension. You can live with quiet power.

The law of God created you and created me. Every once in a while you ought to look at yourself and say, "Think of the complexity of this body with which I am blessed." And it functions perfectly when kept in harmony with His law. But if your attitudes become contentious, selfish, hostile; or if you take this wonderful instrument and drive it too hard, then tension, stress, and anxiety take over. But when you bring yourself back into harmony with God's law, the tension abates and good health returns. The law of God is the law of organization, of harmony, of control.

LIFE LIFTER: *Many people live needlessly ineffective lives because they won't let go of the weight of sin. But if we freely confess to Him our wrongdoing and ask forgiveness, Jesus Christ will forgive us and cleanse us from sin.*

<table>
<tr><td>DAY
4</td><td>*And he said, I heard thy voice in the garden, and I was afraid, because I was naked; and I hid myself.*   GENESIS 3:10</td></tr>
</table>

If any man is honest with himself he knows the sin that is in him, he knows the weakness that is in him. And he ought also to know he should confess it to God and ask Him to forgive him and release him from it. And the Lord who loves him will respect him for his honesty. So will any good minister respect him. I've had the worst things confided to me by people who conclude by saying, "You'll never speak to me again. You thought I was a fine person."

"I think you're finer now than I ever thought you were before, because you have the sincerity and courage to come clean about your wrongdoing and want God to change you," I say to them.

So don't be defeated, don't be weak; don't be wicked. Remember there is the power of God to help you follow through on your prayers. If a person will really pray and will surrender up the evil things that he thinks and does and says, it is incredible what can happen to him.

LIFE LIFTER: *The forgiveness of sins is one of the most majestic of all biblical promises. The great promise is that if we believe in the atoning power of Christ's death on our behalf, we shall not perish when we die, but have everlasting life.*

<table>
<tr><td>

DAY

5

</td><td>

And said, I cried by reason of mine affliction unto the Lord, and he heard me; out of the belly of hell cried I, and thou heardest my voice.　　　　　JONAH 2:2

</td></tr>
</table>

Vincent Tracy did more good for alcoholics than almost any man I know. He and I were together for a Christmas night radio program and he said to me, "Back in 1948, life and my weaknesses were more than I could take. I started across the Brooklyn Bridge and headed for the Bowery, where I could get a handout. On the bridge I stopped and looked down at the cold water. The urge to jump was strong. But something kept saying to me, 'Keep on across the bridge.' And over on the Bowery, I suddenly started praying: 'Please dear Lord, won't You come to me and help me?' Instantly a great light burst into my mind. I walked away from the Bowery saying the Lord's Prayer, with my hand in the hand of Jesus. And I've been walking along the road with Him," he concluded, "ever since. Without Him I wouldn't be anything."

"With Him, Vincent," I said, "you're a very great deal." Vincent Tracy was humble enough to be wise. He came to Jesus and became a wiser wise man.

PRAYER: *Our Heavenly Father, help us to remember that when things go wrong it could very well be that we are wrong ourselves. Make us right. Through Jesus Christ, our Lord. Amen.*

DAY 6

I can do all things through Christ which strengtheneth me. PHILIPPIANS 4:13

I read about a young man who suddenly found himself at the top of his class in college, whereas previously he had been rattling around near the bottom. Somebody asked him how he had done this. He replied, "I went to a handwriting expert who told me I was a natural-born extrovert. When he told me that, on the basis of his science, I was an extrovert, I believed what he said. I began to act like an extrovert. That is why I'm no longer near the bottom of the class."

You may say that is superficial. It isn't superficial at all. Paul, in his letter to the Philippians, affirms, "Christ gives me the strength to face anything." You have heard that for years. If you really believe it, then you know that spiritually you are a released extrovert. Go out and be that. It is an old and thrilling theme that I just love. No one has ever changed my opinion that a human being has in him illimitable powers. He usually lives and dies without ever bringing more than a tiny fraction of his potential into action.

LIFE LIFTER: *Visualize God, who created you, as constantly re-creating you in every element of being. Try living one day without any unhealthy thoughts. It may be very difficult, but try another day, until it becomes habitual, and life will move in the direction of becoming healthy, vital, and alive.*

DAY 7

Thou shalt guide me with thy counsel, and afterward receive me to glory. PSALM 73:24

In the seventy-third Psalm we read these words: "Your advice has been my guide, and later you will welcome me in glory." There are many things you and I do not understand. But if you live with Him so that He guides you with His counsel, you will find your destination in eternal life.

God gives Christians a deep, sensitive perceptiveness and understanding of truth. This is what a Christian has that makes him different from other people. He has truth. Error is reduced in him. The great issue of life is: How much error have you; how much truth have you? If you live by error you will go wrong and come to wrong ends. Error means that which is wrong. Truth means that which is right. To people who love Him, who study Him, who live with Him, Jesus gives a sensitive, keen perceptiveness of truth. That means you don't need to go stumbling through life ineptly, failing at what you try, miserable and helpless. You have available to you the answers that answer.

LIFE LIFTER: *It is not always easy to stay on a high level. But God renews our hearts and keeps us going and holds us up. He helps us to "be strong like eagles soaring upward on wings" (Isaiah 40:31). Just keep on keeping on in goodness and great blessings shall be yours.*

<table>
<tr><td>DAY
8</td><td>*And I heard a loud voice saying in heaven,
Now is come salvation, and strength, and the
kingdom of our God, and the power of his
Christ: for the accuser of our brethren is cast*</td></tr>
</table>

down, which accused them before our God day and night.

REVELATION 12:10

I received a letter from a man who told me that he was
just five years old—that he had been resurrected that
many years ago. "I've been around for fifty-one years,"
he wrote, "but I was dead for all but the last five of
them." And he went on to explain, "Some years ago I
was making a good deal of money in real estate, but I
started drinking. I lost everything. I became a bum.
One day I stopped at the clubroom of Alcoholics
Anonymous. I found one of your sermons lying on a
table. I stuck it in my pocket and shuffled out. Passing a
park bench, I sat down and read that sermon. You said
that Jesus Christ was greater than any human weakness.
I thought about that and found myself saying, 'Jesus
Christ, change me!' I went back to my room and slept
twelve hours. When I woke up, I was free of my
weakness. It was that simple. I am a resurrected person.
Once again, I've become a successful businessman."

PRAYER: *Our Heavenly Father, we give You thanks for
the everlasting Gospel which, when we take it into our
hearts, enables us to live joyously, no matter what. Help us to
accept it and live by it. Through Jesus Christ, our Lord. Amen.*

<table>
<tr><td>DAY
9</td><td>Remembering without ceasing your work of faith, and labor of love, and patience of hope in our Lord Jesus Christ, in the sight of God and our Father.   I THESSALONIANS 1:3</td></tr>
</table>

To be a true optimist you have to be rugged and tough in mind. An optimist is a person who believes in a good outcome even when he can't yet see it. He is a person who believes in a greater day when there is yet no evidence of it. He is one who believes in his own future when he can't see much possibility in it.

You know, a lot of people do live under a cloud. But up above the clouds, the sun is always shining. Down here, on the surface of the earth, groping around in the shadows under a low ceiling, a person may not feel optimistic. But you ought to begin to practice optimism. Send up into the mass of dark clouds bright, powerful optimistic thoughts, a bright optimistic faith. By so doing, you can actually dissipate the clouds and have an entirely different life. Constantly send up into the overcast blanketing your mind bright thoughts of faith, love, hope, thoughts of God, thoughts about the greatness of life.

PRAYER: *Our Heavenly Father, we know that You want us to be not only good and decent, but also alive and vital. Help us to come to know Jesus, that we may know this great secret of dynamic, exciting living. Through Jesus Christ, our Lord. Amen.*

DAY 10

My soul longeth, yea, even fainteth for the courts of the Lord: my heart and my flesh crieth out for the living God.   PSALM 84:2

I once spoke with a gentleman who seemed to be on top of the world. His attitude astonished me somewhat, because I knew how much trouble he had been through. You've heard it said, "It never rains, but it pours." Well, it really poured on him. But he endured it all, and more than that, he came through victoriously. "You are a remarkable, indefatigable human being," I told him. "You really are something special. How come?" He grinned and said, "The answer is: Years ago, I discovered a philosophy that will stand up under anything. Nothing can break it—and I mean nothing. And it can be stated in five words: Keep believing— never lose faith."

The writer of Psalm 84:2 knew the same truth: "Deep in my heart I long for Your temple, and with all that I am, I sing joyful songs to You." What a picture! Here is a man who was really up against it and would have folded had he not been able to see that, despite how bad everything was, the goodness of the Lord prevails!

LIFE LIFTER: *When you think you are down for good, simply start affirming: "What an advantage to have hit bottom. The bottom is as far down as I can go. The only direction from there is up. And up I am going."*

<table>
<tr>
<td>

DAY
11

</td>
<td>

And he shall bring a ram without blemish out of the flock, with thy estimation, for a trespass offering, unto the priest: and the priest shall make an atonement for him concerning his

</td>
</tr>
</table>

ignorance wherein he erred and wist it not, and it shall be forgiven him.

LEVITICUS 5:18

I sometimes read the obituary notices in the papers. The obituary notices do not have the romance they once had. When I was a boy growing up in Ohio towns, the obituaries used to fill three or four columns. They told the most interesting things about people. From reading those notices you could pick up some wisdom.

Well, some years back, the New York papers carried the obituary of Mrs. Knox of the Knox Gelatin Company. She evidently ran the business herself. She must have been a dynamic and intelligent lady, but rather cryptic, too, and perhaps a bit difficult to work with, for she had a sign in her office warning people about making mistakes. And this is the way it read: "He who stumbles twice on the same stone deserves to break his own neck." Well, that is pretty hard-boiled. Let us everlastingly be thankful to the Good Lord that He has more patience than Mrs. Knox.

LIFE LIFTER: *The secret of changing one's personality, regardless of the problem, is to think in new categories. Empty out old dead thoughts and be reborn in mind and spirit. Let God take over your life and run it. He knows how.*

<table>
<tr>
<td>
DAY

12
</td>
<td>

There is one alone, and there is not a second; yea, he hath neither child nor brother: yet is there no end of all his labor; neither is his eye satisfied with riches; neither saith he, For
</td>
</tr>
</table>

whom do I labor, and bereave my soul of good? This is also vanity, yea, it is a sore travail.   ECCLESIASTES 4:8

A man offered to drive me to the airport if I would talk with him about a personal problem. On the way there, he confided all his troubles, worries, disappointments, unhappiness compounded.

I said to him, "The only way to free yourself from it is to stand up against it now and practice happiness."

"How do you practice happiness?" he asked.

I cited the example of John Wesley who, in his maturity, was one of the greatest men of faith in all the world. At an earlier time in his life Wesley had no faith whatsoever. So he hit upon the device of acting as though he did have faith. And in due time he did have faith. You can bring about the ideal condition by persistently acting as though that ideal condition already existed.

PRAYER: *Our Heavenly Father, we thank You that within each of us is a divine potential. This is put into us to assure a wonderful life. Grant that we may find an answer, that we may be willing to yield ourselves to God. Then certainly there will be good days ahead. Through Jesus Christ, our Lord. Amen.*

<table>
<tr><td>DAY
13</td><td>*Then Uzziah was wroth, and had a censer in his hand to burn incense: and while he was wroth with the priests, the leprosy even rose up in his forehead before the priests in the*</td></tr>
</table>

house of the Lord, from beside the incense altar.

II CHRONICLES 26:19

One morning after I preached in a church in New Jersey there suddenly appeared in front of me a woman who bluntly demanded, "Tell me why I itch all the time."

I talked with her at some length. It gradually came out that this woman's father had provided in his will that his estate was to be divided equally between his two daughters. Later this woman got the idea that her sister had "double-crossed" her and so she built up an enormous resentment and a terrible sense of guilt.

Fortunately, she was a strong person, with the wisdom to insist, "I am my own sickness. I must get myself healed." And that is exactly what she did. She took love and forgiveness and goodwill into her, and the hatred went and so did the itching.

Know the truth about yourself and know the truth about God, and you will be set free and become an entirely different person.

LIFE LIFTER: *Every night empty your mind of unhappy thoughts as you empty your pockets, and come alive. Pray for people you do not like or who have mistreated you. Resentment blocks spiritual power.*

| DAY **14** | *And he said, Oh let not the Lord be angry, and I will speak yet but this once: Peradventure ten shall be found there. And he said, I will not destroy it for ten's sake.* GENESIS 18:32 |

Prayer can change your life. I strongly recommend that you learn the art or science of prayer and put it to work in your life. Now this may seem to you to be just one more religious idea, without much life or sparkle to it. But that is where you would be wrong. It is the way to life itself.

When I say this of prayer I do not speak of the mere mumbling of words. I do not mean formal affirmations either, although formal prayers sometimes help and some formal prayers are touched with the glory of God. What I mean is a deep, fundamental, powerful relationship of the individual to God whereby his whole mind and heart become changed and he receives power from God within himself. I have seen such prayer change the lives of many.

> **LIFE LIFTER:** *Make a list of all the people who have hurt and mistreated you, or those whom you do not like. Then pray for each by name and sincerely forgive each one. Ask the Lord to bless them. Repel the thought that you are "justified" in your resentment. Speak kindly about these persons to others. Go out of your way to help them. This will break down many barriers. It will clear the path by which spiritual power comes to you.*

| DAY 15 | *For God, who commanded the light to shine out of darkness, hath shined in our hearts, to give the light of the knowledge of the glory of God in the face of Jesus Christ.* |

II CORINTHIANS 4:6

Years ago, I spoke with a chaplain who had returned from a year in Vietnam. As chaplain, it was his duty to go out and bring back the wounded men. One time, he was crawling through the mud toward one man, when his strength suddenly left him. He felt he could not go any farther.

"But just at that instant," he said, "a long shaft of sunlight came down to a spot just in front of me and rested upon a flower. It was the only vegetation left. There came to me in that instant," he continued, "that Scripture in II Corinthians where it says, 'God is shining in our hearts to let you know that His glory is seen in Jesus Christ.' New heart came to me, new strength filled my body, a new determination made me know I could bring back that wounded man."

Every one of us knows that deep trouble of the human spirit known as disheartenment. But just then, if you will look for it, God will repeat His miracle. He will shine in your heart.

LIFE LIFTER: *Practice hope. As hopefulness becomes a habit, you can achieve a permanently happy spirit. Do not let circumstances defeat you. You can if you think you can.*

> **DAY 16**
>
> *Then Saul fell straightway all along on the earth, and was sore afraid, because of the words of Samuel; and there was no strength in him; for he had eaten no bread all the day, nor all the night.*
>
> I SAMUEL 28:20

A famous physician has said that fear is the commonest and subtlest of all human diseases. And an equally famous psychologist has declared that fear is the most deteriorating enemy of human personality. Now these men, being scientists, are referring not to normal fear, but to abnormal fear. Normal fear is both proper and desirable. It is a mechanism designed by the Creator for our protection.

Abnormal fear is another matter. If you step over the line that separates it from the normal, you find yourself in a region of grotesque shadows and darkness, obsessions, and mental distortions.

But Almighty God never intended that anyone should live like that, and He has provided an approach by which you can have so much faith that you can live unafraid. There is a power by which you rise above the dangers and uncertainties of human existence and have power over them.

LIFE LIFTER: *Know that there is no death, that all life is indivisible, that the here and hereafter are one, that time and eternity are inseparable, that this is one unobstructed universe. We are citizens of eternity.*

| DAY 17 | *He that covereth his sins shall not prosper: but whoso confesseth and forsaketh them shall have mercy.* PROVERBS 28:13 |

There is nothing that can keep you or keep me out of the glorious new world of Christianity-in-depth—save our own reluctance to embrace it.

"Well," I can hear someone say, "my trouble isn't as serious as that. But I'm not a good person. So how do you expect me to step into that new world? I must confess to you, sir, that there is a great deal of sin in my life. I'm weak. I'm a pushover for temptation. I haven't got the strength to give myself as you say I must in order to enter into this experience. I can assure you that in the depths of my heart I desire it. But what about all these blemishes in my conduct, all these sins, all this hate, all this lust, all this dishonesty? How can I separate myself from these?"

How? By changing, that's all. Anyone can change if he has the desire to change and the will to change and will let Jesus Christ bring about that change.

LIFE LIFTER: *There is a reason why you do what you do and it is an important day in your life experience when at last you discover the reason. Self-knowledge is the beginning of self-correction. Don't shy off real spiritual faith. Through study and practice, develop intensity of belief, in-depth faith, as contrasted with the nominal variety.*

DAY 18

Great is our Lord, and of great power: his understanding is infinite.   PSALM 147:5

One day, a radio and television producer that I know was sitting in the Pittsburgh airport reading the New Testament. A soldier sitting next to him said, "You know, I don't think Jesus ever lived at all. It's all a myth and a fairy tale. He never lived."

"It's funny you would say that," the producer said, "because He was with me here just a minute ago."

"He was with you a minute ago?" asked the soldier. "Is that why you look so peaceful and so happy?"

"Yes, and you, too, can be peaceful and happy if you will let Him help you get rid of your conflicts and fears. He loves you as much as He loves me."

The soldier stood up and cleared his throat. He took my friend's hand and he said, "Okay, mister. I think maybe you've got something there. I'll try."

Now that is all any of us can do, is to try. And as we try, God will meet our feeble efforts much more than halfway. He will give us the power to stand up against fears, disappointments, frustration, opposition, misunderstanding—everything—and we will walk with our heads above it all into victory.

> **LIFE LIFTER:** *Practice kindly affection. Practice being considerate. Courtesy has amazing power to dissipate ill will. Free your heart of jealousy and resentment. The love you give will return to you, and lift your spirit to new levels.*

| DAY 19 |

This is the day which the Lord hath made; we will rejoice and be glad in it. PSALM 118:24

Isn't it wonderful to meet a person who is really alive? Not long ago I found myself talking with a man who positively sparkled with vitality. "Tell me," I said, "where did you get so much faith and enthusiasm?"

"I heard you speak at a meeting," he explained. "There was something in your talk that day that changed my life. It was a single sentence."

The sentence that had done so much for him was Psalm 118:24: "This day belongs to the Lord! Let's celebrate and be glad today."

"And in what way has this changed your life?" I asked.

"Saying that verse helped me realize that if I take just this one day and do my best with it, then when night comes I can give thanks to God and go to sleep, knowing that He watches over me."

Not every day is going to be a pleasant day. Not every day is going to be an easy one. Life brings to each of us some share of pain, struggle, sorrow, heartache. But even in a day that is full of suffering and difficulty, there lies hidden a nugget of something good.

PRAYER: *Our Heavenly Father, we thank You for all the days You have given us. Grant, O Lord, that we may demonstrate in our living that every day, be it dark or sunlit, can be a good day. Through Jesus Christ, our Lord. Amen.*

<table>
<tr><td>

DAY

20

</td><td>

So Joab came to the king, and told him: and when he had called for Absalom, he came to the king, and bowed himself on his face to the ground before the king: and the king kissed

</td></tr>
</table>

Absalom.   II SAMUEL 14:33

Some years ago, I received a call to come to a hospital to see a patient—a medical doctor. On my way to the hospital I remembered that a doctor by this name had been mixed up in some crooked business. I went into the hospital room and asked, "I don't know you, do I?"

"No," he replied. "But I know you. I want you to get me out of this place. I have a stomach condition, and it has developed because I hate so many people. I want you to operate on me and get this hate out of me."

"Doctor, I have a suspicion about you," I said. "What have you got on your conscience besides hate?"

After a pause he admitted, "Doctor Peale, I am absolutely full of rottenness and sin."

He told me all the dirty things he had done and there were plenty. He wanted to change. And before we got finished in that hospital room he did just that, for he said to the Lord Jesus Christ, "I will go with You all the rest of the way." And he did, too. He got the error out of him and got the truth in him.

 LIFE LIFTER: *Remember that you will never be spiritually blessed until you forgive. Goodwill cannot flow toward you unless it flows from you.*

<table>
<tr><td>

DAY

21

</td><td>

I know thy works, that thou art neither cold nor hot: I would thou wert cold or hot. So then because thou art lukewarm, and neither cold nor hot, I will spew thee out of my mouth.

REVELATION 3:15–16

</td></tr>
</table>

Charles M. Schwab, one of the great American industrialists, said: "A man can succeed at almost anything for which he has unlimited enthusiasm." My friend Raymond Thornburg gave me a wonderful quotation from Anatole France, who said, "I prefer the folly of enthusiasm to the indifference of wisdom." George Matthew Adams said, "Enthusiasm is a kind of faith that has been set afire." Sir Edward V. Appleton, the Scottish physicist whose scientific discoveries made worldwide broadcasting possible and won him a Nobel prize, was asked the secret of his achievements. Now what would you think a scientist of that caliber might say? Well, Sir Edward V. Appleton answered, "It was enthusiasm. I rate enthusiasm even above professional skill." It is a fact that people who do not have the skill of the professional, but have enthusiasm that the professional lacks, achieve things. They have the motivational force.

LIFE LIFTER: *The secret of successful living is to get turned on with self-repeating enthusiasm, and to keep the positive principle going. If you are out of enthusiasm, get reborn spiritually. It will make you come alive.*

<table>
<tr><td>DAY
22</td><td>*And now, Israel, what doth the Lord thy God require of thee, but to fear the Lord thy God, to walk in all his ways, and to love him, and to serve the Lord thy God with all thy heart*</td></tr>
</table>

and with all thy soul. DEUTERONOMY 10:12

I remember a sign I saw back at the time when I lived in Syracuse, New York. The winters in upstate New York are rugged, and the spring thaws break up the roads very badly. One spring, near Watertown, I actually saw a sign some farmer had put up that said, "Choose your rut well. You'll be in it for the next twenty-five miles." When people get into ruts in living it's for longer than twenty-five miles. But you don't have to stay in a rut. You can get out of it.

Each of us, I believe, should at intervals restudy his activities and redefine his goals. At times, a person ought to appraise carefully what he is doing and ask himself the question, "Why am I doing this?" We do our work each day, and maybe we do it the best we can. But why are you doing that particular work? What are your objectives, your goals? Could you tell me what your goal is? Or is it fuzzy, hazy? We need to sharpen our thinking and bring our goals into focus.

> **LIFE LIFTER:** *You can reach your goal, your best dreams can come true, you can get where you want to go—only if you know what your goal is. Be somebody. Practice the principle of the possible (Matthew 17:20).*

<table>
<tr><td>DAY
23</td><td>*And the seventh angel sounded; and there were great voices in heaven, saying, The kingdoms of this world are become the kingdoms of our Lord, and of his Christ; and*</td></tr>
</table>

he shall reign for ever and ever.   REVELATION 11:15

A good friend of mine thinks of the world as "God's tumbling barrel." A tumbling barrel is an industrial device for smoothing pieces of metal. It's a revolving drum into which workers put shaped metal pieces that have burrs or rough edges and an abrasive.

The barrel is then rotated. One piece tumbles against another, and the abrasive rubs steadily against them. After some time, the drum is opened, and the pieces are spilled out. The burrs have disappeared, the rough edges are gone. The metal parts are now in shape to function properly in a finished product.

In my friend's mind, this ingenious process suggests the way human beings are tumbled in God's world. As we move through life we tumble against each other and are rubbed by hardships and difficulties. All this friction smooths our rough edges, rounds our personalities, and forces us to use our minds and make ourselves better people.

LIFE LIFTER: *The tests of life are not to break you but to make you. Stand up to your obstacles and do something about them. You will find that they haven't half the strength you think they have.*

DAY 24

Behold, I set before you this day a blessing and a curse.
DEUTERONOMY 11:26

An old man from a small New York State community appeared on a national television show. The program's host was one of the greatest quipsters in the business, but he nearly lost the show to this old man, who was so full of light and fun that he had everybody rocking with laughter.

The host finally said to him, "Sir, you are the happiest man I ever had on my show. Please tell us how you got to be so happy."

"Why, son," said the old man, "every morning when I wake up I have two choices for the day. One choice is to be unhappy. The other choice is to be happy. So, faced with those two choices, I choose to be happy."

Now what that happy old man was referring to is one of the greatest powers that you and I possess: the power to choose. By the power of choice you can either make your life creative or you can destroy it. Somebody said that history swings on small hinges. Similarly does human life develop according to small decisions. We determine our future by our immense power of choice.

LIFE LIFTER: *To be rid of worries about the past, repeat this daily: "I forget what is behind, and I struggle for what is ahead. I run toward the goal, so that I can win the prize of being called to heaven" (Philippians 3:13–14).*

<table>
<tr><td>

DAY

25

</td><td>

It may be that the house of Judah will hear all the evil which I purpose to do unto them; that they may return every man from his evil way; that I may forgive their iniquity and their sin.

JEREMIAH 36:3

</td></tr>
</table>

A man once wrote, "I was getting near the bottom and couldn't find any way to stop the descent. One day, I went down to the lakeshore and I began to pray. 'God,' I said, 'I need Your help desperately. Please give it to me now. Not later—now.' At that exact moment, I was filled with a sense of incredible peace.

"I'm forty-five years old. I had never really believed in forgiveness. I carried my sins like a sack on my back. I thought it possible that they might be forgiven, but I couldn't believe they could be forgotten. Now it's as though they had vanished. I feel pounds lighter."

This is the reason we believe, with all our hearts, in a Gospel of power that can touch a defeated man and give him power and life again. Believe in God's power, yield yourself to it, and start at once to live differently, in accordance with His will, so that you may be lifted from defeat to victory, from weakness to strength, from sadness to joy.

PRAYER: *Our Heavenly Father, we are grateful that we may come to You and receive the truth by which we can overcome error. Help us, we pray, to live with joyous creativeness. This we ask in His holy name. Amen.*

<table>
<tr><td>DAY
26</td><td>*And he said, Lay not thine hand upon the lad,
neither do thou any thing unto him: for now I
know that thou fearest God, seeing thou hast
not withheld thy son, thine only son, from me.*</td></tr>
</table>

GENESIS 22:12

What we need today is a greater emphasis upon big, strong people. When I was a boy they used to teach us in school that there is a great something a human being can use, which is known as willpower. Later on, a generation of more laid-back educators decided this was corny. But they sure produced a corny situation when they abandoned it! The mental health situation in this country worsened when they abandoned stressing will power.

There is a power in an individual whereby he can decide, "I will. I will it to be. This is my decision. This is it—with the help of God." Naturally, willpower is so much whistling in the dark unless you combine it with God's help. But there are rugged people who with God's help take failure or difficulty or disappointment in their stride, extract from the experience whatever know-how it can give them, then relegate it to oblivion. And these people are inspiring.

LIFE LIFTER: *Take the best into your mind and only that. Nurture it, concentrate on it, visualize it, pray over it, surround it with faith. Spiritually creative mind power, aided by God power, will produce the best.*

| DAY 27 | *Hearken unto me, ye that know righteousness, the people in whose heart is my law; fear ye not the reproach of men, neither be ye afraid of their revilings.* ISAIAH 51:7 |

A young man came to see me. He had been a teacher in a secondary school. He was highly educated, highly trained, scholastically the best. Naturally when the headmaster retired, he thought he would get the job. But the board brought in a man from the outside. Offended and angry, the young man quit.

I said to him, "Look, I understand that you are a man of great potential, great capacity, but you are ruining yourself with resentment. The thing for you to do is to forget the whole incident. Go back and apply for a position on the faculty and go to work."

Well, he never mentioned it again. He went back on that faculty. Later, when a school needed a headmaster, the board chairman recommended him because he had developed so impressively after mastering the art of forgetting—and he became a headmaster.

What misfortune are you nursing in your mind? Forget it. It's a great art. I've seen many people do it. It's difficult. But it's the way to mastery.

PRAYER: *Our Heavenly Father, we thank You for the great truth whereby if we really think, believe, and pray we can find the solution, Your solution, to any problem. For this we give You thanks. Through Jesus Christ, our Lord. Amen.*

DAY **28**	*Therefore whosoever heareth these sayings of mine, and doeth them, I will liken him unto a wise man, which built his house upon a rock.*
	MATTHEW 7:24

Little did the thousands who heard Jesus' words on the hillside that day realize that what they were listening to would be honored by multitudes twenty centuries later. Nor that scholars through the ages would say that these simple statements represented the greatest wisdom mankind would ever hear. As Jesus finished His sermon, He said that a person who had heard and lived by these teachings could be compared to a man who built his house upon a rock. Though all the elements conspired to knock that house down, they could not prevail—it stood, for it was built upon a rock.

Friends, you really listen to something when you listen to that passage of Scripture! Why don't you, this very day, read again the Sermon on the Mount in the Gospel of Matthew? If you read this passage and if you live by it, you will have what it takes, and nothing in this world—and I mean nothing—will be able to beat you down.

LIFE LIFTER: *The Creator built energy into you and me when we were babies. He implanted in us the life force, and true faith can keep this life force alive. Faith is the most powerful of all forces operating in humanity, and when you have it in depth, nothing can get you down. Nothing.*

<table>
<tr><td>DAY
29</td><td>*But Jehoshaphat said, Is there not here a prophet of the Lord, that we may inquire of the Lord by him? And one of the king of Israel's servants answered and said, Here is*</td></tr>
</table>

Elisha the son of Shaphat, which poured water on the hands of Elijah.

II KINGS 3:11

Two gentlemen I knew suddenly found themselves without jobs. What did the two men do? One said to the Lord, "I don't understand why this developed, but I know that You have an answer for me."

Then he made a list of the hundred top executives of great American business organizations. To these men he wrote a letter. He told these presidents exactly what his record was and was absolutely honest. He had seven offers, one of which led him to the very thing in life that he could do best.

The other fellow went all to pieces. And he hasn't made anything of his life even yet, I am sorry to say.

If you adopt the outlook that something great can be done with your trouble, you can do something great. Your outlook determines your future.

PRAYER: *Our Heavenly Father, help us to know that if we see Your goodness it can come to us and if we reorganize ourselves according to Your will, we shall find the kingdom and have all the glorious things it is Your pleasure to give to Your children. Grant that this may come to each of us, through Jesus Christ, our Lord. Amen.*

| DAY **30** | *And she called the name of the Lord that spake unto her, Thou God seest me: for she said, Have I also here looked after him that seeth me?* GENESIS 16:13 |

I wish to remind you of one of the greatest and most helpful facts in this world—namely, you can start life new every morning. This ought to be comforting for everyone who feels discouraged about yesterday or who thinks the future looks hopeless. This assertion is not based on wishful thinking, but upon the solid, factual authority of the Bible itself. In Psalm 90:14 are these sparkling, resplendent, upbeat words: "When morning comes, let your love satisfy all our needs. Then we can celebrate and be glad for what time we have left."

In his poem, "The Song of Diego Valdez," Rudyard Kipling has a line which is a gem. He refers to "The God of Fair Beginnings." It makes no difference to God what mistakes you've made, what failures you have had. He does not hold them against you. He is the God of fair beginnings. God is big. He forgets, He forgives, He writes it off—because He is fair. No matter how badly things have gone, He always makes it possible for you to make a new beginning.

PRAYER: *Our Heavenly Father, we ask Your blessing upon us all. Grant that any problem in anyone's mind may, upon being given to You, break open with answers that truly answer. Through Jesus Christ, our Lord. Amen.*

| DAY **31** | *And there came a fire out from before the Lord, and consumed upon the altar the burnt offering and the fat: which when all the people saw, they shouted, and fell on their faces.* |

LEVITICUS 9:24

There are many people this very day who will die years before they should because they are not masters of themselves mentally and emotionally. For this reason, the subject of how to develop inner calmness may be considered during a service of divine worship. The purposes of worshiping God include pondering His Word and conditioning ourselves to live according to His will. But worship is also part of spiritual healing.

Where is the healthiest place anybody can be on Sunday morning? The highway? Not on your life! A golf course? Well, I'm not going to minimize the health-giving value of golfing, but I have difficulty in understanding why it must be Sunday morning at church time. No, the healthiest place to be Sunday morning is in church where one receives a healing treatment of the mind and of the soul and of the body. Every person should go forth from worship with the peace of God ruling in his heart.

LIFE LIFTER: *God's peace deeply imbedded in your mind can often have a more tranquilizing and healing effect upon nerves and tension than medicine. God's peace is itself medicinal.*

NOVEMBER

DAY
1

*And Elijah said unto her, Fear not; go and do
as thou hast said: but make me thereof a little
cake first, and bring it unto me, and after
make for thee and for thy son.*   I KINGS 17:13

One of the greatest human beings I ever knew was an
old man who lived in Syracuse, New York. One time I
went to him for advice about a problem. And he said,
"Well now, son, tell me all about it." I had no trouble
doing that, because my mind was full of it. When I had
finished he said, "You know, God has a sense of humor.
You know what He does? When He has a wonderful
possibility for you, He buries it at the heart of a big
difficulty and He hands you this difficulty. So if you
know the mind of God you thank Him for the
difficulty because you know that, with His exquisite
sense of humor, He has buried a bright possibility at
the heart of that difficulty."

"But how do you find this bright thing that has
been buried in the difficulty?"

"You surround the difficulty with prayer and faith
and good hard thinking," answered Mr. Andrews, "and
melt it down. And after a while, in the midst of it, you
see this bright, shining thing, this potential good."

> **LIFE LIFTER:** *In every difficult situation is potential
> value. Believe this, then begin looking for it. Say aloud,
> "I don't believe in defeat," until the idea dominates your
> attitudes. You will receive power to handle all your problems.*

> DAY
> **2**

Fear not; for I am with thee: I will bring thy seed from the east, and gather thee from the west. ISAIAH 43:5

Believe the great fact that God is with you. And, with God's help, what can stand in your way? I have no doubt that you believe in God one way or another, but do you really believe that God is with you, on your side, by your side, in you, helping you? When you have this overwhelming faith in God, when you really believe in Him, and then call upon Him, He will answer and show you mighty things, which you never knew.

As you practice this thought, you will become aware that He is also showing you a greater truth. "Don't be afraid! I am with you" (Isaiah 43:5) is probably one of the greatest statements ever made in the history of human life on this earth. "Don't be afraid! I am with you." We are taught this but we do not keep it in mind. Think big. And think the biggest thought of all, that you are not alone, that God will always help you.

LIFE LIFTER: *Take the bright view that if you do your part, the very best you know how, and always think and work positively, bountiful supply and abundant living will come. Start and end every day, and in between times too, by thanking God for everything.*

<table>
<tr>
<td>

DAY

3

</td>
<td>

And I will give unto thee the keys of the kingdom of heaven: and whatsoever thou shalt bind on earth shall be bound in heaven: and whatsoever thou shalt loose on earth shall

</td>
</tr>
</table>

be loosed in heaven.   MATTHEW 16:19

One night I spoke in Webster Groves, Missouri. A man asked if he could drive me back to my hotel. He said, "I want to tell you a story of spiritual victory. I was a failure. I was down, completely down. Then a friend said to me, 'Frank, I want you to read the Bible; stick to Matthew, Mark, Luke and John and when you come to a passage that strikes you, commit it to memory.'

"One day I came upon Matthew 16:19, where Jesus tells Peter, 'I will give you the keys to the kingdom of heaven.' I knew Peter had messed up his life, just as I had. I took it to mean He would give the keys to me, too. Each day in my prayers I unlocked the kingdom of heaven, and blessings started flowing into my life."

That man had had his life changed. He had found Jesus Christ and accepted Him as his Savior. Moreover, he had learned to pray in such a way that he developed perception and understanding. The keys to the kingdom are available to all God's believers.

PRAYER: *Our Heavenly Father, we thank You for the vitality embodied in the Gospel. Help us be willing to endure any sacrifice in order that Your kingdom may come among all people. Through Jesus Christ, our Lord. Amen.*

DAY
4

In thee have they taken gifts to shed blood; thou hast taken usury and increase, and thou hast greedily gained of thy neighbors by extortion, and hast forgotten me, saith the Lord God.

EZEKIEL 22:12

It is said that the United States of America was formed by the convergence of two streams of history. One took its rise in the thinking of the philosophers of classical antiquity: Socrates, Plato, Aristotle, Cicero. These men believed that the human mind must always be free.

The other stream took its rise when Moses addressed a nation of slaves and told them that they were children of God, that other men should not put shackles on their wrists or lay whips to their backs.

The confluence of these two great streams of thought formed a government predicated upon the greatness of the human mind and the sovereignty of the human soul. I have enormous faith in the continuity of these ideals in the American people. You cannot break a nation built upon such foundations, unless that nation becomes arrogant, forgets its great heritage and, worse than all else, turns away from God.

PRAYER: *Our Father, we thank You for Your goodness. Bless our country and all our leaders. Grant that the true principles and ideals of faith, self-reliance, enterprise, virtue, honor, and religion may emerge into the modern world. Through Jesus Christ, our Lord. Amen.*

| DAY 5 |

Because thou hast been my help, therefore in the shadow of thy wings will I rejoice.

PSALM 63:7

Everyone needs to know how to stand up to a tough situation. The answer to this problem may be given in a concise statement. The one sentence is very simple, but if it is believed in and used, it can help you stand up successfully to any tough situation, no matter what kind it may be. This may seem like claiming a great deal, but the claim is a valid one. And we find this great truth in Psalm 63:7: "You have helped me, and I sing happy songs in the shadow of your wings."

We can put this truth another way: Don't struggle so hard. Don't get yourself worked up. Don't fill your life with tension. Do the best you can with any situation and then commit it—that means put it completely in the hands of the Lord, trusting absolutely in Him, and He will bring it to pass in a right and proper manner. This is an old truth, but the wisest and most astute of men and women have believed it, have applied it, and have found it will absolutely, positively work.

> PRAYER: *Our Heavenly Father, we thank You for the great truth that we are not alone, ever, no matter what, that You are always with us and always will be, to the end of our lives and beyond. We give You thanks for this blessing, Your holy presence. Through Jesus Christ, our Lord. Amen.*

<table>
<tr><td>DAY
6</td><td>*And when any will offer a meat offering unto the Lord, his offering shall be of fine flour; and he shall pour oil upon it, and put frankincense thereon.*
LEVITICUS 2:1</td></tr>
</table>

William L. Stidger was a distinctive preacher, but at one time he had a nervous breakdown and sat for months in abysmal gloom. He emerged from this by the practice of thanksgiving.

One day a friend said, "Think of people who have benefited you and ask yourself whether you have ever thanked them." Stidger gave it some thought, then wrote a letter to an old teacher. Presently he received a letter written in the shaky handwriting of an aged lady. "Dear Willy," she wrote, "I taught school for fifty years. Yours is the first letter of thanks I ever received from a student and I shall cherish it until I die."

This brought a ray of sunshine into Stidger's mind and he wrote another letter and another and another, until he had written five hundred letters! In the years that followed, whenever depression began to seize him, he would take out his copies of the letters of thanks he had written to people and the happiness he had felt while doing it would well up in his heart once again.

LIFE LIFTER: *Give thanks daily for your blessings. Get into the habit of thinking happy thoughts. Go out of your way to make other people happy. That is the formula for real happiness and enthusiasm.*

| DAY **7** | *He that handleth a matter wisely shall find good: and whoso trusteth in the Lord, happy is he.* PROVERBS 16:20 |

Happiness is not, as some might carelessly assume, a light or frivolous topic. Many tend to play down happiness as a superficial objective. But such an attitude is contrary to the facts of human nature. To be truly happy is to be drawing upon the essence of life. Furthermore, happiness fosters healthiness.

A physician once said that happiness corrects imbalances in a person's being. Imbalances, he said, tend to produce sickness, weakness, and deterioration. Balance tends to produce health, strength, and growth. Therefore, genuine happiness brings healthiness.

Happiness will not be found in soft sweetness. It will not be found in moonlight and roses. Happiness in depth—and that is the only kind of happiness that will stand despite trials and continue to be happiness—is to be found through struggle, hardship, pain, suffering, difficulty. It is a joy that is bathed with tears and consecrated by effort. If you are experiencing pain today, look carefully in it for a golden nugget called happiness that has been buried there.

LIFE LIFTER: *Learn to love God's ways; your life will be blessed with creative forces. All things will flow toward you. Your efforts will be blessed, and God's bountiful prosperity will be yours. You will live on God's law of supply.*

DAY 8

And Solomon stood before the altar of the Lord in the presence of all the congregation of Israel, and spread forth his hands toward heaven.
I KINGS 8:22

There has never been anyone like Jesus in all the history of mankind. He is incomparable because He had the truth and has it now. He has love for people and a strange, mysterious power to change men—to take the bad out of them and put the good in, to take weakness out of them and put strength in, to take hate out of them and put love in, to take dishonesty from them and make them honest. Jesus can change anyone. Because all of us, wistfully down in our hearts, want to be better than we are, we continue to follow Him, hoping, praying, dreaming. One day we meet Him, and are changed.

It is for this reason that today untold millions around the world shout acclaim to Him. "The sky and the earth won't last forever…" (Matthew 24:35). You shall pass away, I shall pass away. But if we are in Him, none of us will ever pass away. We will be immortalized in His truth, which is deathless.

LIFE LIFTER: *If you love people, you inevitably get love in return and thereby experience a joy that makes you a happy person. To be successful is to be helpful, caring and constructive, to make everything and everyone you touch a little bit better. The best thing you have to give is yourself.*

DAY 9

For both he that sanctifieth and they who are sanctified are all of one: for which cause he is not ashamed to call them brethren.

HEBREWS 2:11

I was once interviewed by reporters from a hometown of mine, Findlay, Ohio. They asked me the usual questions. Finally, one of them asked, "Dr. Peale, have you any advice for young people about how to work for a good future for themselves and, beyond that, how they can help make the world a better place for people everywhere?"

With that question in mind, I would suggest that the essential first step would be to let God release a fuller measure of our potential.

Everyone has potential. God put it in you. That is a tremendous word: potential. Eleven men once got their potential freed and began to use it, and they turned the whole world upside down with their message of Christ. They were so dynamic that wherever they went they turned things upside down, bringing new life, new understanding and new joy. Did anyone ever say that about you? How to release our potential—this is the problem.

PRAYER: *Our Heavenly Father, we pray that Your children everywhere may realize that the one way to real fullness of life is through Jesus Christ, who said, "I am the way, the truth, and the life." In His name we pray. Amen.*

DAY
10

He maketh me to lie down in green pastures: he leadeth me beside the still waters. He restoreth my soul: he leadeth me in the paths of righteousness. PSALM 23:2–3

One can learn various techniques for strengthening one's faith. I think preachers make these concepts so general and abstract sometimes that a person can't quite get hold of them. So I will mention a few specific, simple techniques for faith-building. For example, there was a timid, inferiority-complex-ridden young woman who lived in Brooklyn and worked in Manhattan. She came to our clinic for counseling. "How can I get over these fears?" she wanted to know. The counselor suggested she memorize specific passages in the Bible and say them over to herself from time to time during the day. This she did. On her daily subway trip, she discovered she could repeat Psalm 23 three times and the Lord's Prayer twice. That is how she got her mind imbued with the great presence of God and with the truth, *I won't be afraid. You are with me.* And by this means, she developed faith. If you repeat Psalm 23 every day of your life, paying attention to its meaning, the fears would begin to ease out of your mind.

> **PRAYER:** *Our Heavenly Father, grant that we may have that cast of mind which is the true practicing of joy rather than gloom, and that love of others shall be always in our hearts. Through Jesus Christ, our Lord. Amen.*

<table>
<tr><td>DAY
11</td><td>*And thou shalt go down before me to Gilgal; and, behold, I will come down unto thee, to offer burnt offerings, and to sacrifice sacrifices of peace offerings: seven days shalt thou tarry,*</td></tr>
</table>

till I come to thee, and show thee what thou shalt do.

I SAMUEL 10:8

A story is told of an incident during the Nazi occupation of Denmark in World War II. The Nazis told King Christian that they were going to put the Nazi flag on every building in Denmark, saying he could fly the Danish flag beneath the Nazi banner.

King Christian replied, "If you put a Nazi flag over the Danish flag, in ten seconds a Danish soldier will pull it down and send up the Danish flag."

"That soldier," they threatened, "will be shot."

"All right," said the king, "I will be that soldier."

They never shot him. Then when they were going to proscribe the Jews and make them all wear Star of David armbands, the king put a Star of David band on his own arm and protected his Jewish subjects. There are still people who will risk everything for freedom.

> **PRAYER:** *Our Heavenly Father, we give You thanks for the great truth to be found in these human experiences, that, as we draw near to Jesus and give our lives to God by deep commitment, we gain power to meet the most difficult experiences of this life. For this we give You thanks. Through Jesus Christ, our Lord. Amen.*

DAY
12

At that time when David saw that the Lord had answered him in the threshingfloor of Ornan the Jebusite, then he sacrificed there.
I CHRONICLES 21:28

Many years ago, in a farmhouse in the Midwest, a seventeen-year-old boy was in a coma, desperately ill. The doctor said, "I see no reason why this boy should die. What he needs is a faith transfusion, a desire to live. In some way he is near death because the faith isn't there to pull him through." He said, "If a transfusion like that doesn't happen, he will die before morning."

When the doctor said that, a farmer drew near and started reading to the boy from the Bible. Hour after hour, he drove those healing thoughts into the boy's unconscious mind until near dawn when, suddenly, the boy gave a sigh. His eyes opened, he looked at the man and at all the people in the room—gave them a smile and fell into a deep, untroubled, normal sleep.

The doctor checked his vital signs and said, "The boy will live!" And he did live. Saved by what? By faith and prayer and thought. The problem had its solution right within itself, as all problems do.

> **PRAYER:** *Our Heavenly Father, we thank You that You are related to our health and well-being. Help us to empty out all diseased attitudes, that the great healthy mindedness that comes from You, our Creator, may result in re-creation of our bodies, our minds, and our souls. Amen.*

<table>
<tr>
<td>

DAY
13

</td>
<td>

Thus saith the Lord God; When I shall have gathered the house of Israel from the people among whom they are scattered, and shall be sanctified in them in the sight of the heathen,

</td>
</tr>
</table>

then shall they dwell in their land that I have given to my servant Jacob. EZEKIEL 28:25

I remember an experience of my old friend E. Stanley Jones, the famous missionary. During his first few years in India, he labored under a heavy sense of personal inadequacy. He began to think he would have to give up his missionary career.

At a meeting in Lucknow he had a remarkable experience. He was praying and he seemed to hear a voice asking, "Are you ready for this work to which I called you?" Silently, he confessed that he just didn't seem to have the strength. Then the voice said, "If you will turn it over to Me, I will take care of it."

But there is a catch. You can't expect that God is going to help you repeatedly unless you help Him. The furtherance of His kingdom on earth comes about through human beings trying to help and serve. That is how He ordained it should be. God has to have the love and help of people.

> **LIFE LIFTER:** *When you concentrate on helping people with their difficulties, you will be able to cope with your own more effectively. Somehow, the act of self-giving is a personal power-releasing factor.*

DAY
14

Then touched he their eyes, saying, According to your faith be it unto you. MATTHEW 9:29

Pray big. Think big. Believe big. The gospel of Matthew, chapter 9, verse 29, declares, "Because of your faith, you will be heard." In other words, your life is going to be in proportion to how greatly you believe. Believe little, you get a little life. Believe weak, you get a weak life. Believe fear, you get a life of fear. Believe sickness, you get a sick life. Believe big, and you get a big life. Jesus said, "Anything is possible for someone who has faith!" (Mark 9:23). Which means what? That the person who believes is going to get everything he wants? No, it doesn't say that. But it does mean that if you believe big, you move things out of the realm of the impossible into the realm of the possible. Christianity is the religion of the incredible, the religion of the astonishing, the religion of the breathless. You bring to yourself what you believe.

LIFE LIFTER: *When uncontrolled, your mind can be very damaging to you, but when controlled it can develop unlimited power. Think defeat and you are bound to feel defeated. But practice thinking confident thoughts, and you will develop such a strong sense of capacity that regardless of what difficulties arise you will be able to overcome them. Fear is the most powerful of all thoughts with one exception, and that one exception is faith. Stress the thought of plenty. Thoughts of plenty help create plenty.*

<table>
<tr>
<td>

DAY

15

</td>
<td>

For they all made us afraid, saying, Their hands shall be weakened from the work, that it be not done. Now therefore, O God, strengthen my hands. NEHEMIAH 6:9

</td>
</tr>
</table>

Are your human relationships what you want them to be? Would you like them to be better? Then why aren't they better? Maybe it is because you fail to realize your full capacity. If all the members of some group of, say, several hundred persons would suddenly realize their full capacity, do you know what they could do? They could change this world. If we would just all catch it!

But how do you catch it? How does one get a power that is plenty for the work of God's kingdom? One thing is certain: you can't manufacture it yourself. Human beings are weak. We are only as strong as we are strong in God. God promises you infinitely more strength. But you've got to reach for it. You have to take it. You have to want it. You have to accept it. Then you have the full complement of power.

Surrender yourself completely to Jesus Christ and build your life around Him and live the way He wants you to live, even though it's hard at times. Do this and you will have the power.

LIFE LIFTER: *Thoughts and words form your mental image. And since we become what we picture, be sure your thoughts and words express prosperity and blessing rather than poverty and defeat.*

> DAY **16**

I, even I, am he that blotteth out thy transgressions for mine own sake, and will not remember thy sins. ISAIAH 43:25

Rest in the Lord, wait patiently, have faith in providence and God's love. In this way, you actually get your life under new management. What happens when a business repeatedly fails to show a profit? Usually it gets a new management, doesn't it? A human life that hasn't been going well likewise calls for a new management. Does everything go wrong for you? Why? Poor management. Are you nervous and tense and tired? Why? Poor management. Are you resentful and grumpy and bitter, full of hate and miserable as a result? Why? Poor management. You are making life hard for yourself because you don't think right, you don't act right, you don't plan right. Get your life under new management. Do it by opening your mind and heart to Jesus Christ. Take Him into your thinking and living.

LIFE LIFTER: *The secret of life isn't what happens to you, but what you do with what happens to you. Always remember that problems contain values that have improvement potential. Break the tension of a problem by shifting your thoughts completely from it. Instead, think only about God. When you return to the problem, your insight will sharpen, your understanding deepen.*

| DAY 17 | *I am crucified with Christ: nevertheless I live; yet not I, but Christ liveth in me: and the life which I now live in the flesh I live by the faith of the Son of God, who loved me, and gave* |

himself for me.
                                    GALATIANS 2:20

If you are failing at anything, chances are it is because you have an image of yourself failing. Do you know what you are doing? Hypnotizing yourself with a limiting idea. When you come to church and when you read the Bible and when you listen to Jesus Christ, when you lift up your eyes and look on Him, He eliminates the limitations you have imposed upon yourself. I know this is a fact. It all depends on what you think of yourself. The image you and I have of ourselves determines the actual state of our lives. The Christian religion teaches us not only how to live good moral lives and to have faith so we will be received into eternity, but also how to live as children of God here and now. What Jesus Christ wants to do is to knock the shackles off our minds and remove the limitations of our lives.

LIFE LIFTER: *Set your goal. Hold that goal in consciousness. Keep that image always before you and your goal will materialize. Self-trust is the first secret of success. So believe in and trust yourself. Never forget that all the enthusiasm you need is in your mind. Let it out—let it live—let it motivate you.*

DAY 18

The Lord is good to all: and his tender mercies are over all his works. PSALM 145:9

Many Americans have long since forgotten the romance of the simple basic blessings of this life. A Japanese businessman remarked to me once that his people "still know how to contemplate and love the simple, basic things of human existence." He told me of a Japanese custom called a snow-viewing party. This is usually held on a night when the moon is full, by someone who has a large picture window with a beautiful garden outside. The guests gather. There are no cocktails, there is no hubbub, no empty conversation, no hand-shaking. You sit and look through the picture window at the snow, at the stark, bare trees with little flecks of snow on them, at the great rocks capped with snow. You spend an hour or two, in silence, viewing the snow and thinking and meditating. Then you rise, bow, and you go home. That is all. But you have had an hour of quiet fellowship with sensitive, appreciative people. Life is good; and you walk along thinking long thoughts about how lovely the world is. So let us give thanks for the deep basic things of human existence and for family, friends, and loved ones.

> **LIFE LIFTER:** *Take pleasure in the pattern of the sunlight falling through the trees or the sound of the snow under your foot. Relish these things, which are the essence of life, and they will make your heart sing within you.*

<table>
<tr><td>

DAY

19

</td><td>

For I know the forwardness of your mind, for which I boast of you to them of Macedonia, that Achaia was ready a year ago; and your zeal hath provoked very many.

II CORINTHIANS 9:2

</td></tr>
</table>

After two years of professional baseball with the St. Louis Cardinals, Frank Bettger hurt his arm and had to give up baseball. He spent two years in a dismal job, then he switched to selling life insurance. His first ten months in this new work were the most discouraging months of his life. He would make many calls without selling a single policy.

Finally, Bettger decided to burn up the paths in life insurance just as he had done in baseball. The next day, he sold a policy to his first prospect. That was the beginning of a spectacular career. Insurance people tell me that Bettger is regarded as having been one of the greatest salesmen in the history of life insurance. And on the subject of developing enthusiasm Bettger says, "There is only one rule. To become enthusiastic, act enthusiastic."

LIFE LIFTER: *Practice enthusiasm in even the most commonplace things and presently the immense power of enthusiasm will begin working wonders for you. Dare to be what your best self knows you ought to be; dare to be a bigger human being than you have ever been.*

DAY 20

And for the wood offering, at times appointed, and for the firstfruits. Remember me, O my God, for good. NEHEMIAH 13:31

A young man had told me his grandmother was always doing good, so I decided to look her up. I drove to an unpaved road and found a house with the number the young man had given. Eventually I saw an elderly lady coming down the road, carrying a big basket on her arm. And she was singing—beautifully and melodically—at the top of her voice.

"Are you Mrs. Wright?" I asked.

A big smile crossed her face as she said, "Of course, that's who I am. What do you want to see me about?"

"I had a letter from your grandson and he says that you are an angel on two feet," I explained. "Please tell me how you got to be so happy."

"I just love everyone," she answered. "When you have the Lord Jesus in your heart, you love everyone and it's like birds singing. It's like music all day long."

Jesus said: "I will give you the keys to the kingdom of heaven" (Matthew 16:19). The greatest of all keys to the kingdom of heaven is to have Jesus in your heart. And this is the greatest of all formulas for happiness.

PRAYER: *Our Heavenly Father, we thank You for the glorious gift of happiness offered to all people everywhere by Jesus Christ. Grant that everyone let God fill his life with joy. Through Jesus Christ, our Lord. Amen.*

<table>
<tr><td>DAY
21</td><td>*But ye are a chosen generation, a royal priesthood, an holy nation, a peculiar people; that ye should show forth the praises of him who hath called you out of darkness into his*</td></tr>
</table>

marvelous light.   I PETER 2:9

Do you know what the greatest word in the New Testament is? It's "life." Hunt through the New Testament to find how many times the word life appears and you will be amazed. And associated with the word life is another word—"new." The whole emphasis of the New Testament is on newness. The Bible is the most modern thing in the world. It is more modern than today's newspaper, for it deals with life that is new.

In I Peter 2:9 are the words, "God has brought you out of darkness into his marvelous light." What is light associated with? Morning, the new day. And again, in Ephesians 4:23–24, we are told: "Let the Spirit change your way of thinking and make you into a new person." And, again, the Bible says, "Anyone who belongs to Christ is a new person. The past is forgotten, and everything is new" (II Corinthians 5:17). That is the word: new, new, new! Fresh, new world. New life.

LIFE LIFTER: *The secret of prayer is to find the process that will most effectively open your mind humbly to God. So experiment with fresh prayer formulas. Practice new skills and get new insights.*

<table>
<tr><td>

DAY

22

</td><td>

Behold, I give unto you power to tread on serpents and scorpions, and over all the power of the enemy: and nothing shall by any means hurt you.

LUKE 10:19

</td></tr>
</table>

A man I once knew was always depressed, always discouraged, and had a low opinion of himself. Sometime later, I met him again and I was astonished by the remarkable change in this man. He was full of enthusiasm and vitality and hopefulness. And so I asked him, "How did it happen?"

"When I feel weak and inadequate," he said, "I always say Luke 10:19 to myself: 'I have given you the power…to defeat…your enemy Satan. Nothing can harm you.' When I feel bad in body, mind and spirit, I use John 10:10. When financial troubles come, I repeat Philippians 4:19."

The man's face glowed, his whole personality seemed vibrant, he was on top of things. Why? Because he knew that God was always with him, a great knowledge to have. But you never get it as long as you are constantly passing through your mind thoughts of poverty, weakness, fear and inferiority. Pass these great passages from the Bible through your mind.

PRAYER: *Our Heavenly Father, we thank You for the Gospel of Jesus Christ, which is for people who want to be lifted out of their narrowness. May every individual live at his best. Through Jesus Christ, our Lord. Amen.*

DAY

23

But the eye of their God was upon the elders of the Jews, that they could not cause them to cease, till the matter came to Darius: and then they returned answer by letter concerning this matter.

EZRA 5:5

You may say, "You don't know the difficulties I have. There are so many problems. I have inner conflicts and all kinds of trouble. Yet you tell me not to be depressed." But let me ask you: Would you want all those problems and troubles to be taken away from you? Who made this world? Some whimsical being? Some devilish individual? Or was it Someone with wisdom? You know it was Someone with wisdom because everywhere you find order and law, and wherever you find order and law you are beholding signs of intelligence. This world was created by an intelligent God. He put you in it and He put some trouble in it along with you. Why? Because He wants to make a great person out of you. If He didn't care whether you ever amounted to anything, He wouldn't have put any difficulty in your life.

LIFE LIFTER: *Believe that all the resources you need are in your mind. That is a formula that really works! Try living one day without any unhealthy thoughts. It may be very difficult, but try another day, until it becomes habitual, and life will move in the direction of becoming healthy, vital, and alive.*

DAY
24

And he said, Hearken ye, all Judah, and ye inhabitants of Jerusalem, and thou king Jehoshaphat, Thus saith the Lord unto you, Be not afraid nor dismayed by reason of this great multitude; for the battle is not yours, but God's…. Ye shall not need to fight in this battle: set yourselves, stand ye still, and see the salvation of the Lord with you, O Judah and Jerusalem: fear not, nor be dismayed; tomorrow go out against them: for the Lord will be with you.

II CHRONICLES 20:15, 17

Discouragement is one of the most pernicious diseases of the human spirit. It weighs heavily upon the mind, making its judgments grotesque and unsharp. It saps energy. It destroys creative possibilities. It renders us ineffective.

And, let's face it, oftentimes there is much cause to be discouraged. If I wanted to, I could give you quite a talk on all the things you might find to be discouraged about. But I don't think it's my job to tell you how bad things are. You know that already. My theme is that you can do something about it. You can learn to handle and get above discouragement. Out of discouragement, rightly handled, great things come.

LIFE LIFTER: *Think health, practice health, pray health. Keep thinking, keep praying, keep dreaming. Be mentally sensitive at all times so that the magic word that motivates you may one day speak to your deep inner self.*

DAY **25**	*And I saw a new heaven and a new earth: for the first heaven and the first earth were passed away; and there was no more sea.*

REVELATION 21:1

Jesus promised that if people would believe in Him, really believe in Him, and follow Him, a wondrous thing would happen to them. He told people that they could discover a whole new world of real living. If He were standing among us today, He would say to any of us who feel confused, unhappy, restricted, defeated, depressed, that we need not be this way at all, that if we reorganize our thoughts and affirm our faith, we can discover a marvelous new world of real living. He is the only man in history who has delivered such a promise.

There may be some who say, "I wouldn't want to change my life for the world. It is perfect. I like it just as it is." Don't ever settle for what you already have, no matter how good it may seem to be. No matter how wonderful your life is, it can be more wonderful. You can go from level to level into an ever-new world of real living. This is why Jesus lives and is a real, contemporary personality when all other great figures pass away.

> **LIFE LIFTER:** *To settle for self-limitation is to lock yourself up within yourself and therefore to deny to yourself the God-given opportunity for growth. Have confidence that you can draw the best to yourself.*

<table>
<tr><td>DAY
26</td><td>*And it was so, when Gideon heard the telling of the dream, and the interpretation thereof, that he worshipped, and returned into the host of Israel, and said, Arise; for the Lord*</td></tr>
</table>

hath delivered into your hand the host of Midian.

JUDGES 7:15

I think it may be said that a pastor sees people as they really are. Having had this experience for many years, I have an exalted respect for human beings, because I've seen them struggle against the greatest imaginable odds and gain victories through the power of God.

I've observed one thing that has never ceased to impress me. The person who has a certain great truth in his mind can never be defeated by anything and will ultimately win victories, though he may have to go through the deep waters now and then. That great truth is the belief—the obsessive belief—that God is always with us. When you believe this, that you are not alone, never, under any circumstances, and when you live with this belief, then you are never rejected, you are never forsaken, you never walk by yourself. God is with you—this is the greatest source of strength a human being can have.

LIFE LIFTER: *Go to sleep using the conscious thought and affirmation that whatever you may be called upon to handle the next day, God and you will be able to do together.*

DAY
27

O give thanks unto the Lord; for he is good....
PSALM 136:1

Have you had a hard time this past year?
Psalm 136:1 tells us we should give thanks for it. Hard
times struggled with in the name of Jesus become
victories by and by, and we are stronger people for
wrestling with those problems. Have you had sorrow?
Through your tears, give thanks for it, for it is through
difficult circumstances that souls grow. Whatever life
has brought, the message is: give thanks. And, as you do
so, greater things will come.

We need to recall and give thanks for the gift of life
itself. We're so accustomed to being alive that we take
it for granted. The thrill and the wonderment of it
elude our minds. Do you ever get up in the morning
and look out the window or go to the door and
breathe in the fresh air and go back in and say to your
wife or husband, "Isn't it great to be alive?" Probably if
you did that your spouse would have a heart attack!
But life in itself is so tremendous, such a privilege, that
it should be cause for deep thanksgiving.

PRAYER: *Our Heavenly Father, we know that all
things are a demonstration of the spiritual. Grant that
we may have the wisdom to see this in our lives and fill us
with wonder and joy. Through Jesus Christ, our Lord. Amen.*

DAY 28

Turn us again, O God, and cause thy face to shine; and we shall be saved.   PSALM 80:3

Some years ago, a summer conference of the Fellowship of Christian Athletes drew 2,300 athletes and coaches from all over the United States. One of the speakers was Paul Anderson, an Olympic weight lifting champion, said to be the strongest man in the world. He began by amazing his audience with feats of strength. After he got through these demonstrations, he preached a forceful sermon on the theme that anyone who has filled himself with the love of Jesus Christ can overcome any temptation life may bring him. He said that Christlike love is the greatest power men and women can tap. And, he told the assembled athletes, use it!

Of all the people I have known, the happiest are those who have had lots of trouble, sickness, pain, difficulty, but overcame all these because they had a resource. And the resource they had is an acquaintance with God. They knew that, no matter how dark the shadows, God and Jesus Christ were always there. If you know that, then no matter how much trouble and difficulty you have, you are happy in your heart, because you know that the source of victory is yours.

PRAYER: *Our Heavenly Father, we thank You that the faith we have is a rugged faith, fit for rugged people. We ask that we may not only be equal to tough situations but conquer them. Through Jesus Christ, our Lord. Amen.*

| DAY
29 | *If so be they will hearken, and turn every man from his evil way, that I may repent me of the evil, which I purpose to do unto them because of the evil of their doings.* JEREMIAH 26:3 |

God is so big that He has confidence in His creatures. He gives them the power of private judgment, He makes them free moral agents so that they can do what they want to do—even contrary to His will. That is a big God. If God were a little god He would tell us exactly what to do. But He leaves us free.

You and I repeatedly make a mess of things, that's for sure. To some people, the human picture looks quite hopeless. Life is dark at times. But I hold with the faith expressed by John Greenleaf Whittier in the lines:

I know not where His islands lift

Their fronded palms in air;

I only know I cannot drift

Beyond His love and care.

Beyond this universe, Christianity tells us, is eternal goodness. The conflict between evil and good, between hate and love, goes on and on; but love is fundamental and love underlies the immortality of the soul.

LIFE LIFTER: *Do kindly things for people, for nothing can so completely erase gloom and create new vigor as the practice of caring and goodwill. The most curative thought in the world is the thought of love.*

| DAY **30** | *If there be among you a poor man of one of thy brethren within any of thy gates in thy land which the Lord thy God giveth thee, thou shalt not harden thine heart, nor shut thine* |

hand from thy poor brother. DEUTERONOMY 15:7

Sam Reeve was so poor that the first time he ever wore a suit was the day he graduated from high school, and the suit was given to him by a neighbor. One day, he read this passage in the Bible: "If you give to others, you will be given a full amount in return" (Luke 6:38). Sam decided to predicate his life on this and eventually became an outstandingly successful small businessman. He was invited to a White House conference of small businessmen who had done distinguished jobs. The President asked him, "Sam, how did you do it?"

Sam thought a moment and then answered, "I just tried to give away more than my competitors. I try to find my pleasure in giving," he said, "and let the getting part take care of itself." I tell you, if you really believe in the Bible you've got to believe in this. If you want a life full of blessings, a life out of poverty, a life victorious over difficulties, if you want things to flow your way, you practice that.

PRAYER: *Our Heavenly Father, we ask Your blessing. We pray that we may hold in mind our great expectations in You and that we may live with You. We give You thanks. Through Jesus Christ, our Lord. Amen.*

DECEMBER

<table>
<tr><td>DAY
1</td><td>Howbeit I believed not the words, until I came, and mine eyes had seen it; and, behold, the half was not told me: thy wisdom and prosperity exceedeth the fame which I heard.</td></tr>
</table>

I KINGS 10:7

Christianity is a fountain of power—of the greatest power in the universe. Jesus, after His Resurrection, said to the disciples, "But the Holy Spirit will come upon you and give you power" (Acts 1:8). That was the beginning of the Christian faith, a power promise.

How much power have you? Do you have a great surging river of power or do you have just a little rivulet that carries you through some things but fails you in others? The law of supply is a great concept. And this law of supply is offered to anyone who will practice the magic of believing.

This doesn't mean that you are going to get rich. Christianity isn't designed to make you rich. Christianity isn't interested in whether you are rich or not. The Bible says, "Be generous, and someday you will be rewarded." You shall have every one of your needs satisfied if you practice the magic of believing.

LIFE LIFTER: *Take God as your partner in every enterprise. Every day flush "lack" thoughts out of your mind and refill it with dynamic thoughts of abundance. Expect generous benefits in never-failing supply.*

DAY

2

And thou say in thine heart, My power and the might of mine hand hath gotten me this wealth. DEUTERONOMY 8:17

God knows that human beings need help. No matter how strong they may be or what attainments they may have to their credit, they still are faced with many problems that upset them. Even though their faces may look calm and peaceful, people can be upset in one degree or another.

Only a short time ago, there came to my office a man whose name I think would be known to nearly everyone who has any knowledge of the American business world. He manages a vast industrial empire. He is one of those men born to leadership, a strong, powerful character. And he sat in my office and asked me, "Can I unload my mind to you?"

"Go ahead," I said. And he was with me a long time, for he had lots to unload. There he sat in front of me, a powerful, famous man, but at the same time just a human being whose mind was terribly upset. He had come to talk with me because he wanted me to tell him how Jesus could help him. I was touched. And he was touched. And he was helped.

LIFE LIFTER: *You have qualities within you that can overcome the seemingly impossible. Contact with God establishes within us a flow of the same type of energy that re-creates the world and that renews springtime every year.*

<table>
<tr><td>DAY
3</td><td>Jesus answered and said unto them, Verily I say unto you, If ye have faith, and doubt not, ye shall not only do this which is done to the fig tree, but also if ye shall say unto this</td></tr>
</table>

mountain, Be thou removed, and be thou cast into the sea; it shall be done. And all things, whatsoever ye shall ask in prayer, believing, ye shall receive.

MATTHEW 21:21–22

"If you have faith...you can tell this mountain..." Now what does Jesus mean by "mountain"? Well, obviously, not a mountain made of stone or earth. You couldn't remove such a mountain by faith. Or maybe you could, but there would be no meaning to it. There would be no sense in it. No, what is referred to here are the difficulties of life mountainously piled one upon another. If you have faith and do not doubt it, you can say to those difficulties, "Be removed, be cast into the sea"—which is another way of saying, cast out of sight, gone for good—and they will be. That is what the Bible says. And I personally am simple enough to believe it. I believe it because I have seen this truth demonstrated many times. The believer is conferred power over difficulties.

> **PRAYER:** *Our Heavenly Father, grant us boldness to live in our day and generation heroically, doing the great things You put it in our hearts to do. Grant us courage always. Through Jesus Christ, our Lord. Amen.*

<table>
<tr><td>DAY
4</td><td>*Then said David, Ye shall not do so, my brethren, with that which the Lord hath given us, who hath preserved us, and delivered the company that came against us into our hand.*
I SAMUEL 30:23</td></tr>
</table>

Through extraordinary intelligence, hard work and by the application of the basic laws of successful achievement, W. Clement Stone has made huge sums of money. But I never knew a man who gave so much money so generously as does Mr. Stone. It appears that his chief reason for making money is to help people. For example, he has helped more prisoners to find new life—and more boys to find a future—than anyone I know of. He started life with nothing. He said that the Lord just gave him the gift of making money.

But I've noticed that a lot of people who make money hang on to it. Some of the tightest people I've ever known are people who have made money—they've got the idea that it is for them alone. If you have the ability to acquire wealth you should learn the equally important art of how to give it for mankind. You are a steward of God, who made everything and owns all values of this world.

PRAYER: *Our Heavenly Father, we ask You to bless everyone with a realization that as he opens his purse he will bring upon himself a filling up of his whole life. For this we give You thanks. Through Jesus Christ, our Lord. Amen.*

DAY
5

So they did eat, and were filled: and they took up of the broken meat that was left seven baskets. And they that had eaten were about four thousand: and he sent them away.

MARK 8:8-9

Frank Boyden was headmaster of Deerfield Academy at Deerfield, Massachusetts, for over sixty years. When he first took charge, the Academy was heavily in debt. But if you go there today, you will see the most marvelous campus. I asked Frank Boyden one day, "How did you get this place built up?"

"Whenever I got to rock bottom," he said, "I'd talk to the Lord about it. The Lord would say, 'Frank, give some more.' I would tighten my belt and give more of my own money, more of myself. And the blessings have just rolled in—because I wanted to make good men out of little boys and I gave of myself to do it."

I will tell you this: If you are missing blessings in your life, if the flow of prosperity has been inhibited, the thing to do is start giving! Even when you haven't anything to give, give anyway. This is what is offered you through the law of supply. The law of supply works only as long as you give.

LIFE LIFTER: *The great secret of getting what you want from life is to know what you want and believe you can have it. Always do something for others, then ask God to help you and get at it.*

DAY
6

I likewise, and my brethren, and my servants, might exact of them money and corn: I pray you, let us leave off this usury. Restore, I pray you, to them, even this day, their lands, their vineyards, their oliveyards, and their houses, also the hundredth part of the money, and of the corn, the wine, and the oil, that ye exact of them. NEHEMIAH 5:10–11

Jesus delivered a message that would bring peace, goodwill, happiness, creativity to all the world. And it was as if He said, "This cannot be except by your own choice, for you have been created free moral agents. You can turn it down if you wish. You can support it if you wish. It cannot be realized without you."

Think of all the blessings that ensued from the vast onward march of Christendom over the past two thousand years! But still it is not enough. The forces of materialism and evil grow so fast that we have to keep building our Christianity ever higher and broader and deeper. And the people who will give themselves to this task are going to be the people who see blessings beyond all calculation. You have to give. If a person doesn't give he doesn't get. If he does get and doesn't give, he doesn't keep. It is a spiritual law.

PRAYER: *Heavenly Father, we give thanks to You for our freedom of choice. We know that happiness does not lie on the path of weakness, but on the path of strength. Help us take the path to life. Through Jesus Christ, our Lord. Amen.*

| DAY 7 | *And the whole congregation of the children of Israel murmured against Moses and Aaron in the wilderness.* EXODUS 16:2 |

Prayer is a mental process. Oftentimes a person will complain, "I've prayed and prayed and I didn't get what I wanted." You didn't? Well, who said you were supposed to get what you wanted? Prayer isn't a device to get you what you want. Prayer is a means of bringing you to the point where you will accept what God wants. If you're using it just for getting what you want, you're engaging in an improper and degraded use of it.

The Lord does want good things for us all and if with all your heart you pray for something that is wholesome and constructive, you are likely to receive it. But sometimes the thing you pray for is something you shouldn't have. We are like children—we want what we want when we want it. But to be a Christian means to be a mature person. You learn to say, "This is what I'd like to have, Lord, if You think it's all right for me, but if You don't, then give me what You want me to have or show me what You want me to do."

> PRAYER: *Our Heavenly Father, we know that the only way in which the Kingdom of God within us may be activated and brought to life is by the creative working of God in our lives. Help us to achieve a state where we no longer get in our own way. Through Jesus Christ, our Lord. Amen.*

DAY
8

But I am poor and needy: make haste unto me, O God: thou art my help and my deliverer; O Lord, make no tarrying.

PSALM 70:5

I received a letter from a young man in Texas. He began: "Until about two years ago my life was governed by sick, consuming fear. I prayed for God for help, but when the answer came it was not what I'd had in mind. It was an idea: 'Go to the library and get a book on psychology and find out why you are afraid.'

"I went to the library and what caught my eye that day was something you had written, *A Guide to Confident Living.* Confident living—that's what I needed all right! And the idea of a personal God and His presence in our lives strongly appealed to me. I became a church member. Reading the Bible took on a new meaning. God touched me.

"My life has changed. It is not a bed of roses by any means. But I am calmer now. I know that God never turns His back on anyone who sincerely seeks Him."

This is the key to the formula. Let God touch you and you become a victorious person, whose mind has been freed from fear by being filled with faith.

LIFE LIFTER: *Take a long straight look at your fear and stand firmly up to it. Then practice strong action. If everyone followed the purposes of the Creator, the general thrust of life would be in our favor.*

DAY 9

And with them, by their generations, after the house of their fathers, were bands of soldiers for war, six and thirty thousand men: for they had many wives and sons. I CHRONICLES 7:4

When I first met Paul Chow, he had brought his family from Shanghai to freedom in Hong Kong. He wanted to come to America. Even though I practice positive thinking, I warned him, "It will be difficult for you to get to America."

"I know," he assured me, "but difficulties are the things the Lord handles."

And the day came when, standing in the pulpit at Marble Collegiate Church, I saw a wonderful face and thought, "It looks like Paul Chow." And, sure enough, it was. Well, I found that Paul and his family were living on a street that was more dismal than anything I'd seen in Hong Kong. I exclaimed to my wife, "Imagine a man going to the trouble he went to only to land in a place like this. I won't let them stay there." We found a home for them in Pawling, New York. And the Chows became one of the most beloved families in the community. Against great odds this man became a tremendous person because he had Jesus in his heart.

LIFE LIFTER: *Help other people to cope with their problems, and your own will be easier to cope with. Miracles are not altogether made out of dreams. Often they are put together out of plain, everyday, nonglamorous facts.*

| DAY **10** | *This also cometh forth from the Lord of hosts, which is wonderful in counsel, and excellent in working.* ISAIAH 28:29 |

W. Clement Stone is a philosopher who says you should read the Bible with the idea that God wants to do wonderful things for you. You get exactly what you are looking for, he says. If you seek inspiration, you become inspired. If you seek knowledge, you become informed. If you seek wisdom, you become wise. If you seek health, sickness disappears. Seek good and it comes to you. Seek success and it will come to you. Know specifically what you want and then keep your mind on that which you want—and off the things you don't want. If you keep thinking about what you don't want, you'll get what you don't want. But if you think about what you want, it is likely to come to you.

PRAYER: *Our Heavenly Father, we thank You for the great truths that are given to us out of Your Holy Word. We know that Your great powerful gospel was made for people who can develop a great faith and that the greater the faith, the greater the victory. Help us therefore to commit ourselves to You in completeness and say, "Lord, I want to live on the upthrusting power of Your spirit." And then will come victory after victory. We will not be relieved of difficulties, but we will have the power to overcome them. And for this we give You thanks. Through Jesus Christ, our Lord. Amen.*

DAY
11

Every man of the children of Israel shall pitch by his own standard, with the ensign of their father's house: far off about the tabernacle of the congregation shall they pitch.

NUMBERS 2:2

When an old friend's last will and testament was read, it contained the following declaration:

"I desire to testify and give thanks for the goodness of God, who has blessed me far beyond my merit; for Godly parents; for the patience and devotion of my wife; for the Christian character, love and loyalty of my darling daughter, my son-in-law and their family, my grandchildren; the rich fellowship of my friends; the kindness and cooperation of those with whom I have been associated in business; the opportunities for service in the community and in the church; the strength for daily toil; the joy of living; the inexpressible reward of striving, even in an imperfect way, to follow Christ, and the glorious certainty of life eternal and abundant—these comprise my real possessions."

My friend had so many blessings because he was constantly activating the flow of blessings by giving praise and thanks to the Source of it all.

LIFE LIFTER: *Whatever you do, do not make all your prayers into the form of asking God for something. The prayer of thanksgiving is much more powerful.*

DAY 12	*For the Lord will judge his people, and he will repent himself concerning his servants.*
	PSALM 135:14

The Empire State Building is a marvelous structure. Seeing it reminded me of a boy who lived in downtown New York in devastating poverty. At the age of thirty, he was elected to the New York State Assembly and was assigned to the committee on banking; he had never had a bank account up to that time. He was so discouraged trying to read the bills that came before him that he almost decided to quit.

I am talking about Alfred E. Smith, four times governor of New York state. And he realized his dream of building the tallest building in the world, the Empire State Building. Once I sat with him in that building and said, "Governor, you have had a great career. Tell me about it."

He smiled and replied, "My mother always believed in me. She said there was something in me that God would bring out if I allowed Him to do so."

So, if you are not satisfied with your life, say "Lord, help me to bring out the greatness that is within me." What God can make out of a person is astounding.

LIFE LIFTER: *To be successful is to be helpful, caring and constructive, to make everything and everyone you touch a little bit better. Keep probing for the tremendous quality built into you that has not yet emerged.*

DAY
13

And he went up from thence to Beer-sheba.
GENESIS 26:23

During the Depression of the 1930s, the air was filled with gloom. One night I went out and walked in Walnut Park, with fear clutching at my heart. How were we going to live? How were we going to keep the church going? How were we going to pay bills?

When I came home, my wife said, "Now, look. You are my husband, but you are also my pastor. And you are doing better at the first than you are at the second. I want to tell you something, Norman. All we need to do is to give."

"But we haven't anything to give."

"We will give of what we have. I'll promise you this," she continued—and I can remember looking into her lovely face as she said it—"if you will rededicate yourself to Jesus Christ and if you will give your money, and your time, to God and to the church and to human beings, God will always take care of us. You can forget being afraid." That was a long time ago and He has always taken care of us. We have had blessings. Why? Because I deserve them? No! But that kind of faith will always bring blessings.

LIFE LIFTER: *Each of us has good news deep within ourselves—the fact that with God's help we have what it takes to meet all upsetting situations and to react creatively to them. The spirit of God can revitalize every great thing.*

| DAY 14 |

Rejoice evermore. Pray without ceasing.
I THESSALONIANS 5:16–17

I liked to hear my grandmother, Laura Peale, pray. She could pray as few persons I have ever known on this earth. My brother and I as boys used to spend summers with her and our grandfather. Each night she put us to bed with the Bible and that old Methodist magazine, *The Christian Advocate*. I can see her yet, with those concave glasses people used to wear, reading stories out of a magazine and the Bible. Then she would take us upstairs and put us into a comfortable feather bed.

Then she would blow out the kerosene lamp. She knew we might be afraid in the dark and so she would put one hand on Bob's head and one on mine and say, "Dear Lord, let these boys know that You watch over them all night long. Keep Your eye on their pillows while they sleep tonight." Then we would hear her soft footsteps going downstairs and we would drift off to sleep. As long as I live, I shall remember the sweet, beautiful, loving prayers of my grandmother.

PRAYER: *Our Heavenly Father, we thank You for this message, which comes to us from Your Holy Word, that we are not alone. You did not create us and then set us off to fend for ourselves, but You are with us always, even until the end of the world. For this we give thanks. Through Jesus Christ, our Lord. Amen.*

<table>
<tr><td>DAY
15</td><td>*And all the tithe of the land, whether of the seed of the land, or of the fruit of the tree, is the Lord's: it is holy unto the Lord.*
LEVITICUS 27:30</td></tr>
</table>

Ernest L. Wilkinson wrote a booklet on tithing. One day we got to discussing the subject. He said, "The way to unlock the flow of power is to give." And he told me about a man in Grand Rapids who made furniture.

This man got into difficulties and practically went broke. He was able to save the factory, but his credit was thin. The banks wouldn't loan him money, so a few friends loaned him enough to get started again. Then he got the idea of tithing—giving ten percent of his income and his time to the Lord. When he was ready to start his factory again, he knelt in his office and said, "Lord, this plant, such as it is, is Yours. I accept You now as my Partner and I will give the first ten percent all the rest of my life to You." His business grew and he brought blessings to other people.

The basic spiritual law of the universe, demonstrated by Jesus Christ who gave His life, is that blessings come from giving yourself away. If you can believe this, all things are possible.

LIFE LIFTER: *The positive thinker is a hardheaded, tough-minded, factual realist. He sees all the difficulties clearly, but such a person sees more than difficulties—he or she tries to see the solutions of those difficulties.*

<table>
<tr><td>

DAY
16

</td><td>

*But thou, Bethlehem Ephratah, though thou
be little among the thousands of Judah, yet out
of thee shall he come forth unto me that is to
be ruler in Israel; whose goings forth have*

</td></tr>
</table>

been from of old, from everlasting.   MICAH 5:2

Some years ago, a man named Bob waited for me after
the Sunday service and said, "Tomorrow I have to go to
the hospital. Would you pray for me right now?"

I put my hand on his shoulder and said, "Okay, Bob,
I don't want you to think that the hand on your
shoulder is the hand of Norman Peale. You just believe
that the hand of Jesus is on your shoulder. Will you?"
He looked at me and said, "Yes, I will." I prayed. Then
he said to me, "I give myself to Him."

Later, Bob came along on a trip to the Holy Land.
Looking at Bethlehem from a site known as the
Shepherd's Cave, Bob was so moved he could hardly
speak. He pointed toward the city and said, "Norman,
what would have happened to me had He not been
born? had I not taken Him as my Savior?" I looked
into his face and I thought to myself: The wise men
still come to Bethlehem. And they still find their
answer. They find a power that changes their lives.

> PRAYER: *Our Heavenly Father, help us to see ourselves
> as children of God, not weak, not restricted. Help us to
> be transformed by the renewing of our minds. And for this we
> give You thanks. Through Jesus Christ, our Lord. Amen.*

DAY 17

Then they cried unto the Lord in their trouble, and he delivered them out of their distresses.

PSALM 107:6

We encounter some real troubles in life. Anyone living anywhere on earth will know someone who is having a grievous time with real troubles. I think there are certain basic things we can do when we're in trouble to keep our troubles from overwhelming us. The first is to remember God and have faith in His providence. Look to Him for guidance. And from this there follows a second basic idea: Since we are children of God and can look to Him for help, we ought not to quake in the presence of trouble, nor run away from it, nor pretend it isn't there, but face it, stand up to it, take hold of it, and deal with it. Actually, the more you try to run away from trouble, or evade it, the more overwhelming it becomes; while if only you would boldly take hold of it, you would find it that much easier to handle.

PRAYER: *Our Heavenly Father, we pray that those of Your children who are disturbed today may receive from You deep healing quietness and in that deep pool of quietness let their turmoil be absorbed so that no more shall they be troubled. Through Jesus Christ, our Lord. Amen.*

<table>
<tr><td>DAY
18</td><td>*And yet this was a small thing in thine eyes, O God; for thou hast also spoken of thy servant's house for a great while to come, and hast regarded me according to the estate of a man*</td></tr>
</table>

of high degree, O Lord God.   I CHRONICLES 17:17

When I was a boy, several people told me they didn't think I would be able to make much of anything out of my life. So I was comforted to read an article by Alston J. Smith in which he mentioned a number of distinguished men and women who early in their lives had been the butts of brutally discouraging remarks—including Thomas Edison and Louisa May Alcott.

One of the functions of the church is to help people who have lost faith in themselves, who are overcome with difficulties and problems, by reminding them who they are. There isn't anyone who hasn't within himself tremendous possibilities. You should never let the fact that you have problems and difficulties overcome you. If you have a whole armful of difficulties, you may be sure the Lord likes you. And He knows that you have what it takes to dig down into this difficulty and that problem and come up with bright and shining good.

PRAYER: *Our Heavenly Father, We feel the God-inspired life in our souls. Make it manifest in each of us so that we may go into society and bring to pass the glorious possibles of God. Through Jesus Christ, our Lord. Amen.*

DAY 19

And the governors of Judah shall say in their heart, The inhabitants of Jerusalem shall be my strength in the Lord of hosts their God.

ZECHARIAH 12:5

Some people seem to be afraid to partake of any optimism put to them—as though there were something blasphemous about taking a hopeful view. Pessimism thrives, the intellectuals say, because the world is in so much trouble. Certainly it's in trouble. Since when hasn't it been in trouble? This is the nature of human existence. The bright fellows who think they are going to create a perfect world have a superficial understanding of the nature of life. It always has been a world full of trouble and it always will be. But out of this world of trouble, people rise who live above the trouble.

What is your trouble? It isn't anything you can't rise above. Not by your own strength, but with Him lifting you. There is an old gospel song in which each line of the refrain ends, "He lifted me." Get lifted in the spirit, and life will have great new meaning.

LIFE LIFTER: *Practice excited thinking until you become excited—and exciting. Set aside a few minutes every day to say aloud such words as exciting, dynamic, marvelous, fabulous, terrific. Visualize the Kingdom of God as in you. See yourself as the potential possessor of God's bounty.*

<table>
<tr><td>DAY
20</td><td>*Verily, verily, I say unto you, He that believeth
on me, the works that I do shall he do also;
and greater works than these shall he do;
because I go unto my Father.*   JOHN 14:12</td></tr>
</table>

I read sometime ago that a well-known psychiatrist in France had added a new dimension to the psychological perception of humans. He maintains, it seems, that we have not only the conscious and the unconscious but a superconscious within us. And he refers in this connection to Jesus' words in John 14.12: "I tell you for certain that if you have faith in me, you will do the same things that I am doing. You will do even greater things, now that I am going back to the Father." Does that mean that I can do greater things than Jesus did? Or that you can? Well, that is what Jesus said! The French psychiatrist reasons that it is through the superconscious element in man that this possibility exists. A person can do things incredible to himself when he gets the kind of understanding that is a wellspring of life to those who have it.

PRAYER: *Our Heavenly Father, we ask Your blessing upon us all. Help us to know that we cannot overcome our fears, our weaknesses, and our sins by our own power, but fortunately may receive in us through Jesus Christ Your great power that can set us free of everything that would defeat us. Grant that it may be so in the life of each of us now and always. Through Jesus Christ, our Lord. Amen.*

DAY **21**	*Fear not, little flock; for it is your Father's good pleasure to give you the kingdom.*
	LUKE 12:32

When an individual really gets enthusiasm, you can see it in the flash of the eyes, in an alert and vibrant personality. You can see it in the spring of a step. You can see it in the verve of one's whole being. Enthusiasm makes the difference in our attitude toward other people, toward a job, toward the world. It makes a great big difference in the zest and delight of human existence. Do you have enthusiasm? Or have you grown dull? Lackadaisical? Indifferent? Has the zest gone out of you? Well, remember what is said in Luke 12:32: "Your Father wants to give you the kingdom." And that implies that a person gains an enthusiastic participation in life.

LIFE LIFTER: *Life's blows cannot break a person whose spirit is warmed at the fire of enthusiasm. Enthusiasm lifts living out of the depths and makes it mean something. Play it cool and you may freeze. Play it hot and even if you get burned, at least you will shed warmth over a discouraged and bewildered world.*

| DAY 22 | *He hath made the earth by his power, he hath established the world by his wisdom, and hath stretched out the heaven by his understanding.* JEREMIAH 51:15 |

In his early life, Abraham Lincoln traveled the court circuit and stayed overnight, as was his custom, with an old Illinois farmer. One night the farmer witnessed the spectacular phenomenon known as "shooting stars." He thought the end was at hand and he got scared. Then he remembered Lincoln was asleep upstairs. He dashed up the stairs crying, "Abe, Abe, get up! The heavens are falling! The world is coming to an end!"

Lincoln got out of bed and looked out the window. He stepped back into the room, put his hand on the shoulder of his frightened friend and said to him, "Don't you be afraid, Bill. Even if there are some shooting stars, the great constellations are still there."

When difficulties rain down upon you it is easy to become bewildered and frightened. But if you look behind this rain of difficulties into the eternal verities and see that the great God is still there, then you realize you need not be afraid. Because of His presence, you have what it takes to face up to anything.

LIFE LIFTER: *Quiet your mind so that inspirations may rise from its depths. An inflow of new thoughts can remake you regardless of every difficulty you may now face, and I repeat—every difficulty.*

<table>
<tr><td>DAY
23</td><td>*For whatsoever is born of God overcometh the world: and this is the victory that overcometh the world, even our faith.*   I JOHN 5:4</td></tr>
</table>

Over and over again, I have seen what can happen when a person who has been defeated becomes conscious of the words of Jesus. They cast out all weakness. Life is rebuilt around a substantial center. That is the reason you should go to church and read the Bible—to expose yourself to the powerful words of Scripture.

We need to realize that the difficulties inherent in this life are not without value, and that every defeating situation has within it a potential victory. Almighty God buries at the heart of every difficulty a nugget of gold. Overwhelmed by difficulty, a person may throw up his hands, not knowing that at the very heart of this crisis is some great value in life for which he seeks. So, when a difficulty faces you, don't be appalled by it but say, "I wonder what God has put into this difficulty for me. By His grace I am going to find it."

PRAYER: *Our Heavenly Father, we ask You to bless every human being. You understand us, even when we don't understand ourselves. If we are weak, You can make us strong. If we are lacking in love, You can give us that love. And if we need more power to live, You can give it to us. For this we give You thanks. Through Jesus Christ, our Lord. Amen.*

<table>
<tr><td>DAY
24</td><td>*Therefore the Lord himself shall give you a sign; Behold, a virgin shall conceive, and bear a son, and shall call his name Immanuel.*
ISAIAH 7:14</td></tr>
</table>

One bitterly cold, snowy Christmas Eve, Fred Henderson was sadly making his way home. A series of blows in his business had him literally reeling. Then he saw the lights of home. Fred didn't feel up to the festivities, but he thought, "I must pull myself together. I must not let anyone know what has happened."

He put on a good act. At length, the family prepared to hear the Christmas story and Fred opened the Bible to the first chapter of Matthew. Reading, he came to verse 23: "He will be called Immanuel, which means 'God is with us.'" When he had finished, Fred went out to clear the snow from the walks. As he dug into the drifts he found himself saying, "God is with me." Peace came over him. And with it came a firm conviction that a solution would be found to his problem.

God is with you and with me. This means you can be strong enough to handle any problem that will ever come to you, strong enough to meet any difficulty, take any disappointment, bear up under any reversal.

PRAYER: *Our Heavenly Father, we thank You for the birth of our Lord Jesus Christ in Bethlehem of Judea long ago. Help us to reconsecrate ourselves today to living as He taught. Through Jesus Christ, our Lord. Amen.*

DAY **25**	*And the angel said unto them, Fear not: for, behold, I bring you good tidings of great joy, which shall be to all people.* LUKE 2:10

The great word at Christmas is joy. The old carol says, "Joy to the world! The Lord is come." "Don't be afraid," said the angel. "I have good news for you, which will make everyone happy." All the bright colors, all the lilting music of Christmas bear out the joy with which the season is filled.

It was Jesus who brought the emphasis of joy into our human experience. When I went into the ministry years ago, a friend of mine rather sneeringly asked, "Norman, why do you want to be a preacher? I'm surprised! Are you going to be one of those sanctimonious joy-killers?" Well, not long ago the same man, after all these years, said to me, "I tried to kid myself for years that I was happy, but really I wasn't. Finally, I reorganized my life around Jesus Christ. Then I became and have remained a happy man." He added, "Why was I so dumb for so long? Why did it take me so long to get wise to myself and realize that true happiness is in Jesus?"

> **PRAYER:** *Our Heavenly Father, we give You thanks for the Christmas message. What a wonderful story it is, so simple that even in the midst of life's complexities every one of us can find the way into glorious living. We give You thanks. Through Jesus Christ, our Lord. Amen.*

DAY 26

And Moses sware on that day, saying, Surely the land whereon thy feet have trodden shall be thine inheritance, and thy children's for ever, because thou hast wholly followed the Lord my God.

JOSHUA 14:9

I would like to advance the theory that a Christian should never really be discouraged. There are some who will say I am not being realistic. Well, it depends on how you define discouragement and how you define a Christian. There is superficial Christianity and there is Christianity in depth. When an individual becomes identified with Jesus Christ, surrenders his life to Him, accepts Him as Savior and lives with Him and walks with Him, then Jesus Christ confers upon him the power to rise above discouragement.

This doesn't imply that you are going to turn your back on the world and let it go. The true Christian is a person who participates in the world's work. He is the kind of person who says, "Sure, here's a situation. So what! Let's go to work and bring the power of God to bear upon it." He brings the same approach to his personal problems. And he discovers he need never be a victim of discouragement.

LIFE LIFTER: *How you think about a problem is more important than the problem itself—so always think positively. Be humble, be big in mind and soul, be kindly; you will like yourself that way and so will other people.*

<table>
<tr><td>

DAY

27

</td><td>

Beloved, I wish above all things that thou mayest prosper and be in health, even as thy soul prospereth. III JOHN 1:2

</td></tr>
</table>

It is good to talk about the spirit, because this language confers the sacredness and the inherent greatness of the individual. I went through the Bible asking God's guidance on the subject of the human spirit and came upon this verse, "I pray that all goes well for you. I hope that you are as strong in body, as I know you are in spirit" (III John 1:2). God is a generous God. Abundance is His word. Why, then, do we live in poverty and in want?

I read about a man in Oklahoma who was low financially. But he had a big soul, he loved God, and he had some insights. He took some pieces of paper and put these in his wallet. When things weren't going well, he would take out these slips of paper, on which were written verses such as II Corinthians 9:8: "God can bless you with everything you need, and you will always have more than enough to do all kinds of good things for others." So don't think I'm not preaching out of the Bible when I say there is a law of supply.

LIFE LIFTER: *Know for a fact that you are never alone. A great Someone is with you always. Keep the positive principle going by visualizing energy and vitality continuously at work within you. Go at life with abandon; give it all you've got. And life will give all it has to you.*

<table>
<tr><td>DAY
28</td><td>*And he said, The things which are impossible with men are possible with God.*   LUKE 18:27</td></tr>
</table>

The Bible is filled with astonishing passages. One of them can be found in Luke 18:27, where it says, "There are some things that people cannot do, but God can do anything." Now, of course, on the surface this means that God can do things man cannot do, which is a fact that goes without question. But it seems that this verse implies that if people are identified with God in a special way, the power of God to change impossibles into possibles becomes associated with those people. This, of course, is an enormous assumption. But the Bible deals in enormous assumptions.

You, too, have it in you, as do I, to do (using an ordinary phrase) the things that cannot be done. But there is a tendency in human nature to emphasize the seemingly impossibles in life, to underscore them, to build them up. This is one reason why the life accomplishment of many of us falls at a far lower level than God ever intended it to be. To the degree that we identify ourselves with Him, we gain power over the seemingly impossible.

LIFE LIFTER: *Remind yourself that nothing is too good to be true. Expect great things to happen. Confidently receive God's blessings. Think prosperity, abundance, the best of everything. God wants to give to you, His child, every good thing. Don't hinder His generosity.*

DAY 29

Did not he that made me in the womb make him? and did not one fashion us in the womb?
JOB 31:15

The individual who finds something useful to do beyond himself, who gives himself, knows joy of the deepest kind. Jesus Christ stimulates people to have a meaningful life.

After a speech I made in Indiana, a man drove me to the train station. During our drive, he told me about himself and said, "I'm not happy. Why is it that, having all these things, I'm not happy?"

At the railroad station I said to him, "You have great ability. You have capacity. But you have never found any use big enough for it. Why don't you give yourself to Jesus Christ and help Him build His Kingdom?"

We continued to talk, and sitting there with me beside a couple of mail trucks this man spoke to Jesus saying, "I'll give You my life. I'll do Your job." And since that time, I have followed his activities in the area where he lives. He has been a benediction. He has uplifted young people, saved marriages, and put power in the church. And he has put joy into his own life. That is how Jesus even now brings joy to this world.

LIFE LIFTER: *Motivation puts the fire within you that gets the inner power going. To keep motivation going, begin at once the mental practice of seeing yourself as an individual who is always vital, vigorous and excited.*